I see maths

Delivers ALL the objectives in the KS3 Framework for Teaching Mathematics

Year 7

Sue Jennings and Richard Dunne

Letts

www.letts-education.com/iseemaths

Contents

Year 7 Framework objectives covered	Levels				Page
	3	4	5	6	

Objectives are numbered consecutively within each topic as laid out in the Mathematics Framework, pages 6–11.

Letts **I See Maths** Year 7

Addition and subtraction

Essential exercises

1 Complete the following table.

+ 555 →

400	325	111	323	555					
					955	888	768	597	602

− 555

2 Complete the following sentences.
(a) The sum of 48 and 93 is … .
(b) The difference between 23 and 59 is … .
(c) The total of 126, 472 and 864 is … .
(d) 386 plus 674 plus 227 is … .
(e) 752 subtract 138 is … .
(f) 9238 and 517 take away 916 is … .
(g) 230 take away 30 add 540 add 720 is … .
(h) 985 take away 465 plus 515 is … .

3 What is the number?
(a) Start at 45. Add 36. Subtract 33. Add 29. Add 87. Subtract 55.
(b) Start at 66. Double it. Add 405. Subtract 207. Halve it.
(c) Think of a number. Double it. Add 15. Subtract 7. Add 9. Subtract 17. Halve it.
(d) Think of a number. Add 500. Take away 200. Add 700. Take away the number you first thought of.

4 Complete the following table.

x	60		82	24		47
y		30			35	
$x + y$	100	100	100	100	100	100

5 Complete the following table.

x	12·6	8·4		10·7		25·76
y	5·3		1·9		18·45	
$x + y$		23·6	3·6	33·9	46·37	63·09

6 Complete the following table.

x	16·6	42·8	67·9			60·04
y	6·6	3·7		24·7	72·7	35·03
$x − y$			34·5	12·6	17·5	

Addition and subtraction

Challenging exercises

7 Work out the value of x in each of the following equations.

(a) $35 + x = 67$ (b) $105 - x = 42$ (c) $364 + x = 676$
(d) $x + 99 = 200$ (e) $x - 54 = 33$ (f) $x - 341 = 146$

8 Complete the pyramid below.

$a + b$ over a, b

Pyramid values: 39, 55, 23, 15, 18

9 Complete the magic squares below.

Square 1: 6, 3, _ / _, 4, _ / _, 5, _

Square 2: 14, _, 17 / _, _, 12 / _, _, 16

Square 3: _, _, 110 / _, 107, _ / 104, _, 108

Problem-solving exercises

10 Toby was about to start at his new school. His mum took him shopping to buy some of his kit. They chose some great trainers for £45·34 and shorts and a shirt for £37·25. Then they bought him a pencil case and geometry set for £17·46. They saw a calculator for £8·25 and Toby's mum said that, if there was any money left from the £120 she had brought to the shops, then he could buy it. Did Toby get the calculator and, if so, how much money was left after buying it?

11 The Jones family were going on holiday to Cornwall. They worked out that they had to drive 254 miles to get there. They stopped after 103 miles at a motorway service station. How much further did they have to go?

Homework

Tell some real-life stories for the following maths stories.

(a) $36 + 24 - 15 = 45$ (b) $147 + 256 + 194 = 597$ (c) $36·4 + 28·2 = 64·6$

Letts **I See Maths** Year 7

Key Stage 2 Review

5

Extending the multiplication tables

Essential exercises

1 Complete the following table.

× 5	4	6	9	5	8						÷ 5
						50	20	35	55	100	

2 Complete the following sentences.

(a) Nine times eight is … .
(b) Ninety times eight is … .
(c) Nine times eight hundred is … .
(d) Nine hundred times eight thousand is … .
(e) Nine thousand times eighty is … .
(f) Seventy-two divided by eight is … .
(g) Seventy-two divided by nine is … .
(h) Seven hundred and twenty divided by nine is … .

3 Given that $7 \times 6 = 42$, use this fact to work out the following.

(a) 70×6 (b) 7×600 (c) 7000×6
(d) 700×60 (e) 7000×6000 (f) $70 \times 6\,000\,000$
(g) $0 \cdot 7 \times 6$ (h) $7 \times 0 \cdot 6$ (i) 0.7×60
(j) $\frac{7}{10} \times 6$ (k) $42 \div 6$ (l) $42 \div 7$
(m) $420 \div 6$ (n) $4200 \div 7$ (o) $42\,000 \div 60$

4 Complete the following equations.

(a) $2 \times 3 \times 4 =$ (b) $5 \times 10 \times 2 =$ (c) $8 \times 4 \times 100 =$
(d) $7 \times 9 \times 6 \times 0 =$ (e) $1 \times 8 \times 1 \times 1 =$ (f) $2 \times 2 \times 2 \times 2 =$
(g) $8 \times 6 \div 4 =$ (h) $144 \div 9 \div 2 =$ (i) $3 \times 5 \times 3 \times 5 =$

5 Complete the grids below.

x	9	8			400	2000
y	4		11	5		
$x \times y$		56	77	4500	12 000	16 000

x	63	490			350	1600
y	7		720	60		
$x \div y$		70	9	300	50	140

Letts I See Maths Year 7

Extending the multiplication tables

Challenging exercises

6 Work out the value of x in each of the following equations.

(a) $3x = 27$ (b) $5x = 40$ (c) $6x = 600$

7 Use the '65 times' table to complete the following equations.

$65 \times 0 = 0$	
$65 \times 1 = 65$	
$65 \times 2 = 130$	
$65 \times 3 = 195$	
$65 \times 4 = 260$	
$65 \times 5 = 325$	
$65 \times 6 = 390$	
$65 \times 7 = 455$	
$65 \times 8 = 520$	
$65 \times 9 = 585$	

(a) $65 \times 8 =$ (b) $65 \times 600 =$

(c) $650 \times 5 =$ (d) $6 \cdot 5 \times 9 =$

(e) $520 \div 65 =$ (f) $390 \div 6 =$

(g) $19\,500 \div 650 =$ (h) $13\,000 \div 200 =$

(i) $58 \cdot 5 \div 9 =$ (j) $65 \div 65 =$

(k) $2 \times 65 + 9 \times 65 =$ (l) $15 \times 65 =$

(m) $65 \times 21 =$ (n) $650 \div 65 + 455 \div 65 =$

(o) $975 \div 65 =$ (p) $65 \times 6 \times 10 =$

Problem-solving exercises

8
(a) Work out the area of a rectangle with width 6 cm and length 8 cm.
(b) Work out the area of a triangle with base 10 cm and height 7 cm.
(c) The area of a triangle is 63 cm² and its height is 9 cm. What is the length of its base?
(d) Work out the volume of a cuboid with side lengths 5 cm, 8 cm and 9 cm.
(e) A cuboid has volume 420 cm³ and height 10 cm. What is the area of its base?

9 At my local shop loaves of bread cost 80p each. I bought seven loaves and put them in the freezer. What did I pay for the loaves?

10 An athlete ran one 3000 m race in seven international events. What was the total distance he ran?

11 Mandy went for a long walk. She walked non-stop for twelve miles. It took her three hours. What was her average speed in miles per hour?

Homework

Write real-life stories for the following maths stories.

(a) $50 \times 70 = 3500$ (b) $4 \times 6000 = 24\,000$ (c) $6 \times 8 \times 9 = 432$

(d) $10 \times 7 \div 5 = 14$ (e) $2 \times 2 \times 2 \times 2 \times 2 = 32$ (f) $8 \times 0 = 0$

Addition and subtraction of fractions

Essential exercises

1 Complete the following equations.

(a) $\frac{2}{5} + \frac{1}{5} =$ (b) $\frac{3}{5} + \frac{7}{5} =$ (c) $\frac{16}{5} - \frac{11}{5} =$ (d) $\frac{17}{5} + \frac{31}{5} =$

(e) $\frac{103}{5} + \frac{274}{5} =$ (f) $\frac{363}{5} - \frac{121}{5} =$ (g) $\frac{5}{7} - \frac{3}{7} =$ (h) $\frac{14}{25} + \frac{51}{25} =$

2 Complete the following equations.

(a) $\frac{3}{5} + \frac{4}{5} + \frac{7}{5} =$ (b) $\frac{9}{5} + \frac{11}{5} + \frac{23}{5} =$ (c) $\frac{39}{5} + \frac{42}{5} - \frac{78}{5} =$

(d) $\frac{8}{5} + \frac{47}{5} - \frac{16}{5} + \frac{17}{5} =$ (e) $\frac{26}{9} + \frac{84}{9} + \frac{44}{9} - \frac{16}{9} =$ (f) $\frac{15}{37} + \frac{8}{37} + \frac{19}{37} =$

3 Complete the following equations.

(a) $\frac{5}{10} - \frac{3}{10} =$ (b) $\frac{7}{10} + \frac{8}{10} =$ (c) $\frac{41}{100} + \frac{63}{100} =$

(d) $\frac{6}{5} + \frac{9}{5} - \frac{4}{5} =$ (e) $1\frac{2}{5} + 3\frac{4}{5} =$ (f) $15\frac{3}{4} + 10\frac{1}{4} - 7\frac{3}{4} =$

4 Complete the grids below.

x	$\frac{4}{8}$	$\frac{15}{23}$		$\frac{72}{83}$		$2\frac{35}{150}$
y	$\frac{7}{8}$		$\frac{65}{101}$	$\frac{72}{83}$	$\frac{23}{16}$	
$x + y$		$\frac{53}{23}$	$\frac{125}{101}$		$\frac{59}{16}$	$5\frac{140}{150}$

x	$\frac{4}{3}$	$\frac{3}{4}$		$1\frac{3}{5}$	$5\frac{2}{10}$	$\frac{67}{40}$
y	$\frac{5}{3}$	$\frac{9}{4}$	$\frac{14}{7}$		$4\frac{8}{10}$	
z	$\frac{7}{3}$		$\frac{21}{7}$	$3\frac{2}{5}$		$\frac{72}{40}$
$x + y + z$		$\frac{18}{4}$	10	$7\frac{1}{5}$	$13\frac{4}{10}$	$\frac{210}{40}$

Challenging exercises

5 True or false?

(a) $\frac{11}{11} = 1$ (b) $\frac{0}{7} = 0$ (c) $\frac{17}{1} = 17$

6 True or false?

(a) When you add fractions with the same denominator, you add together all the numerators then you add together all the denominators.

(b) When you add fractions with the same denominator, you add together all the numerators. The denominator does not change.

7 Solve the following equations. Write down the values of x.

(a) $\frac{2}{7} + x = \frac{9}{7}$ $x =$

(b) $x - \frac{5}{11} = \frac{13}{11}$ $x =$

(c) $\frac{7}{24} + x = \frac{31}{24}$ $x =$

8 In each triangle below, the area shown in colour is a fraction of the area of the whole triangle. Find the fraction.

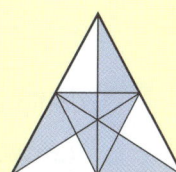

Problem-solving exercises

9 When I set off for work in my car, there were fifteen litres of fuel in the tank. The journey used two and three-quarters litres of fuel. How much fuel was left?

10 Jasmin, Errol and Sanjit have a litre bottle of lemonade between them. Jasmin drinks two-tenths of a litre, Errol drinks three-tenths and Sanjit drinks four-tenths. What fraction of the lemonade is left? How many millilitres is this?

11 Aisha made a drink using a fruit concentrate. One-tenth was concentrate and the rest was water. What fraction of the drink was water? What percentage of the drink was water?

Homework

Complete this pyramid. Add pairs of adjacent numbers to make the number in the box above them.

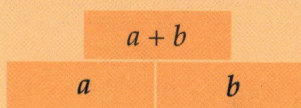

$a + b$	
a	b

$\frac{6}{15}$	$\frac{14}{15}$	1	$\frac{3}{15}$	$\frac{13}{15}$

The distributive law

Definition Multiplication is distributive over addition and subtraction.
The distributive law can be used to make some calculations easier.
$$k(a + b) = ka + kb \qquad \text{and} \qquad k(a - b) = ka - kb$$

Example $9 \times 36 = 9 \times (30 + 6) = 9 \times 30 + 9 \times 6 \qquad 9 \times 36 = 9 \times (40 - 4) = 9 \times 40 - 9 \times 4$

Essential exercises

1 **Example**
20×53 can be worked out using a grid like this.

×	50	3	
20	1000	60	1060

$$\begin{aligned} 20 \times 53 &= 20 \times (50 + 3) \\ &= 20 \times 50 + 20 \times 3 \\ &= 1000 + 60 \\ &= 1060 \end{aligned}$$

Use a grid to work out each of the following multiplications.

(a) 40×37 (b) 60×28 (c) 50×85
(d) 64×30 (e) 700×92 (f) 85×4000
(g) 400×94 (h) 29×40 (i) 600×49

2 See how the distributive law can be used to make calculations easy to work out.

Example
$$\begin{aligned} 243 \times 12 &= 243 \times (10 + 2) \\ &= 243 \times 10 + 243 \times 2 \\ &= 2430 + 486 \\ &= 2916 \end{aligned}$$

Example
$$\begin{aligned} 31 \times 576 + 69 \times 576 \\ = (31 + 69) \times 576 \\ = 100 \times 576 \\ = 57\,600 \end{aligned}$$

Example
$$\begin{aligned} 323 \times 19 &= 323 \times (20 - 1) \\ &= 323 \times 20 - 323 \times 1 \\ &= 6460 - 323 \\ &= 6137 \end{aligned}$$

Use the distributive law to help with these calculations.

(a) 124×12 (b) 245×101 (c) 25×15
(d) 334×22 (e) 425×19 (f) 156×18
(g) 44×99 (h) 532×999 (i) 721×21
(j) 426×11 (k) $43 \times 631 + 57 \times 631$ (l) $89 \times 698 - 79 \times 698$

3 **Example**
23×54 can be worked out using a grid like this.

×	50	4	
20	1000	80	1080
3	150	12	162
		Answer	1242

Use a grid to work out each of the following multiplications.

(a) 65×27 (b) 37×42 (c) 48×56
(d) 39×64 (e) 78×26 (f) 35×35
(g) 402×24 (h) 203×32 (i) 47×508

Challenging exercises

4 Calculate each of the expressions below using a single multiplication.

(a) $257 \times 56 + 257 \times 44$ (b) $16 \times 3 \cdot 5 + 11 \cdot 5 \times 16$

(c) $17 \times 2 \cdot 3 + 17 \times 6 \cdot 5 + 17 \times 1 \cdot 2$ (d) $39 \times 275 - 39 \times 25$

(e) $19 \times 22 \cdot 3 + 19 \times 22 \cdot 6 + 19 \times 5 \cdot 1$ (f) $25 \times 17 \cdot 5 - 25 \times 2 \cdot 5$

(g) $64 \cdot 7 \times 2 \cdot 4 + 6 \cdot 47 \times 76$ (h) $28 \cdot 9 \times 7 - 89 \times 0 \cdot 7$

(i) $8 \cdot 27 \times 89 - 82 \cdot 7 \times 7 \cdot 9$ (j) $30 \cdot 08 \times 167 - 0 \cdot 67 \times 3008$

5 Complete the grid below.

a	b	c	ac	bc	$(a+b)c$	$ac+bc$
40	30	53				
7	8		35			
		3	36	45		
20			60		150	
	16			64		136

Problem-solving exercises

6 The Smith family were touring France. They took a train to Bordeaux, drove from Bordeaux to Poitiers (161 miles), Poitiers to Tours (64 miles), and Tours to Paris (146 miles), and then took a train back home. Work out how many kilometres they drove (1 mile = 1609 m).

7 Work out the area of a rectangle of width 29 cm and length 34 cm.

8 Work out the area of a triangle of base 36 cm and perpendicular height 27 cm.

Homework

Write real-life stories for the following maths stories.

(a) $56 \times 11 = 616$ (b) $23 \times 99 = 2277$ (c) $45 \times 54 = 2430$

(d) $608 \times 304 = 184\,832$ (e) $37 \times 42 \times 56 = 87\,024$ (f) $365 \times 28 = 10\,220$

Comprehension 1

Planning a holiday in America

Jasmin is going on holiday to the USA with her family and a small group of family friends. Altogether five children and four adults are going. They are thinking of booking their holiday through Law's Tours because the company is offering a special deal: adults can buy one child's place at half the full price. To groups of over eight people, Law's are giving an extra discount of 10% off the final price. The full price for this holiday is £1200 per person.

Jasmin and her older sister are looking through the holiday brochures. They think they've found a better deal with Havell's Travels. Havell's have the same full price, of £1200 per person for the same holiday. Children's places are 50% of the full price, and children under two go free. Jasmin's friends have a little boy who is only twelve months old. Jasmin's brother says that with the money they save they should be able to hire a car for some of the holiday. Car hire is £60 a day.

They decide to book the holiday with Havell's. Jasmin is starting to save her pocket money so that she will have something to spend on holiday.

1.
   (a) How many children and how many adults are going on holiday?
   (b) How much is the full price of the holiday with Law's Tours?
   (c) What would be the cost of the holiday with Law's Tours if everyone in the group had to pay the full price?
   (d) What is the cost of the holiday with Law's Tours' special deal?
   (e) What savings are made with the special deal?
   (f) What is the cost of the holiday with Havell's Travels?
   (g) How much cheaper is this than the special deal with Law's Tours?

2. Look in holiday brochures or on the internet and work out the cost of different holidays for Jasmin's group.

Pocket money survey

3 **Drum Bridge's School**

Pupils in Y7 of Drum Bridge's School collected the following data about weekly pocket money (£x). The survey was conducted in 2002.

	$x < 2$	$2 \leq x < 5$	$5 \leq x < 10$	$10 \leq x < 15$	$15 \leq x$
Y7	34	53	140	15	3
Y8	9	64	145	18	4
Y9	4	55	156	23	4
Y10	0	42	160	32	5
Y11	0	35	154	45	5

(a) How many pupils in each year group answered the questions in the survey?
(b) How many pupils in total answered the questions in the survey?
(c) Decide on the best way to represent this information and draw appropriate diagrams.
(d) What was the most common amount of weekly pocket money for each year group?
(e) What fraction of pupils in Y7 had weekly pocket money of £5 or more, but less than £10?
(f) Write the answer to (e) as a percentage.
(g) What percentage of Y11 had weekly pocket money of £15 or more?

4 **Springfield School**

	$x < 2$	$2 \leq x < 5$	$5 \leq x < 10$	$10 \leq x < 15$	$15 \leq x$
Y7	45	95	83	10	0
Y8	23	76	126	12	1
Y9	10	64	132	12	1
Y10	5	43	150	14	2
Y11	2	21	163	16	2

Compare this pocket money survey with that in Drum Bridge's School.

Homework

Ask your family or friends what pocket money they had when they were your age. Compare this with either Drum Bridge's School or your own school survey.

Multiplication and division

Essential exercises

1

Example Given that $3 \times 4 = 12$, we know that $12 \div 3 = 4$ and $12 \div 4 = 3$.

(a) Given that $7 \times 9 = 63$, write down $63 \div 7$ and $63 \div 9$.
(b) Given that $8 \times 7 = 56$, write down $56 \div 8$ and $56 \div 7$.
(c) Given that $17 \times 11 = 187$, write down $187 \div 17$ and $187 \div 11$.
(d) Given that $67 \times 83 = 5561$, write down $5561 \div 67$ and $5561 \div 83$.

2

Example Work out $462 \div 3$. Use the '3 times' table.

$$3\overline{)462} \qquad \longrightarrow \qquad 3\overline{)\begin{array}{l}300\\150\\12\end{array}} \qquad \longrightarrow \qquad \begin{array}{r}3 \times 100\\3 \times 50\\3 \times 4\\\hline 3 \times 154\end{array}$$

Answer: $462 \div 3 = 154$

Example Work out $462 \div 5$. Use the '5 times' table.

$$5\overline{)462} \qquad \longrightarrow \qquad 5\overline{)\begin{array}{l}450\\10\\2\end{array}} \qquad \longrightarrow \qquad \begin{array}{r}5 \times 90\\5 \times 2\\\text{remainder } 2\\\hline 5 \times 92 \text{ remainder } 2\end{array}$$

Answer: $462 \div 5 = 92$ remainder 2 or $92\frac{2}{5}$ or $92 \cdot 4$

Use the multiplication tables to work out the following.

(a) $462 \div 4$ (b) $462 \div 6$ (c) $462 \div 7$ (d) $462 \div 8$ (e) $462 \div 9$
(f) $879 \div 3$ (g) $879 \div 5$ (h) $879 \div 4$ (i) $879 \div 7$ (j) $879 \div 8$

3 Use the multiplication tables to work out the following.

(a) $925 \div 5$ (b) $925 \div 3$ (c) $726 \div 3$ (d) $726 \div 7$ (e) $656 \div 8$
(f) $656 \div 4$ (g) $656 \div 7$ (h) $541 \div 3$ (i) $882 \div 6$ (j) $937 \div 5$
(k) $1264 \div 4$ (l) $2435 \div 7$ (m) $3009 \div 5$ (n) $4070 \div 6$ (o) $1991 \div 11$

Letts **I See Maths** Year 7

Challenging exercises

4 Write out the '17 times' table. Use this table to work out the following.

(a) 5508 ÷ 17   (b) 8704 ÷ 17   (c) 2960 ÷ 17

(d) 10 477 ÷ 17   (e) 3831 ÷ 17   (f) 5638 ÷ 17

5 Write the following numbers as the product of their prime factors.

> **Example** $24 = 2 \times 2 \times 2 \times 3$

(a) 36   (b) 48   (c) 53   (d) 87   (e) 64   (f) 91   (g) 100

6 Given that $43 \times 27 = 1161$, work out the following.

(a) 430×27 (b) 4300×270 (c) $4 \cdot 3 \times 27$ (d) $4 \cdot 3 \times 2 \cdot 7$

(e) $43\,000 \times 270$ (f) $1161 \div 27$ (g) $1161 \div 43$ (h) $116\,100 \div 27$

(i) $116\,100 \div 430$ (j) $1\,161\,000 \div 27\,000$ (k) $0 \cdot 43 \times 27$ (l) $4 \cdot 3 \times 0 \cdot 27$

7 Complete the grid below.

x	63	490	800		252		760
y	7			18	12	11	19
$x \div y$		70	50	15		18	

Problem-solving exercises

8 (a) Calculate the mean height of eight people if the sum of their heights is 1248 cm.

(b) Calculate the mean mass of six people if the sum of their masses is 374 kg.

9 (a) The area of a rectangle is 414 cm². The width is 9 cm. What is its length?

(b) The area of a triangle is 91 cm². Its perpendicular height is 7 cm. What is the length of the base?

Homework

Write some real-life stories for the following maths stories.

(a) 435 ÷ 3 = 145   (b) 345 ÷ 5 = 69   (c) 595 ÷ 7 = 85

(d) 1968 ÷ 8 = 246   (e) 648 ÷ 12 = 54

Symmetry and area

Essential exercises

1 Copy the shapes below onto squared paper and reflect them in the mirror lines.

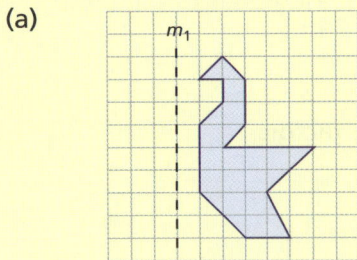

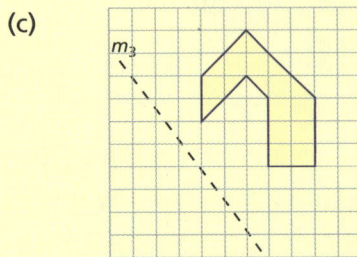

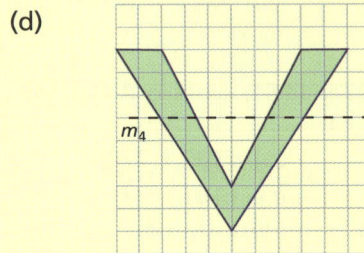

(a)

(b)

(c)

(d)

2 Calculate the areas of the following shapes.

(a)

(b)

3 Calculate the areas of the shaded parts of the following shapes.

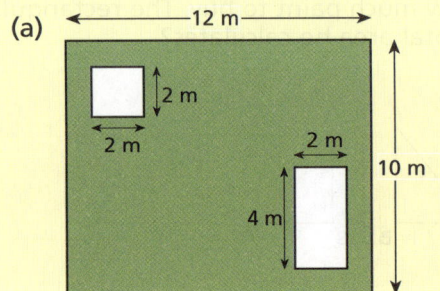

(a)

(b)

Letts **I See Maths** Year 7

Key Stage 2 Review

Challenging exercises

4 Imagine that the figure below is a scale drawing of the surface of a swimming pool (1 square = 1 m²). Work out the area of the swimming pool's surface by looking for the shapes that make it up. Calculate the area of each shape then write it in the table. Add the areas together.

Shape	Area in m²
square ABJI	
triangle FAI	
triangle BCJ	
rectangle IJDE	
triangle FIE	
triangle JCD	
Total	

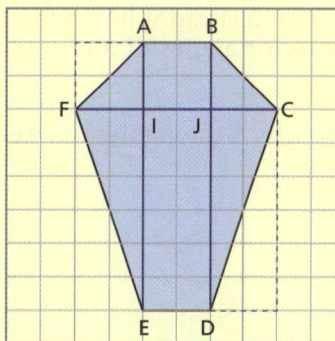

5 The plan represents a garden containing four identical rectangular lawns with these dimensions: width x m, length y m.

(a) Calculate the length x.

(b) Calculate the length y.

(c) A border of shrubs surrounds each lawn, so there are lawn edges to be cut. What is the total length of lawn edge?

(d) The area surrounding the lawns is paved. What is the total surface area of the paving?

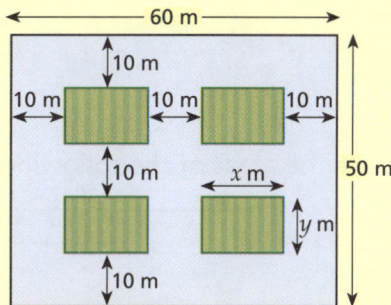

Problem-solving exercises

6 Mr Jones is putting down a path around the outside of three sides of his rectangular garden, which measures 9 metres by 6 metres. The path will be 1 metre wide and he needs to order some gravel to put down on it. The gravel is sold according to the number of square metres that need covering. What is the area of his path, in square metres?

7 Mr Jones is going to paint a room. He will paint the walls and ceiling a lovely shade of blue. He will put on two coats of paint. He works out the total area of the walls and ceiling (ignoring windows and doors) so that he knows how much paint to buy. The rectangular room measures 5 metres by 3 metres. What is the total area he calculates?

Homework

Inspect this reflection.

Use the words 'vertices', 'mirror line', 'reflected', 'equal distance' and 'perpendicular' to write some sentences about this reflection.

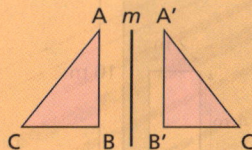

Angles, lines and triangles

Essential exercises

1 Complete the following sentences.

(a) One full turn is equal to .... degrees.
(b) A half turn is equal to .... degrees.
(c) Angles at a point add up to .... degrees.
(d) Angles on a straight line add up to .... degrees.
(e) The interior angles of a triangle add up to .... degrees.

2 Calculate each of the angles marked with a letter.

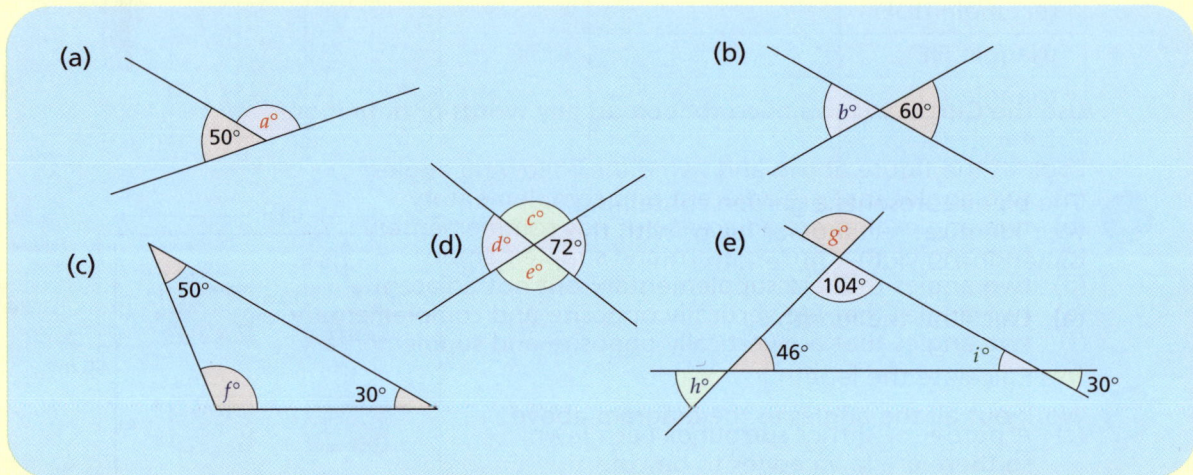

3 For each set of lines write 'parallel' or 'not parallel'.

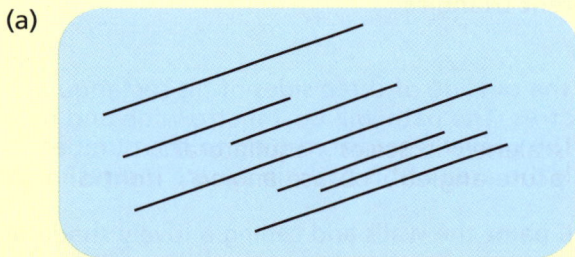

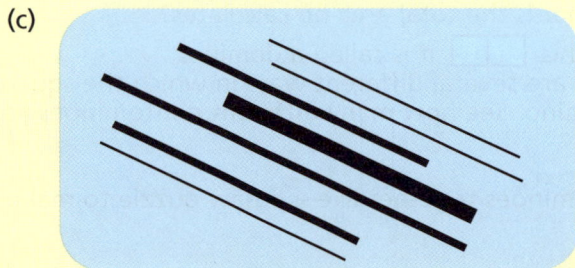

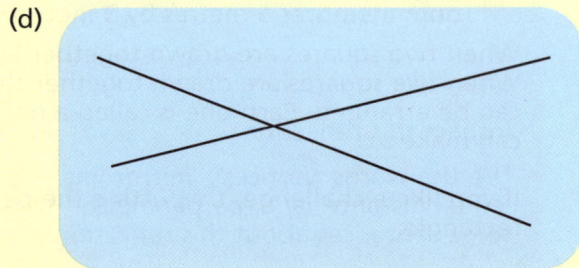

Letts I See Maths **Year 7**

Challenging exercises

4

Use the Glossary if you need to look up any words or definitions.

Look at the figure above and name the following angles:
(a) two angles that are adjacent and complementary
(b) two angles that are adjacent but not complementary
(c) two angles that are adjacent and supplementary
(d) two angles that are supplementary but not adjacent
(e) two angles that are vertically opposite and complementary
(f) two angles that are vertically opposite and supplementary.

5 Work out all the angles in the diagram above.

Problem-solving exercise

6 (a)

Using a grid like this,
how many **different** triangles
can you make?

(b) Name each triangle using the words 'scalene', 'isosceles', 'equilateral'.
(c) Name each triangle using the words 'acute-angled', 'obtuse-angled', 'right-angled'.
(d) Work out the area of each triangle.

Homework

When two squares are drawn together like this □□ it is called a domino.
When five squares are drawn together there are several different ways in which the squares can be arranged. Each one is called a pentomino. See how many **different** pentominoes you can make.

If you like a challenge, try putting the pentominoes together like a jigsaw puzzle to make a rectangle.

Key Stage 2 Review

Reading scales and graphs

Essential exercises

1

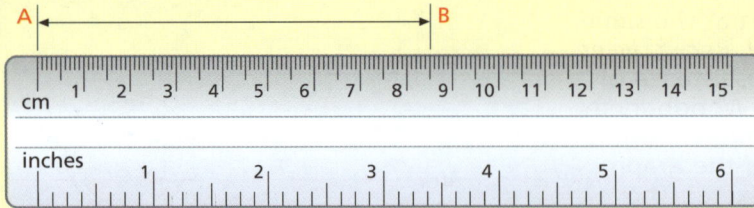

Write down the length of AB:

(a) in centimetres   (b) in metres

(c) in millimetres   (d) in inches.

2

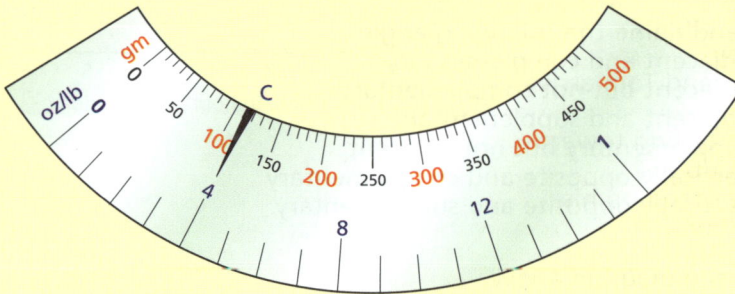

Write down the mass as measured on the scales above by the pointer C:

(a) to the nearest five grams   (b) as a fraction of a pound

(c) in kilograms to two decimal places   (d) in ounces.

3

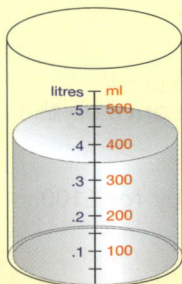 container D

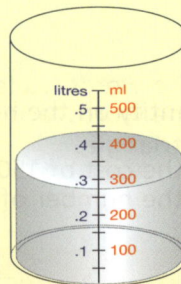 container E

Write down the volume of liquid in container D:

(a) in millilitres   (b) in litres.

Write down the volume of liquid in container E:

(c) in millilitres   (d) in litres.

Challenging exercise

4 This graph records the cycle rides of two children. Their journeys start at the same time and use the same road. Becky cycles from Exeter to Woodbury, a distance of 10 miles. Tom sets off from Woodbury in the direction of Exeter then turns round and goes back. The y-axis of the graph shows their distance from Exeter. The x-axis shows how much time has passed.

(a) How far does Becky cycle in the first hour?
(b) How long is Becky's first stop?
(c) How long after leaving Exeter does Becky pass Tom? Is he cycling in the same direction as her?
(d) Becky stops at a café seven miles from Exeter. When does she arrive? How long does she stay?
(e) At what time do Becky and Tom arrive in Woodbury?
(f) Does Tom travel faster cycling towards Exeter or towards Woodbury?
(g) What is Tom's average speed on his journey back to Woodbury?

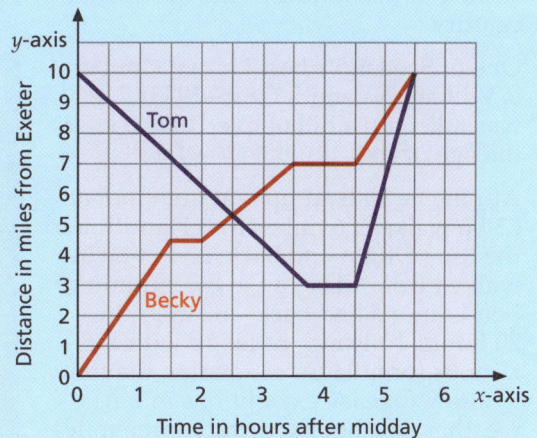

Problem-solving exercise

5 The fuel that Mr Jones uses in his car costs 90 pence per litre.
(a) Complete the following table.

Quantity in litres	1	10	50	100	200	500	1000
Price in pence	90						

(b) Draw a graph with the quantity on the horizontal axis and the price on the vertical axis.
(c) Use the graph to estimate the cost of 150 litres.
(d) Use the graph to estimate the number of litres Mr Jones can buy for £100.

Homework

Draw a distance–time graph to show one of the following:
(a) your journey to school
(b) your journey to go on holiday
(c) your journey visiting a friend or relative
(d) your journey on a trip or visit.

Comprehension 2

Climbing in Scotland

Scottish mountaineering has always been different from alpine climbing. The first Scottish climbing clubs were started in the middle of the nineteenth century.

One of Scotland's best-known climbers is William Naismith (1856–1935). He was taken up a hill of over 1000 feet at the age of six.

At nine he walked up Ben Lomond, at 23 he walked 56 miles from Hamilton to the top of Tinto and back, and at 60 he walked from Glasgow to the summit of Ben Lomond and back – 62 miles in 20 hours. Naismith came up with this famous formula for estimating the time to allow for easy expeditions in fair weather: one hour for every three miles on the map plus one hour for every 2000 feet of ascent.

From 1880, Ben Nevis quickly developed as one of Scotland's finest climbing grounds. Every year, on the first Saturday in September, a race is held here. Over 400 men and women run to the summit then back to Fort William along 14 miles of tourist paths. The first record for the course, set in 1895, was 2 hours 41 minutes. Women were allowed to race from 1902, when Lucy Cameron completed the women's course in 2 hours 3 minutes.

In 1911, a Model T Ford was driven up Ben Nevis as a publicity stunt. The ascent took several days, and the car had to be rescued three times. The descent took just two and a half hours.

1
(a) Write down a date in the middle of the nineteenth century.
(b) How old was William Naismith in the year that he died?
(c) Is 1000 feet more or less than a mile?
(d) What was Naismith's average speed when he walked to the summit of Ben Lomond and back at the age of 60?
(e) Using Naismith's formula, how long would it take to walk 60 miles on the map whilst ascending 6000 feet?
(f) How much faster did the first woman complete the Ben Nevis race in 1902 than the first man in 1895?
(g) What was the average speed of the first record for the course, to the nearest mile per hour?

2 Use an atlas or the internet to look up Ben Nevis on a map.

(a) How high is Ben Nevis in metres?
(b) What is the highest mountain in Scotland?
(c) What is the highest mountain in England?

The Mississippi

People lived in North America long before Europeans began emigrating there. These people are called native Americans. The Mississippi River got its name from one of their tribes, the Chippewa, who called it 'Misi Sipi', meaning 'Big Water'. This is a good name, because the Mississippi is long and wide. It winds for nearly 3800 km (2375 miles) through the USA, starting at Lake Itasca (near the Canadian border) and flowing into the Gulf of Mexico. Although the Mississippi is a small stream to begin with, by the time it has reached halfway to the sea it is nearly 1.5 km wide.

The Mississippi's main tributary is the Missouri. The Missouri rises high in the Rocky Mountains and travels nearly 4000 km (2500 miles) to join the Mississippi just north of St Louis. Together, the Mississippi and the Missouri make up what many claim to be the longest waterway in the world.

The first European to see the Mississippi was Hernando de Soto in 1541. He had landed in Florida with an army and was making his way west in search of gold and precious stones.

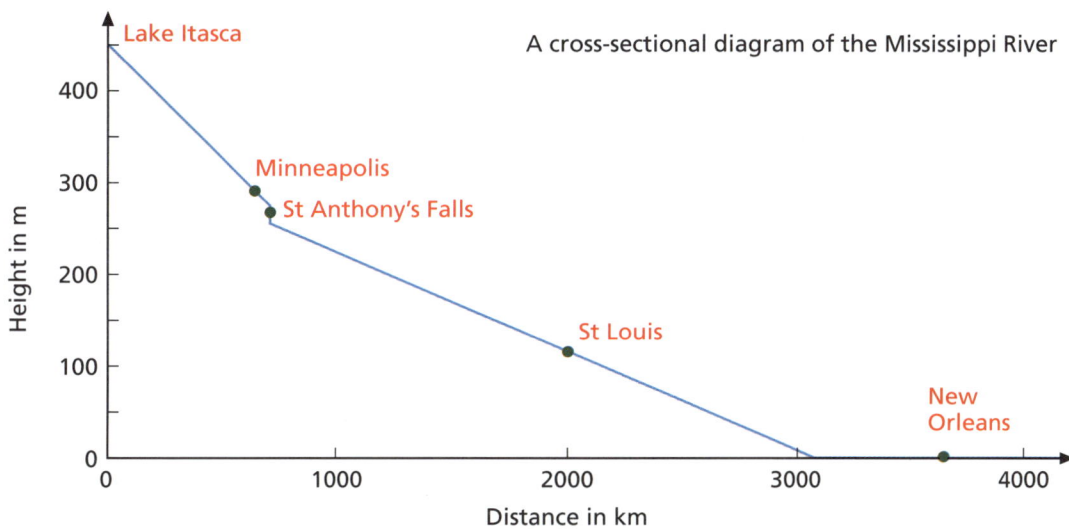

A cross-sectional diagram of the Mississippi River

3 (a) How long is the Mississippi?
   (b) How wide is the Mississippi when it has reached halfway to the sea?
   (c) How far does the Missouri travel to join the Mississippi?
   (d) In which century did the first European see the Mississippi?
   (e) At what height is Lake Itasca?
   (f) Estimate the height of St Louis, to the nearest 10 metres.
   (g) What is the difference in height between Minneapolis and St Louis, to the nearest 10 m?

Homework

Find out which is the highest mountain in the world. What is its height in feet and in metres?

Fractions 1

Goals

By the end of this lesson you will be able to answer questions such as these:

👁 Complete the following equations.

$$\frac{5}{10} + \frac{6}{10} = \qquad \frac{328}{100} + \frac{145}{100} = \qquad \frac{3}{10} + \frac{8}{10} + \frac{14}{10} =$$

$$\cdot 5 + \cdot 6 = \qquad 3 \cdot 28 + 1 \cdot 45 = \qquad \cdot 3 + \cdot 8 + 1 \cdot 4 =$$

👁 Look at ·517. How much is there here: ·5̲17?

Starter

1 Act out with cups.

(a) $6 + 2 - 1 = 7$

(b) $6 - 2 + 1 = 5$

(c) $6 - 2 - 1 = 3$

(d) $6 - (2 - 1) = 5$

(e) $6 - (2 + 1) = 3$

2 Act out with cards.

(a) $\frac{6}{5} + \frac{2}{5} - \frac{1}{5} = \frac{7}{5}$

(b) $\frac{6}{5} - \frac{2}{5} + \frac{1}{5} = \frac{5}{5}$

(c) $\frac{6}{5} - \frac{2}{5} - \frac{1}{5} = \frac{3}{5}$

(d) $\frac{6}{5} - (\frac{2}{5} - \frac{1}{5}) = \frac{5}{5}$

(e) $\frac{6}{5} - (\frac{2}{5} + \frac{1}{5}) = \frac{3}{5}$

Demonstration 1

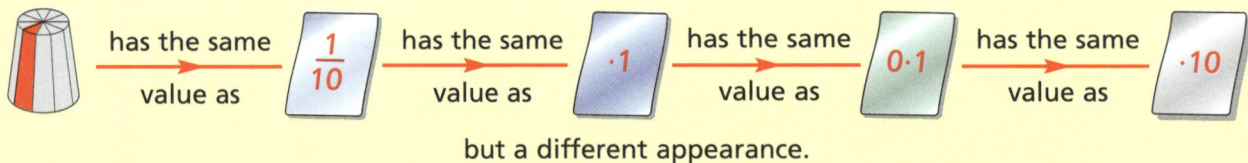

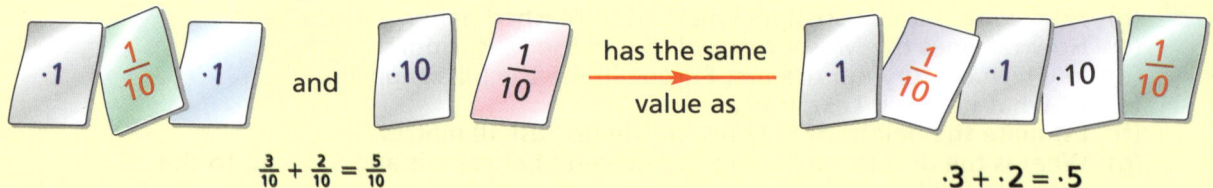

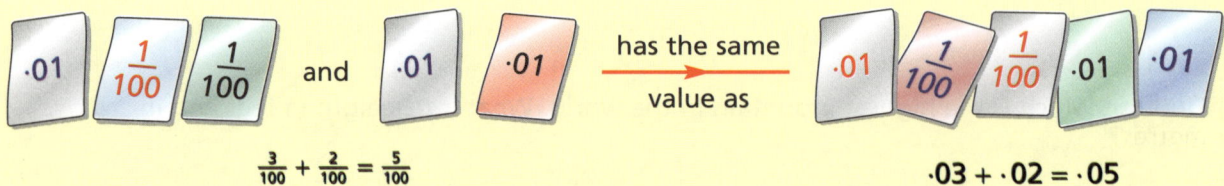

has the same value as $\frac{1}{10}$ has the same value as ·1 has the same value as 0·1 has the same value as ·10 but a different appearance.

·1 $\frac{1}{10}$ ·1 and ·10 $\frac{1}{10}$ has the same value as ·1 $\frac{1}{10}$ ·1 ·10 $\frac{1}{10}$

$$\frac{3}{10} + \frac{2}{10} = \frac{5}{10} \qquad\qquad \cdot 3 + \cdot 2 = \cdot 5$$

·01 $\frac{1}{100}$ $\frac{1}{100}$ and ·01 ·01 has the same value as ·01 $\frac{1}{100}$ $\frac{1}{100}$ ·01 ·01

$$\frac{3}{100} + \frac{2}{100} = \frac{5}{100} \qquad\qquad \cdot 03 + \cdot 02 = \cdot 05$$

Number and Algebra

Number and Algebra

Letts I See Maths Year 7

24

Demonstration 2

·14 → has the same value as → ·1 ·04

$·14 = \frac{1}{10} + \frac{4}{100}$ $·14 = ·1 + ·04$

has the same value as

Look at the decimal fraction:

·73

There is $\frac{7}{10}$ here.
There is $\frac{3}{100}$ here.
There is $\frac{73}{100}$ here.

Look at the mixed number:

4·73

There is 4 here.
There is $\frac{7}{10}$ here.
There is $\frac{3}{100}$ here.
There is $\frac{473}{100}$ here.

Key words   decimal fraction   mixed number   vulgar fraction

---

Worked example

Exercise bank 👉

1 Complete the following equations.

(a) $\frac{5}{10} + \frac{3}{10} = \frac{8}{10}$

$·5 + ·3 = ·8$

(b) $\frac{27}{10} + \frac{41}{10} = \frac{68}{10} = 6\frac{8}{10}$

$2·7 + 4·1 = 6·8$

(c) $\frac{42}{100} + \frac{35}{100} = \frac{77}{100}$

$·42 + ·35 = ·77$

(d) $\frac{648}{100} - \frac{317}{100} = \frac{331}{100}$

$6·48 - 3·17 = 3·31$

Plenary

👁 Inspect the first set of questions in the Goals. Can you see the relationship between fractions and decimals? Answer all the questions and show them to your teacher.

👁 Look at ·738.
How much is there here: ·738?
How much is there here: ·738?
How much is there here: ·738?
How much is there here: ·738?
How much is there here: ·738?
How much is there here: ·738?

Letts I See Maths Year 7

Fractions 1

Essential exercises

1 Complete the following table.

$+\frac{3}{5}$

$\frac{2}{5}$	$\frac{7}{5}$	$\frac{11}{5}$	$\frac{27}{5}$	$\frac{156}{5}$					
					$\frac{6}{5}$	$\frac{3}{5}$	$\frac{23}{5}$	$\frac{107}{5}$	$\frac{201}{5}$

$-\frac{3}{5}$

2 Complete the following sentences. (The first one has been done for you.)

$\frac{2}{10}$ has the same value as, but a different appearance from ·2.

(a) $\frac{7}{10}$ has the same value as, but a different appearance from ... .

(b) $\frac{19}{10}$ has the same value as, but a different appearance from ... .

(c) $\frac{4}{100}$ has the same value as, but a different appearance from ... .

(d) $\frac{27}{100}$ has the same value as, but a different appearance from ... .

(e) $\frac{254}{100}$ has the same value as, but a different appearance from ... .

3 Complete the following equations.

(a) $\frac{2}{10} + \frac{3}{10} =$

·2 + ·3 =

(b) $\frac{7}{10} + \frac{4}{10} =$

·7 + ·4 =

(c) $\frac{12}{10} + \frac{33}{10} =$

1·2 + 3·3 =

(d) $\frac{19}{100} + \frac{56}{100} =$

·19 + ·56 =

(e) $\frac{72}{100} + \frac{85}{100} =$

·72 + ·85 =

(f) $\frac{421}{100} + \frac{529}{100} =$

4·21 + 5·29 =

4 Complete the grid below.

x	$\frac{3}{7}$	$\frac{5}{9}$		$\frac{32}{67}$	$\frac{35}{100}$		·44	·75
y	$\frac{4}{7}$		$\frac{6}{10}$			·56	·66	
$x + y$		$\frac{11}{9}$	$\frac{14}{10}$	$\frac{105}{67}$	$\frac{224}{100}$	·89		2·36

5 Complete the grid below.

x	$\frac{8}{11}$	$\frac{14}{15}$	$\frac{9}{10}$	$\frac{19}{73}$			1·23	
y		$\frac{12}{15}$			$\frac{6}{100}$	·33		1·61
$x - y$	$\frac{5}{11}$		$\frac{2}{10}$	$\frac{13}{73}$	$\frac{22}{100}$	·45	·14	3·94

Letts I See Maths **Year 7**

Number and Algebra

Challenging exercises

6 Work out the value of x in each of the following equations.

(a) $\frac{4}{5} + x = \frac{13}{5}$ (b) $\frac{8}{9} - x = \frac{4}{9}$ (c) $x + \frac{5}{6} = \frac{13}{6}$ (d) $9 \cdot 3 - x = 6 \cdot 1$

7 Complete the pyramid here.
Add pairs of adjacent numbers to make the number in the box above them.

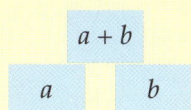

$a + b$

a b

$\frac{13}{7}$ $\frac{25}{7}$

$\frac{9}{7}$ $\frac{12}{7}$

$\frac{4}{7}$

8 Complete these magic squares.

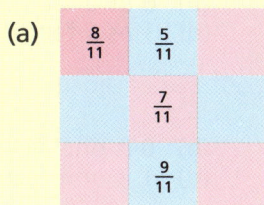

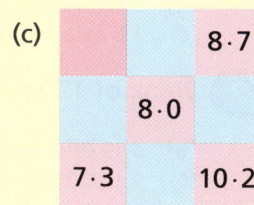

(a)
$\frac{8}{11}$	$\frac{5}{11}$	
	$\frac{7}{11}$	
	$\frac{9}{11}$	

(b)
$\frac{5}{25}$		$\frac{4}{25}$
		$\frac{7}{25}$
		$\frac{7}{25}$

(c)
		8·7
		8·0
7·3		10·2

Problem-solving exercise

9 Calculate the perimeters of the following shapes.

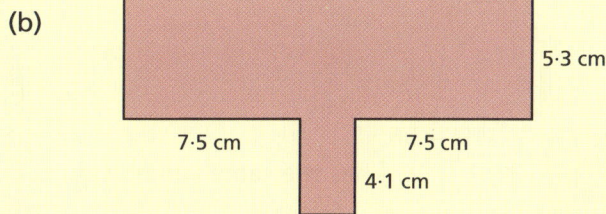

(a)
10 cm
6·8 cm
3·2 cm
14·5 cm

(b)
17·4 cm
5·3 cm
7·5 cm 7·5 cm
4·1 cm

Homework

Put the signs + or − in the blank boxes to make the equations true for both rows and columns.

$\frac{3}{10}$		$\frac{16}{10}$		$\frac{4}{10}$	=	$\frac{15}{10}$
$\frac{21}{10}$		$\frac{7}{10}$		$\frac{6}{10}$	=	$\frac{8}{10}$
=		=		=		=
$\frac{24}{10}$		$\frac{9}{10}$		1	=	2·3

Fractions 2

Goals

By the end of this lesson you will be able to answer questions such as these:

👁 Complete the following equations.

(a) $\frac{5}{6} = \frac{}{24}$ (b) $\frac{4}{3} = \frac{}{300}$

👁 Write the vulgar fraction $\frac{37}{9}$ as a mixed number.

👁 Reduce the fraction $\frac{35}{63}$ to its simplest form.

Starter

1 Work out a number that has both:

(a) 3 as a factor and 4 as a factor   (b) 6 as a factor and 5 as a factor
(c) 11 as a factor and 5 as a factor   (d) 1 as a factor and 7 as a factor.

2 Think of 12 as the product of two factors.

(a) 3 is one factor; what is the other?   (b) 6 is one factor; what is the other?
(c) 4 is one factor; what is the other?   (d) 1 is one factor; what is the other?

Demonstration 1

Same value: different appearance

$\frac{1}{6}$ has the same value as $\frac{2}{12}$

You can think of $\frac{5}{6}$ as twelfths.

Look at $\frac{5}{6}$. Say 'five-sixths'. This tells us the denomination is 'sixth'.

Speak the same value with 'twelfth' as the denomination:

One-sixth has the same value as two-twelfths: $\frac{1}{6} = \frac{2}{12}$

Five-sixths has the same value as ten-twelfths: $\frac{5}{6} = \frac{10}{12}$

Visualise the cups!

Letts I See Maths Year 7

Demonstration 2

Look at the cup.
Think of 'fifths'.
Think of 'fifteenths'.

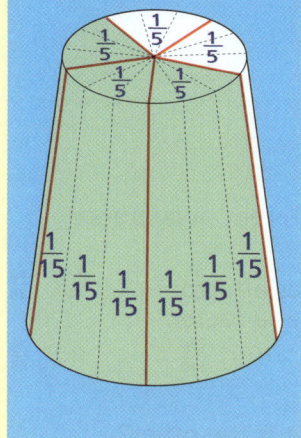

When you see $\frac{3}{15}$ you are looking at $\frac{1}{5}$.

When you see $\frac{6}{15}$ you are looking at $\frac{2}{5}$.

When you see $\frac{9}{15}$ you are looking at $\frac{3}{5}$.

$\frac{9}{15}$ and $\frac{3}{5}$ have the same value but a different appearance.

$\frac{9}{15}$ and $\frac{3}{5}$ are equivalent fractions.

Think of the quantity $\frac{9}{15}$.

We say $\frac{3}{5}$ is its simplest form.

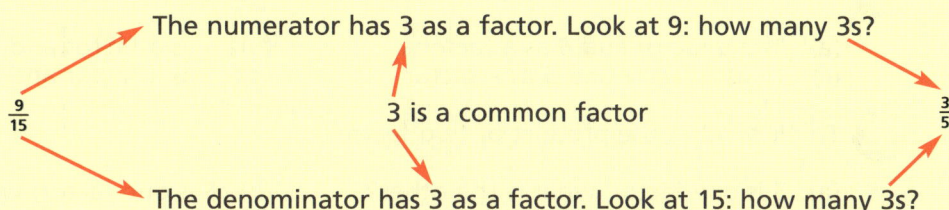

$\frac{9}{15}$

The numerator has 3 as a factor. Look at 9: how many 3s?

3 is a common factor

The denominator has 3 as a factor. Look at 15: how many 3s?

$\frac{3}{5}$

Key words   denomination   denominator   equivalent   factor   numerator

Worked examples

Exercise bank

1 Find three fractions with the same value as $\frac{3}{7}$.

$\frac{3}{7} = \frac{6}{14}$ and $\frac{9}{21}$ and $\frac{12}{28}$.

2 Write these fractions in their simplest form.

(a) $\frac{15}{25} = \frac{3}{5}$ (b) $\frac{15}{60} = \frac{3}{12} = \frac{1}{4}$ (c) $\frac{40}{60} = \frac{2}{3}$

Plenary

◉ Remember the phrase 'same value: different appearance'. $\frac{3}{5}$ has the same value as $\frac{12}{20}$ but a different appearance. Think about this phrase as you answer all the questions in the Goals.

◉ Invent new examples of your own.

◉ Discuss the decimal fraction that has the same value as the vulgar fraction $\frac{238}{1000}$.

Letts **I See Maths** Year 7

Fractions 2

Essential exercises

1 Complete the following equations.

(a) $\frac{2}{3} = \frac{}{9}$ (b) $\frac{4}{5} = \frac{}{25}$ (c) $\frac{1}{7} = \frac{}{28}$

(d) $\frac{3}{20} = \frac{}{100}$ (e) $\frac{3}{4} = \frac{}{76}$ (f) $\frac{2}{9} = \frac{}{72}$

2 Look at the list of fractions below.
Write down the pairs of fractions that have the same value but a different appearance.

(a) $\frac{3}{7}$ (b) $\frac{25}{35}$ (c) $\frac{17}{10}$ (d) $\frac{3}{4}$ (e) $\frac{5}{6}$ (f) $\frac{7}{12}$ (g) $\frac{40}{48}$

(h) $\frac{75}{100}$ (i) $\frac{2}{3}$ (j) $\frac{9}{21}$ (k) $\frac{18}{27}$ (l) $\frac{5}{7}$ (m) $\frac{170}{100}$ (n) $\frac{28}{48}$

3 Find the fractions in the list below that have the same value as $\frac{2}{5}$ but a different appearance. Write them down.

(a) $\frac{6}{9}$ (b) $\frac{50}{125}$ (c) $\frac{14}{35}$ (d) $\frac{10}{20}$ (e) $\frac{6}{15}$ (f) $\frac{22}{55}$ (g) $\frac{20}{50}$

(h) $\frac{40}{100}$ (i) $\frac{4}{10}$ (j) $\frac{12}{30}$ (k) $\frac{102}{105}$ (l) $\frac{18}{45}$ (m) $\frac{18}{40}$ (n) $\frac{8}{20}$

4 Reduce each of the following fractions to its simplest form.

(a) $\frac{6}{8}$ (b) $\frac{15}{20}$ (c) $\frac{24}{36}$ (d) $\frac{16}{64}$ (e) $\frac{9}{12}$ (f) $\frac{21}{28}$ (g) $\frac{18}{45}$

5 The vulgar fraction $\frac{13}{5}$ can be written as the mixed number $2\frac{3}{5}$. Write the following vulgar fractions as mixed numbers.

(a) $\frac{17}{5}$ (b) $\frac{23}{7}$ (c) $\frac{14}{9}$ (d) $\frac{15}{6}$ (e) $\frac{42}{20}$ (f) $\frac{35}{4}$ (g) $\frac{92}{25}$

(h) $\frac{40}{9}$ (i) $\frac{58}{8}$ (j) $\frac{320}{50}$ (k) $\frac{280}{40}$ (l) $\frac{130}{25}$ (m) $\frac{231}{100}$ (n) $\frac{450}{200}$

Number and Algebra

Letts **I See Maths Year 7**

Challenging exercises

6 Find the value of the integer x to satisfy each of the following inequalities. Explain your answers.

(a) $\frac{x}{9} < \frac{7}{x} < \frac{x}{6}$

(b) $\frac{3}{x} < \frac{x}{7} < \frac{4}{x}$

7 Find the value of the number x such that $\frac{4}{x} = \frac{x}{9}$.

8 Find three decimal fractions x such that $2\cdot3 < x < 2\cdot4$.

9 What is the biggest fraction you can make that is less than 1 and has a single digit in the numerator and the denominator?

10 Is the following statement true? $\frac{1}{3} < \frac{13}{30} < \frac{1}{2}$

Problem-solving exercises

11 In a survey of pupils in 7H, $\frac{3}{4}$ of the pupils liked football, $\frac{2}{3}$ liked tennis and $\frac{4}{5}$ liked swimming. Which activity is most popular?

12 Six cars, A, B, C, D, E and F, were tested for economy of fuel. Each car was given 42 litres of fuel. Here are the results.

Car	A	B	C	D	E	F
Distance travelled with 42 litres (in km)	581	593	611	605	584	601
Distance travelled with 1 litre (in km)	$\frac{581}{42}$					

Which was the most economic car?

Homework

(a) Write down all the fractions with the same value as $\frac{24}{16}$, where the denominator is a number between 1 and 19.

(b) Write down all the fractions less than 1, where the sum of the numerator and the denominator is equal to 11. Write these fractions in ascending order.

Fractions 3

Goals

By the end of this lesson you will be able to answer questions such as this:

👁 Complete the following equations.

(a) $\frac{7}{3} + \frac{5}{3} + \frac{1}{3} =$

(b) $\frac{9}{7} - \frac{4}{7} =$

(c) $\frac{3}{8} + \frac{6}{8} - \frac{5}{8} =$

(d) $\frac{4}{5} + \frac{2}{3} =$

(e) $\frac{4}{6} - \frac{2}{5} =$

(f) $\frac{3}{4} + \frac{1}{3} - \frac{2}{5} =$

(g) $2\frac{2}{5} + 3\frac{1}{4} =$

(h) $\frac{4}{9} + ? = \frac{13}{9}$

(i) $\frac{11}{8} - ? = \frac{3}{8}$

Starter

1 What is the denominator of each of these fractions?

(a) $\frac{11}{7}$ (b) $\frac{3}{2}$ (c) $\frac{2}{5}$ (d) $\frac{3}{4}$ (e) $\frac{17}{100}$ (f) $\frac{53}{87}$ (g) $\frac{9}{10}$

2 What is the denomination of each of the above fractions?

3 Look at each pair of fractions. Jot down the denominators of each pair.
What number has both denominators as a factor?
Write down the denomination that has this number as a denominator.

(a) $\frac{2}{3}, \frac{1}{2}$ (b) $\frac{11}{7}, \frac{4}{11}$ (c) $\frac{5}{13}, \frac{2}{3}$ (d) $\frac{2}{5}, \frac{3}{10}$

Demonstration 1

Think of fractions of denomination 'seventh'.

Think of 'sevenths'   as cards like this

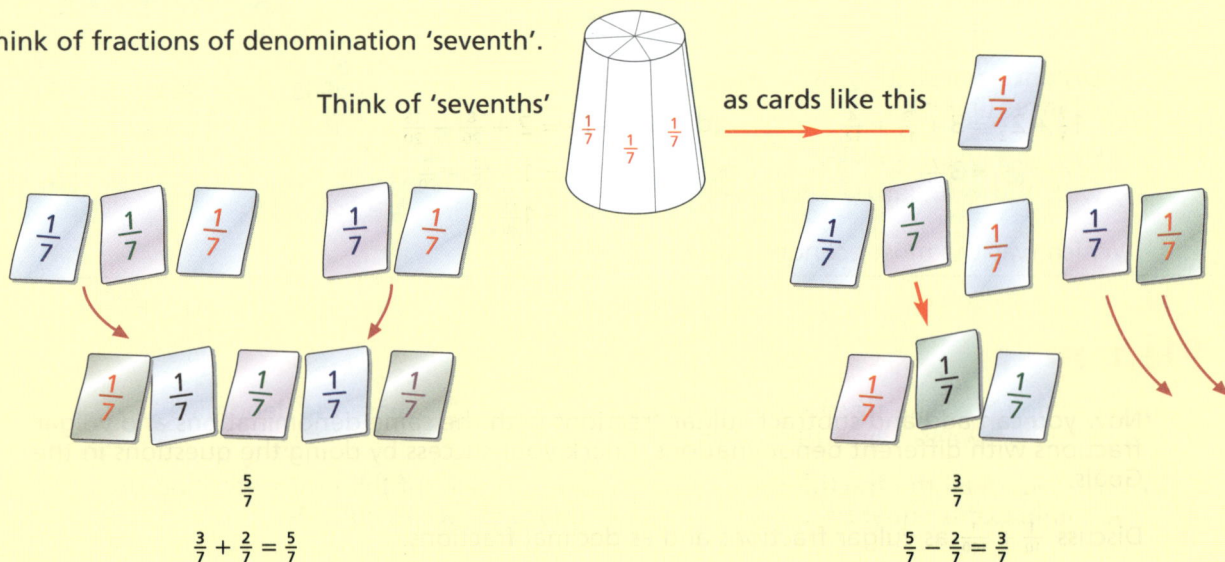

$$\frac{3}{7} + \frac{2}{7} = \frac{5}{7}$$

$$\frac{5}{7} - \frac{2}{7} = \frac{3}{7}$$

Letts **I See Maths** Year 7

Number and Algebra

Demonstration 2

$\frac{2}{3} + \frac{3}{4}$

and

and

$= \frac{8}{12} + \frac{9}{12}$

$= \frac{17}{12}$

$= 1\frac{5}{12}$

and

Worked example

Exercise bank ☞

1 Complete the following equations.

(a) $\frac{2}{5} + \frac{1}{3} = \frac{6}{15} + \frac{5}{15}$

$= \frac{11}{15}$

(b) $\frac{4}{7} - \frac{1}{2} = \frac{8}{14} - \frac{7}{14}$

$= \frac{1}{14}$

(c) $1\frac{1}{4} + 2\frac{1}{3} = 3 + \frac{3}{12} + \frac{4}{12}$

$= 3\frac{7}{12}$

(d) $3\frac{2}{5} - 1\frac{3}{4} = 2 + \frac{8}{20} - \frac{15}{20}$

$= 1 + \frac{20}{20} - \frac{7}{20}$

$= 1\frac{13}{20}$

Plenary

👁 Now you can add and subtract vulgar fractions with the same denominations and vulgar fractions with different denominations. Check your success by doing the questions in the Goals.

👁 Discuss $\frac{1}{10} + \frac{1}{100}$ as vulgar fractions and as decimal fractions.

Letts **I See Maths** Year 7

Fractions 3

Essential exercises

1 Complete the following table.

$+\frac{3}{5}$

$\frac{1}{2}$	$\frac{2}{3}$	$\frac{4}{7}$	$\frac{7}{10}$	$\frac{3}{8}$					
					$\frac{9}{10}$	$\frac{3}{4}$	$\frac{7}{8}$	$\frac{5}{6}$	$\frac{7}{9}$

$-\frac{3}{5}$

2 Complete the following equations.

(a) $\frac{4}{7} + \frac{5}{7} + \frac{2}{7} =$

(b) $\frac{7}{9} - \frac{2}{9} + \frac{4}{9} =$

(c) $\frac{9}{10} - \frac{3}{10} - \frac{2}{10} =$

(d) $\frac{4}{5} + \frac{3}{4} =$

(e

$\frac{5}{6} + \frac{2}{7} =$

(f) $\frac{7}{8} - \frac{2}{3} =$

(g) $\frac{2}{5} + \frac{1}{4} + \frac{2}{3} =$

(h) $\frac{1}{2} + \frac{3}{8} - \frac{1}{4} =$

(i) $\frac{7}{10} - \frac{1}{5} + \frac{3}{4} - \frac{1}{3} =$

3 Complete the following equations.

(a) $2\frac{4}{5} + 3\frac{2}{5} =$

(b) $5\frac{3}{7} + 6\frac{2}{7} =$

(c) $1\frac{4}{10} - \frac{6}{10} =$

(d) $1\frac{2}{3} + 3\frac{3}{4} =$

(e) $7\frac{2}{5} - 4\frac{1}{3} =$

(f) $4\frac{1}{4} - 1\frac{3}{5} =$

(g) $29\frac{14}{100} + 36\frac{23}{100} - 25\frac{21}{100} =$

(h) $2\frac{3}{87} + 5\frac{44}{87} =$

(i) $19\frac{6}{23} - 14\frac{15}{46} =$

4 Complete the grid below.

x	$\frac{1}{2}$	$\frac{4}{5}$	$\frac{3}{4}$		$\frac{7}{10}$	$\frac{33}{100}$
y	$\frac{3}{10}$	$\frac{5}{6}$		$\frac{4}{7}$	$\frac{4}{5}$	$\frac{4}{25}$
$x + y$			$\frac{17}{12}$	$\frac{15}{14}$		

5 Complete the grid below.

x	$\frac{5}{2}$	$\frac{7}{9}$	$\frac{6}{5}$		$1\frac{3}{8}$	$2\frac{1}{6}$
y	$\frac{3}{4}$	$\frac{3}{8}$		$\frac{2}{5}$	$\frac{3}{4}$	$1\frac{1}{3}$
$x - y$			$\frac{4}{10}$	$\frac{4}{15}$		

Number and Algebra

Letts I See Maths Year 7

Challenging exercises

6 Work out the value of x in each of the following equations.

(a) $\frac{3}{7} + x = \frac{16}{21}$ (b) $\frac{5}{8} - x = \frac{22}{24}$ (c) $x + \frac{3}{4} = \frac{9}{8}$

(d) $x - \frac{3}{10} = \frac{3}{10}$ (e) $1\frac{1}{4} + x = 2\frac{1}{2}$ (f) $3\frac{4}{5} - x = 1\frac{1}{10}$

7 Calculate the number in each blank box by adding the four shaded numbers surrounding it.

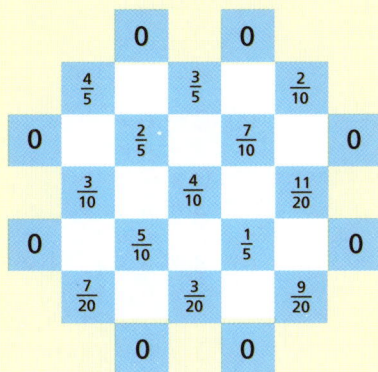

		0		0		
	$\frac{4}{5}$		$\frac{3}{5}$		$\frac{2}{10}$	
0		$\frac{2}{5}$		$\frac{7}{10}$		0
	$\frac{3}{10}$		$\frac{4}{10}$		$\frac{11}{20}$	
0		$\frac{5}{10}$		$\frac{1}{5}$		0
	$\frac{7}{20}$		$\frac{3}{20}$		$\frac{9}{20}$	
		0		0		

Problem-solving exercises

8 One week Paula spent two-fifths of her pocket money on sweets and a quarter on clothes. She saved what was left. What fraction of her pocket money did she save?

9 In a box of sweets one-sixth was brown, one-fifth was yellow and one-third was red. The rest were blue. What fraction of sweets was blue?

10 A map has different countries shaded in pink, green and blue. Two-sevenths of the map is pink and a half is green. What fraction of the map is blue?

Homework

Put the signs + or − in the blank boxes to make the equations true for both rows and columns.

$\frac{4}{5}$		$\frac{3}{10}$		$\frac{1}{5}$	=	$\frac{9}{10}$
	✕		✕		✕	
$\frac{9}{10}$		$\frac{1}{5}$		$\frac{7}{10}$	=	0
=	✕	=	✕	=	✕	=
$\frac{17}{10}$		$\frac{1}{10}$		$\frac{9}{10}$	=	$\frac{9}{10}$

Goals

By the end of this lesson you will be able to answer questions such as these:

👁 Complete the following equations.

(a) $\frac{4}{7} \times 6 =$ (b) $\frac{2}{3} \times 500 =$

👁 Look at $\frac{14}{5}$. How many $\frac{1}{5}$ can you see?

👁 Look at $\frac{14}{5}$. How many $\frac{2}{5}$ can you see?

Starter

1 Complete these equations.

(a) $3000 \times 8 =$

(b) $3 \times 400 =$

(c) $300 \times 4 =$

(d) $3 \times 9000 =$

(e) $300 \times 2000 =$

(f) $30 \times 6 =$

(g) $3 \times 9 =$

(h) $3000 \times 80 =$

(i) $3 \times 2 \times 4 =$

(j) $300 \times 20 \times 4000 =$

$$
\begin{aligned}
3 \times 0 &= 0 \\
3 \times 1 &= 3 \\
3 \times 2 &= 6 \\
3 \times 3 &= 9 \\
3 \times 4 &= 12 \\
3 \times 5 &= 15 \\
3 \times 6 &= 18 \\
3 \times 7 &= 21 \\
3 \times 8 &= 24 \\
3 \times 9 &= 27 \\
3 \times 10 &= 30
\end{aligned}
$$

Demonstration 1

Look at the 'three times' table. Say:

- three times nought equals nought
- three times one equals three
- three times two equals six
- three times three equals nine
- three times four equals twelve

$$
\begin{aligned}
3 \times 0 &= 0 \\
3 \times 1 &= 3 \\
3 \times 2 &= 6 \\
3 \times 3 &= 9 \\
3 \times 4 &= 12
\end{aligned}
$$

and know that:

- three-*fifths* times nought equals nought-*fifths*
- three-*fifths* times one equals three-*fifths*
- three-*fifths* times two equals six-*fifths*
- three-*fifths* times three equals nine-*fifths*
- three-*fifths* times four equals twelve-*fifths*

You can visualise $\frac{3}{5} \times 2 = \frac{6}{5}$ as putting $\frac{1}{5}$ $\frac{1}{5}$ $\frac{1}{5}$ on the maths table twice.

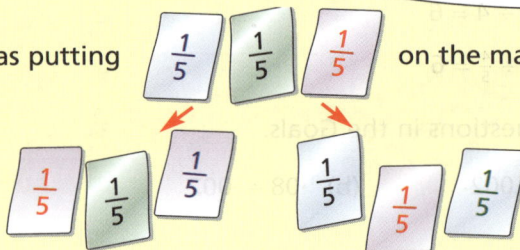

$\frac{1}{5}$ $\frac{1}{5}$ $\frac{1}{5}$ $\frac{1}{5}$ $\frac{1}{5}$ $\frac{1}{5}$

Demonstration 2

$\frac{8}{10} \div \frac{2}{10}$

Think of cups.

Think of $\frac{8}{10}$. ⟶

Look at it and wonder how many piles of $\frac{2}{10}$ you can see.

4

So: $\frac{8}{10} \div \frac{2}{10} = 4$

Think of cards.

Put $\frac{8}{10}$ on the table.

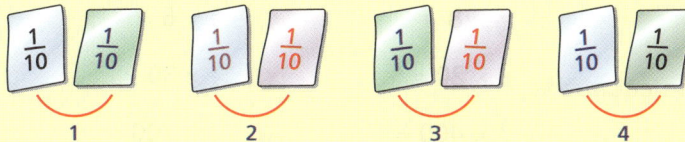

$\frac{1}{10}$ $\frac{1}{10}$	$\frac{1}{10}$ $\frac{1}{10}$	$\frac{1}{10}$ $\frac{1}{10}$	$\frac{1}{10}$ $\frac{1}{10}$
1	2	3	4

Look at it and wonder how many $\frac{2}{10}$ you can see: $\frac{8}{10} \div \frac{2}{10} = 4$

> **Key word**   quotient

Worked example

Exercise bank 👉

1 Complete the following equations.

(a) $\frac{3}{5} \times 2 = \frac{6}{5}$

(b) $\frac{3}{5} \times 12 = \frac{36}{5}$

(c) $\frac{9}{5} \div \frac{3}{5} = 3$

(d) $\frac{16}{7} \div \frac{2}{7} = 8$

Plenary

👁 Division is the inverse operation of multiplication.

$4 \times 6 = 24$ $24 \div 4 = 6$

$\frac{4}{5} \times 6 = \frac{24}{5}$ $\frac{24}{5} \div \frac{4}{5} = 6$

👁 You can now do the questions in the Goals.

👁 Discuss: (a) $\cdot008 \div \cdot002$ (b) $\cdot08 \div \cdot002$

Letts **I See Maths** Year 7

Fractions 4

Essential exercises

1 Complete the following table.

$\times 4$

$\frac{2}{5}$	$\frac{1}{3}$	$\frac{3}{4}$	$\frac{4}{7}$	$\frac{5}{8}$					
					$\frac{12}{5}$	$\frac{24}{9}$	$\frac{40}{11}$	$\frac{8}{3}$	$\frac{80}{10}$

$\div 4$

2 Use the '3 times' table to help you answer these questions on the '$\frac{3}{5}$ times' table.

(a) $\frac{3}{5} \times 5 =$ (b) $\frac{3}{5} \times 8 =$ (c) $\frac{3}{5} \times 6 =$

(d) $\frac{3}{5} \times 9 =$ (e) $\frac{3}{5} \times 20 =$ (f) $\frac{3}{5} \times 50 =$

(g) $\frac{3}{5} \times 4 =$ (h) $\frac{3}{5} \times 400 =$ (i) $\frac{3}{5} \times 700 =$

$3 \times 0 = 0$
$3 \times 1 = 3$
$3 \times 2 = 6$
$3 \times 3 = 9$
$3 \times 4 = 12$
$3 \times 5 = 15$
$3 \times 6 = 18$
$3 \times 7 = 21$
$3 \times 8 = 24$
$3 \times 9 = 27$

3 Visualise the following and answer the questions.

(a) Look at $\frac{12}{5}$. How many $\frac{1}{5}$ can you see? (b) Look at $\frac{12}{5}$. How many $\frac{2}{5}$ can you see?

(c) Look at $\frac{12}{5}$. How many $\frac{3}{5}$ can you see? (d) Look at $\frac{12}{5}$. How many $\frac{4}{5}$ can you see?

(e) Look at $\frac{12}{5}$. How many $\frac{6}{5}$ can you see? (f) Look at $\frac{12}{5}$. How many $\frac{12}{5}$ can you see?

4 Visualise the following and answer the questions.

(a) Look at $\frac{8}{7}$. How many $\frac{2}{7}$ can you see? (b) Look at $\frac{6}{11}$. How many $\frac{3}{11}$ can you see?

(c) Look at $\frac{4}{9}$. How many $\frac{4}{9}$ can you see? (d) Look at $\frac{9}{15}$. How many $\frac{3}{15}$ can you see?

(e) Look at $\frac{1}{2}$. How many $\frac{1}{2}$ can you see? (f) Look at $\frac{8}{3}$. How many $\frac{4}{3}$ can you see?

5 Complete the grid below.

x	$\frac{2}{3}$	$\frac{3}{4}$		$\frac{4}{7}$	6	
y	5		4	8		$\frac{5}{11}$
$x \times y$		$\frac{18}{4}$	$\frac{8}{5}$		$\frac{42}{9}$	$\frac{50}{11}$

6 Complete the grid below.

x	$\frac{8}{5}$	$\frac{10}{3}$	$\frac{21}{10}$		$\frac{15}{2}$	$\frac{18}{11}$
y	$\frac{2}{5}$			$\frac{3}{7}$		
$x \div y$		2	3	9	5	9

Letts I See Maths **Year 7**

Challenging exercises

7 Work out the value of x in each of the following equations.

(a) $3x = \frac{15}{6}$

(b) $5x = \frac{20}{13}$

(c) $7x = \frac{21}{5}$

(d) $x \div \frac{2}{5} = 6$

(e) $x \div \frac{3}{7} = 9$

(f) $\frac{24}{30} \div x = 3$

8 Visualise the following and answer the questions.

(a) Look at $\frac{1}{2}$. How many $\frac{1}{4}$ can you see?

(b) Look at $\frac{2}{5}$. How many $\frac{1}{10}$ can you see?

(c) Look at $\frac{4}{5}$. How many $\frac{2}{10}$ can you see?

(d) Look at $\frac{3}{4}$. How many $\frac{2}{8}$ can you see?

9 Visualise the following and answer the questions.

(a) Look at 0·3. How many $\frac{1}{10}$ can you see?

(b) Look at 0·5. How many $\frac{1}{100}$ can you see?

(c) Look at 0·24. How many $\frac{4}{100}$ can you see?

(d) Look at 0·4. How many $\frac{1}{5}$ can you see?

Problem-solving exercises

10 Robin was collecting money for his favourite charity. His friends each promised to give him £5 if he could eat six large pizzas in one week. He managed to eat four-fifths of a pizza every day for seven days. Did his friends give him the money?

11 On a school trip the teacher took twelve bottles of lemonade. She gave everyone a quarter of a bottle of lemonade each. How many quarter bottles were there altogether?

Homework

Put the signs × or ÷ in the blank boxes to make the equations true for both rows and columns.

$\frac{2}{5}$		3		$\frac{1}{5}$	=	6
$\frac{1}{5}$		$\frac{1}{5}$		5	=	5
=		=		=		=
2		15		1	=	30

Fractions, ratio, decimals and percentages

▶ Goals

By the end of this lesson you will be able to answer questions such as these:

👁 Which of the following numbers have the same value as 3 ÷ 4?

0·75, $\frac{3}{4}$,   ·7500, $1\frac{1}{3}$,   1·3,   75%,   3·4%,   3 : 4

👁 Write each of the following numbers as a percentage: 0·32, 2 ÷ 8, $\frac{3}{10}$.

▶ Starter

1 Say 'vulgar fraction', 'decimal fraction', 'ratio' or 'percentage' for each of these.

(a) $\frac{6}{7}$

(b) ·32

(c) 0·3

(d) 2 : 5

(e) $\frac{11}{8}$

(f) 19·6%

(g) 1 : 7

(h) ·07

(i) $\frac{57}{83}$

(j) $\frac{83}{57}$

(k) 7%

(l) $\frac{1}{2}$

(m) ·001

(n) $\frac{109}{76}$

▶ Demonstration 1

Compare ╱ to ╱ smaller

Using ╱ as the unit of measure, the comparison is '2 to 3'.

The ratio is 2 : 3. The vulgar fraction is $\frac{2}{3}$.

The same comparison using ╱ as the unit of measure is '4 to 6'.

The ratio is 4 : 6. The vulgar fraction is $\frac{4}{6}$.

$\frac{2}{3}$ and $\frac{4}{6}$ have the same value (because they are the same comparison)

– but they have a different appearance.

Fractions, ratio, decimals and percentages

► ## Demonstration 2

Compare ▐▐▐▐▐▐▐▐▐▐▐▐▐▐▐

to ▐▐▐▐▐▐▐▐▐▐▐▐▐▐▐▐▐▐▐▐▐▐▐▐▐▐▐▐▐▐▐▐▐▐ *smaller*

It is 35 : 100 or $\frac{35}{100}$.

When you see $\frac{35}{100}$ you can write 35%.

> **% means 'compared to 100'**

35% is 'smaller'. It is a comparison.

·35 has the same value (different appearance) as 35% because $\frac{35}{100}$ = ·35.

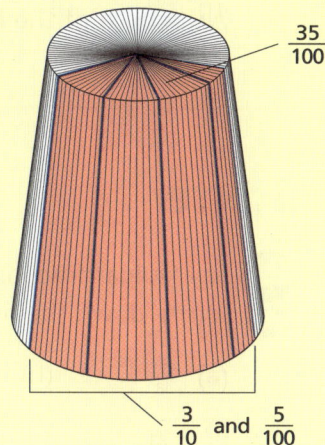

Think of cups!

$\frac{35}{100}$

$\frac{3}{10}$ and $\frac{5}{100}$

> **Key words**   comparison   percentage   ratio

► ## Worked examples

Exercise bank

1 Write a decimal fraction, a percentage and a ratio that have the same value as $\frac{2}{5}$.

0·4 and 40% and 2 : 5.

2 Write each of these numbers as a percentage.

(a) $\frac{1}{5} = \frac{20}{100} = $ **20%**

(b) $3 : 10 = \frac{30}{100} = $ **30%**

(c) $1·7 = \frac{170}{100} = $ **170%**

(d) $\frac{3}{1000} = \frac{·3}{100} = $ **·3%**

► ## Plenary

👁 Do you still remember the phrase 'same value: different appearance'? See how this phrase helps you to answer the questions in the Goals.

👁 Discuss the comparison 1 : 1000.

Number and Algebra

Fractions, ratio, decimals and percentages

Essential exercises

1 Look at the list of numbers below.

Write down the pairs of numbers that have the same value.

(a) $\frac{2}{5}$ (b) $\frac{3}{4}$ (c) $\frac{7}{10}$ (d) 0.25 (e) $4:9$ (f) $\frac{2}{7}$ (g) $\frac{1}{2}$ (h) $4 \div 3$

(i) 3% (j) 50% (k) $\frac{4}{3}$ (l) $\frac{3}{8}$ (m) $\frac{2}{100}$ (n) 0.7 (o) $\frac{15}{40}$ (p) $\frac{1}{6}$

(q) $1:6$ (r) $\frac{4}{9}$ (s) $1:50$ (t) 75% (u) $\frac{6}{21}$ (v) 25% (w) 0.4 (x) $\frac{3}{100}$

2 Write down the numbers from the list below that are equal in value to $6 \div 10$.

(a) $\frac{3}{5}$ (b) $\frac{5}{3}$ (c) 1.6 (d) 0.6 (e) $\frac{18}{30}$ (f) 60% (g) 6.1

3 Study the statements below and say whether they are true or false.

(a) $\frac{3}{4}$ has the same value as 75%.

(b) $\frac{2}{3}$ has the same value as 60%.

(c) 0.33 has the same value as $\frac{1}{3}$.

(d) $1:5$ has the same value as $\frac{1}{5}$.

4 Write each of the following numbers as a percentage.

(a) $\frac{1}{2}$ (b) 0.25 (c) $3 \div 4$ (d) $\frac{9}{10}$ (e) $\frac{18}{100}$ (f) $1:4$ (g) 0.8

(h) 1.2 (i) $\frac{15}{20}$ (j) $\frac{150}{100}$ (k) $\frac{3}{2}$ (l) $\frac{4}{5}$ (m) $\frac{2}{1000}$ (n) 0.005

5 Write the following numbers in ascending order.

$\frac{7}{10}$ 0.5 0.38 68% $1:4$ $\frac{3}{4}$

Letts **I See Maths** Year 7

Challenging exercises

6 (a) Look carefully at the sequence below. Is it true that:

$$\frac{1}{1} = 1, \quad \frac{1}{2} = \frac{2}{1+3}, \quad \frac{1}{3} = \frac{3}{1+3+5}, \quad \frac{1}{4} = \frac{4}{1+3+5+7} \ ?$$

(b) If it is true, then write $\frac{1}{5}$ and $\frac{1}{6}$ in this form and check that they are correct.

7 (a) Show that:

$$\frac{1+2+3}{1+2+3+4} = \frac{3}{5} \quad \text{and} \quad \frac{1+2+3+4}{1+2+3+4+5} = \frac{4}{6} \quad \text{and} \quad \frac{1+2+3+4+5}{1+2+3+4+5+6} = \frac{5}{7}.$$

(b) Evaluate $\frac{1+2+3+\cdots+11}{1+2+3+\cdots+12}$ and verify your result.

8 (a) Is it true that: $\frac{1}{11-2} = \frac{12}{111-3} = \frac{123}{1111-4} = \frac{1234}{11111-5} \ ?$

(b) Give two other fractions equal to the fraction in part (a).

Problem-solving exercises

9 In a survey of 50 cars, 18 were counted as white.
(a) What fraction of cars are white?
(b) Write this as a percentage.
(c) 12% of the cars are green. How many cars is this?

10 'Bicycle' appears as one-eighth of a pie chart about preferred forms of travel. What percentage of people chose to travel by bicycle?

Homework

Complete the following probability scale.

Description	Fraction	Decimal	Percentage
certain	1	1	100%
very likely			75%
likely			
equally likely	$\frac{1}{2}$		
unlikely		0·25	
very unlikely			
impossible	0	0	0

Fractions and ratio

Goals

By the end of this lesson you will be able to answer questions such as this:

👁 Complete the following equations.

(a) $\frac{3}{8}$ of **40** =   (b) 8 of **40** =   (c) $\frac{7}{10}$ of **80** =

Starter

$2 \times 5 = 10$ means | Put 2 cups on the table. Do the same lots of times. Do it 5 times. I can see 10 cups.

1 Speak accurately what each of these means:

(a) $200 \times 5 = 1000$ (b) $2 \times 500 = 1000$ (c) $200 \times 500 = 100\,000$

2 Say what multiplication you can 'see' here:

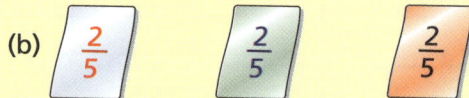

(a) (b) $\frac{2}{5}$ $\frac{2}{5}$ $\frac{2}{5}$

Demonstration 1

1 Look at these cups.

Compare the red pile to the blue pile.	smaller	$\frac{3}{5}$ or 3 : 5
Compare the blue pile to the red pile.	bigger	$\frac{5}{3}$ or 5 : 3
Compare the red pile to all the cups.	smaller	$\frac{3}{8}$ or 3 : 8
Compare all the cups to the blue pile.	bigger	$\frac{8}{5}$ or 8 : 5
Compare the red pile to the red pile.	same	$\frac{3}{3}$ or 3 : 3

2 Look at this pile of cups.

Compare red cups to blue cups.	bigger	3 : 2
Compare blue cups to all cups.	smaller	2 : 5
Compare all cups to red cups.	bigger	5 : 3

Number and Algebra

Demonstration 2

$\frac{2}{3}$ of 12 = 8 means:

Start with 12 cups on the table.

smaller

Every time you see 3 cups

replace with 2 cups.

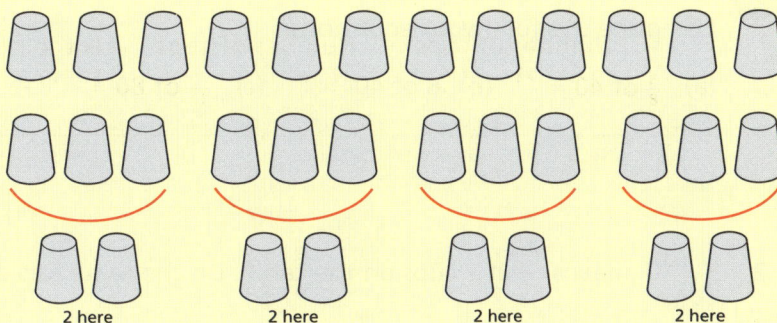

2 here   2 here   2 here   2 here

$\frac{2}{3}$ of 12 = 8 $2 \times 4 = 8$

Key words   compare   multiplication

Worked example

Exercise bank

1 Complete the following equations.

(a) $\frac{3}{5}$ of 20 = 3 × 4 = 12

(b) $\frac{3}{7}$ × 28 = 3 × 4 = 12

(c)   1 : 20 of 100 = 1 × 5 = 5

Plenary

👁   Look at the ratio 2 : 3. It has the same value as $\frac{2}{3}$ but a different appearance.

Look at the fraction $\frac{2}{3}$. This is a number. It is an object.

Look at '$\frac{2}{3}$ of …'. This is an operator. It is telling you to do a job.

Look at '$\frac{2}{3}$ × …'. This is also an operator. It does the same job as '$\frac{2}{3}$ of …'.

$\frac{2}{3}$ of 9 = 6 $\frac{2}{3}$ × 9 = 6

👁   Now do the questions in the Goals.

👁   How many 7s can you see here?

(a)   7 × 6   (b)   7 × 121   (c)   14   (d)   21   (e)   7   (f)   0

Fractions and ratio

Essential exercises

1 Complete the table.

	Number of cups in Set A	Number of cups in Set B	Is the number in A bigger, smaller or the same as the number in B?
(a)	3	6	
(b)	9	4	
(c)	7	7	
(d)	12	13	
(e)	2	15	
(f)	23	14	
(g)	104	96	
(h)	37	37	

2 Complete the table.

	Number of cups in Set A	Number of cups in Set B	Ratio of number in A : number in B	Ratio in its simplest form
(a)	5	10		
(b)	6	9		
(c)	14	7		
(d)	8	8		
(e)	12	16		
(f)	75	100		
(g)	200	100		
(h)	3	24		

3 Complete the following questions.

(a) 2 : 3 of 9　　(b) $\frac{2}{3}$ of 15　　(c) $\frac{2}{3} \times 24$　　(d) $\frac{2}{3}$ of 90

(e) 2 : 3 of 36　　(f) $\frac{2}{3}$ of 27　　(g) $\frac{2}{3} \times 66$　　(h) $\frac{2}{3} \times 42$

4 Complete the following questions.

(a) $\frac{3}{4}$ of 100　　(b) 4 : 1 of 7　　(c) $\frac{1}{2} \times 50$　　(d) $\frac{3}{5} \times 25$

(e) $\frac{1}{7}$ of 49　　(f) $\frac{2}{9} \times 18$　　(g) $\frac{3}{11} \times 33$　　(h) $\frac{5}{9}$ of 90

(i) 1 : 50 of 600　　(j) $\frac{5}{6}$ of 36　　(k) $\frac{7}{8} \times 56$　　(l) $\frac{2}{5} \times 40$

Challenging exercises

5 Write the following ratios in the form $1 : n$.

(a) 5 : 100   (b) 6 : 300   (c) 7 : 28   (d) 100 : 50   (e) 60 : 20   (f) 120 : 160

6 The scale on a map is 1 : 50 000. Work out the actual distance in kilometres if the distance on the map is:

(a) 1 cm   (b) 2.5 cm   (c) 3.75 cm   (d) 10 cm   (e) 12.5 cm   (f) 0.5 cm.

7 Complete the following table as an aid to reading pie charts.

	Angle of sector at centre of circle	Angle as fraction of the whole circle	Fraction written as a percentage
(a)	180°		
(b)	90°		
(c)	45°		
(d)	30°		
(e)	10°		
(f)	1°		
(g)	270°		
(h)	60°		

Problem-solving exercise

8 In class 7B there are 30 pupils. There are 12 boys in the class. (Write each ratio in its simplest form.)

(a) How many girls are in class 7B?   (b) What is the ratio, boys : girls?

(c) What is the ratio, boys : whole class?   (d) What is the ratio, girls : whole class?

(e) What percentage of the class is girls?

Homework

For each of the shapes below, write down:
(a) the ratio, black parts : white parts. (b) the ratio, black parts : total number of parts.

Number and Algebra

Percentages

Goals

By the end of this lesson you will be able to answer questions such as this:

👁 Complete these equations.

(a) 25% of £28 =

(b) 16% of £90 =

(c) 7% of £35 =

(d) 19% of 300 =

(e) 82% of 450 =

(f) 9% of 46 =

Starter

1 Discuss 'same value: different appearance' for each of these.

(a) $16 \times 6 = 8 \times 12$

(b) $\frac{1}{2} \times 28 = 1 \times 14$

(c) $1\,000\,000 \times 10 = 1000 \times 10\,000$

(d) $76 \times 3 \cdot 4 = 7 \cdot 6 \times 34$

(e) $\cdot 2 \times 30 = 2 \times 3$

(f) $1 \times 1 = \cdot 1 \times 10$

Demonstration 1

17% of 200 has the same value as $\frac{17}{100}$ **of 200.**

Think of 200 cups.
Replace with 'smaller'.

200

Every time you see 100 cups

100   100

replace with 17 cups.

17   17

$17 \times 2 = 34$

17 here   17 here

So: 17% of 200 = 34

Think again about 17% of 200.

It means:

Look at 200 cups. For every 100 you can see (2 of them) replace with 17.
$17 \times 2 = 34$
So: 17% of 200 = 34

Letts **I See Maths Year 7**

48

Number and Algebra

Demonstration 2

Think of 17% of 254.

It means:

Look at 254 cups. Think how many hundreds you can see.

You can see 2 and a bit of them. You can see a hundred, a hundred, and a bit of a hundred.

You can see $2\frac{54}{100}$ batches of 100.

You can see 2·54 batches of 100.

Replace every 100 with 17.
(Remember: You can see more than two of them but less than three of them.)

You can see 17 × 2·54.
17 × 2·54 = 43·18

So: 17% of 254 = 43·18

> **Key word**   percentage

Worked example

Exercise bank

1 Complete the following equations.

(a) 21% of 300
= 21 × 3
= 63

(b) 13% of 70
= 13 × ·7
= 9·1

(c) 17% of 416
= 17 × 4·16
= 70·72

Plenary

◉ 25% has the same value as $\frac{25}{100}$ has the same value as 0·25 has the same value as $\frac{1}{4}$.
See if you can do the questions in the Goals in your head. Can you explain your methods?

◉ Read and discuss:
I have 28 cups on the table.
I want to see how many hundreds I have. I have more than zero hundreds.
I have less than one hundred. I have not got a complete hundred.

Compare 28 to 100. It is smaller. It is a comparison of $\frac{28}{100}$. It is ·28.

I do not have one hundred. I have a bit of a hundred. I have a fraction of a hundred.

I have $\frac{28}{100}$. I have ·28.

Letts **I See Maths Year 7**

Percentages

Essential exercises

1 (a) Complete the following table.

Percentage	£1	£5	£10	£20	£50	£75	£100
1%							
5%							
10%							
20%							
50%							
75%							

(b)   Use the table above to answer the following questions.

(i)   15% of £20

(ii)   70% of £50

(iii) 10% of £30

(iv)   30% of £45

(v)   15% of £15

(vi)   65% of £75

(vii) 17% of £25

(viii) 37% of £60

2   **Same value: different appearance**

15% of $\frac{15}{100} \times$ $0.15 \times$ 'for every 100 replace with 15'

Complete the following questions.

(a) 15% of 200

(b) $\frac{15}{100} \times 300$

(c) 0.15×600

(d) 15% of 60

(e) $\frac{15}{100} \times 40$

(f) 0.15×70

3   Using a calculator – '9% of' means 'enter $0.09 \times$'
                        – '3.5% of' means 'enter $0.035 \times$'
                        – '17% of' means 'enter $0.17 \times$'

Use a calculator to answer the following questions.

(a) 17% of 45

(b) 29% of 84

(c) 37% of 23

(d) 46% of 95

(e) 18% of 172

(f) 62% of 424

(g) 19% of 503

(h) 6.5% of 45

(i) 17.5% of 86

Number and Algebra

Letts I See Maths **Year 7**

Challenging exercises

4 What percentage of the number 300 is represented by each of the following numbers?

(a) 30 (b) 15 (c) 150 (d) 90 (e) 210

5 Complete the phrases below.

(a) … % of 250 is 50. (b) … % of 840 is 210.
(c) … % of 100 is 73. (d) … % of 138 is 69.

6 A floor is built of 248 red tiles and 372 white tiles. What percentage of the floor is red tiles?

Problem-solving exercises

7 After deductions, Mr Jones receives a monthly income of £1800. Of this, 32% pays for his mortgage, 20% for other bills and 10% for food.

(a) What percentage is left after paying each of these?

(b) How much is this?

8 Complete the table below, which shows a survey of 3600 people.

Age range in years	Percentage of people	Number of people
10–16	12%	
17–25	18%	
26–40	24%	
41–55	21%	
56–70	19%	
Over 70	6%	
Total		

Homework

Inspect this pie chart representing preferred forms of travel. 144 people took part in the survey.

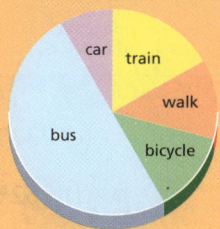

Complete the table below.

Form of travel	Fraction of total	Percentage of total	Number of people
bus			
train			
walk			
car			
bicycle			

Number and Algebra

Negative numbers 1

Goals

By the end of this lesson you will be able to answer questions such as this:

👁 Complete the following equations.

(a) $^-5 + {}^-7 =$

(b) $^-9 + {}^-21 =$

(c) $^-76 + {}^-54 =$

(d $^-999 + {}^-999 =$

(e) $^-5 + 12 =$

(f) $15 + {}^-61 =$

(g) $^-43 + 33 =$

(h) $^-999 + 999 =$

Starter

$3 + 2 - 1$ This says: ◁ Three plus two minus one.

$3 - 2 + 1$ This says: ◁ Three minus two plus one.

$^-3 + 1$ This says: ◁ Negative three plus one.

1 Read these accurately:

(a) $^-3 + 2 + {}^-1 - 2 - {}^-2 + 7 - 3$

(b) $^-200 - 347 + 2·5 - {}^-1·7$

Demonstration 1
The garden story

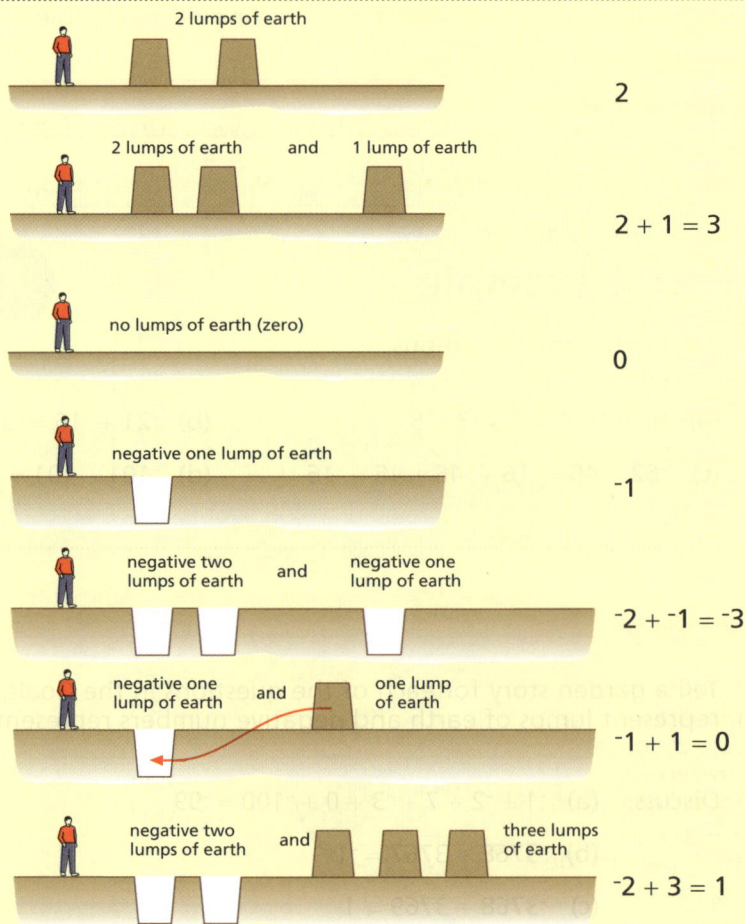

2 lumps of earth

2

2 lumps of earth   and   1 lump of earth

$2 + 1 = 3$

no lumps of earth (zero)

0

negative one lump of earth

$^-1$

negative two lumps of earth   and   negative one lump of earth

$^-2 + {}^-1 = {}^-3$

same value: different appearance

negative one lump of earth   and   one lump of earth

$^-1 + 1 = 0$

negative two lumps of earth   and   three lumps of earth

$^-2 + 3 = 1$

Number and Algebra

► Demonstration 2

Think of a lump of earth like this $\boxed{1}$ and a hole (negative one lump of earth) like this $\boxed{^-1}$

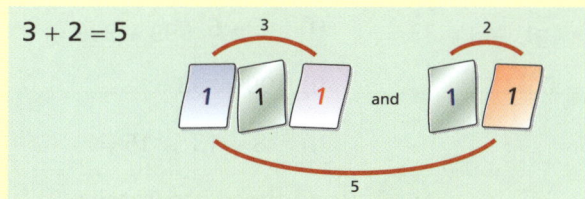

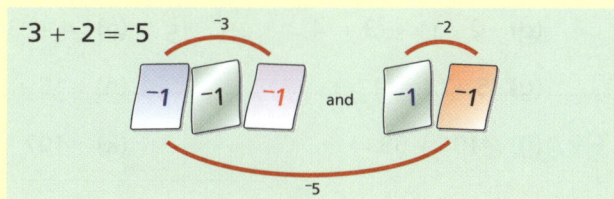

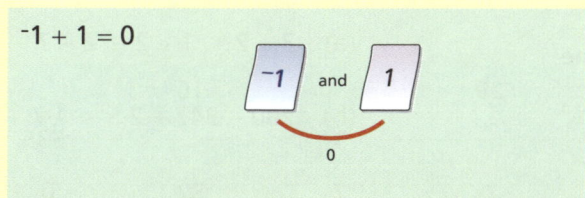

$3 + 2 = 5$

$^-3 + ^-2 = ^-5$

$^-1 + 1 = 0$

$^-4 + 3 = ^-1$

Key words   minus   negative

► Worked example

Exercise bank 👉

1 Complete these equations.

(a) $8 + ^-3 = 5 \quad 3 + ^-3 = 5$

(b) $^-21 + ^-16 = ^-37$

(c) $^-62 + 46 = ^-16 \quad ^-46 + 46 = ^-16$

(d) $^-101 + 101 = 0$

► Plenary

👁 Tell a garden story for each of the questions in the Goals. Remember that positive numbers represent lumps of earth and negative numbers represent missing lumps of earth (or holes).

👁 Discuss: (a) $^-1 + ^-2 + 7 + ^-3 + 0 + ^-100 = ^-99$

(b) $^-3768 + 3767 = ^-1$

(c) $^-3768 + 3769 = 1$

Essential exercises

1 Tell a garden story for each of the following expressions and use them to help you complete the equations.

(a) $4 + 6 =$

(b) $^-1 + {}^-2 =$

(c) $^-1 + {}^-1 + {}^-1 =$

(d) $^-2 + {}^-1 + {}^-3 + {}^-4 =$

(e) $4 + {}^-3 =$

(f) $^-6 + 6 =$

(g) $5 + {}^-8 + {}^-1 =$

(h) $^-15 + {}^-25 + 0 =$

(i) $99 + {}^-98 =$

(j) $^-101 + 99 =$

(k) $^-107 + 95 =$

(l) $^-8 + 13 + {}^-15 =$

2 Complete the grid below.

x	6	3		$^-99$		$^-16$	
y	$^-6$		45		$^-3$		$^-535$
$x + y$		$^-3$	$^-50$	2	$^-7$	$^-32$	0

3 Complete the puzzle below.

To calculate the number in each blank space add the four blue boxes around it.

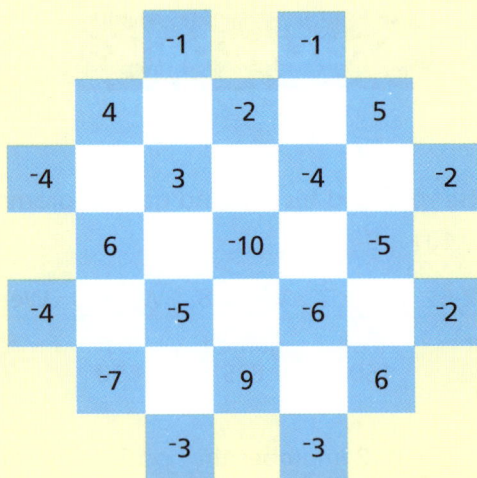

4 Complete the following equations.

(a) $^-2 + {}^-5 + 3 + 8 + 0 + {}^-6 + {}^-10 + 12 =$

(b) $^-6 + {}^-6 + {}^-6 + 5 + 5 + 5 =$

Number and Algebra

Challenging exercises

5 Complete the magic squares below.

6 Find the value of the number x such that the sum of the numbers situated along each line is the same. The number a is any number.

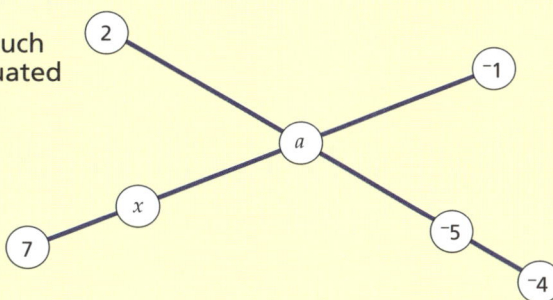

7 (a) Find the value of the number x such that the sum of the three numbers at the vertices of each triangle are the same. The numbers a and b are any numbers.

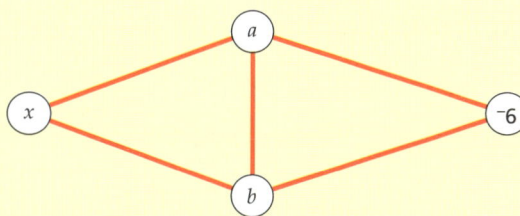

(b) How did you know how to find the value for x?

Problem-solving exercise

8 Mr Jones was on a diet. He wanted to lose 6 kg. He recorded his loss and gain in grams each week for ten weeks. Did he reach his goal?

Week 1	Week 2	Week 3	Week 4	Week 5	Week 6	Week 7	Week 8	Week 9	Week 10
lost 870	lost 800	lost 650	gained 500	lost 750	lost 940	lost 1500	gained 825	lost 650	lost 945

Homework

Write garden stories for the following equations.
(a) 4 + ⁻3 = 1
(b) ⁻2 + ⁻5 = ⁻7
(c) ⁻6 + 6 = 0
(d) ⁻50 + 49 = ⁻1
(e) 100 + ⁻99 = 1
(f) 1000 + ⁻1000 = 0

Negative numbers 2

Goals

By the end of this lesson you will be able to answer questions such as this:

👁 Find the missing number in each of the equations.

(a) $^-8 + ? = {}^-17$ (b) $^-14 + ? = {}^-30$ (c) $? + {}^-25 = {}^-100$ (d) $? + {}^-999 = {}^-1000$
(e) $^-17 + ? = 0$ (f) $15 + ? = {}^-15$ (g) $? + {}^-44 = 5$ (h) $^-81 + ? = 20$

Starter

1 What is the value of each of these?

(a) $3 + 1$ (b) $^-3 + 1$ (c) $4 + {}^-4$ (d) 0

(e) $2 + {}^-1 + 7$ (f) $^-3 + {}^-2 + {}^-100$ (g) $100 + {}^-99$ (h) $^-100 + 99$

(i) $^-9{\cdot}7 + 9{\cdot}7$ (j) $^-1 + {}^-1 + {}^-1 + {}^-1$

Demonstration 1

Visualise $2\frac{1}{2}$ as $\boxed{1}$ $\boxed{1}$ $\boxed{\frac{1}{2}}$ or

Visualise $^-2\frac{1}{2}$ as $\boxed{^-1}$ $\boxed{^-1}$ $\boxed{\frac{^-1}{2}}$ or

Visualise $^-2{\cdot}5$ as $\boxed{^-1}$ $\boxed{^-1}$ $\boxed{^-{\cdot}5}$ or

$\cdot 5 + {}^-{\cdot}5 = 0$ $\boxed{{\cdot}5}$ and $\boxed{^-{\cdot}5}$ or

$1 + {}^-\frac{1}{2} = \frac{1}{2}$ $\boxed{1}$ and $\boxed{\frac{^-1}{2}}$ or

Letts **I See Maths** Year 7

Demonstration 2

1 $3\frac{1}{2} + {}^{-}1\frac{1}{2} = 2$

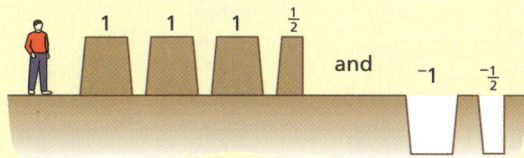

2 $^{-}100 + 98 = {}^{-}2$ There are one hundred of these $^{-}1$ and ninety-eight of these 1.

There are more holes than lumps, so there are lots of 0 and two $^{-}1$.

3 $^{-}2 + 5 + 2 + {}^{-}3 + 1 = 3$

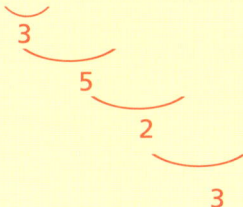

Worked examples

Exercise bank

1 Write down questions to give an answer of (a) 4 (b) $^{-}1 \cdot 8$.

(a) $^{-}2 + 6$ or $8 \cdot 1 + {}^{-}4 \cdot 1$ or $2 \cdot 9 + 1 \cdot 1$

(b) $^{-}1 + {}^{-} \cdot 8$ or $^{-}6 + 4 \cdot 2$

2 From the list below, find pairs of expressions that have the same value.

| $8 + {}^{-}2$ | $99 + {}^{-}102$ | $15 + {}^{-}9$ | $^{-}14 \cdot 2 + {}^{-}8 \cdot 9$ | $^{-}2 + {}^{-}1$ | $^{-}25 + 1 \cdot 9$ |

$8 + {}^{-}2 = 6$ and $15 + {}^{-}9 = 6$

$^{-}2 + {}^{-}1 = {}^{-}3$ and $99 + {}^{-}102 = {}^{-}3$

$^{-}25 + 1 \cdot 9 = 23 \cdot 1$ and $^{-}14 \cdot 2 + {}^{-}8 \cdot 9 = {}^{-}23 \cdot 1$

Plenary

👁 Work like a detective! Find the missing numbers in the questions in the Goals.

👁 Discuss: (a) $^{-}2 + {}^{-} \cdot 1$ (b) $^{-}2 \cdot 1$ (c) $^{-}2 + \cdot 1$ (d) $^{-}2 + \frac{1}{2}$ (e) $^{-}2 + {}^{-}\frac{1}{2}$ (f) $2 + {}^{-}\frac{1}{2}$

Negative numbers 2

Essential exercises

1 Find a set of three cards whose sum is zero. Find as many sets as you can.

1	3	⁻12	56	⁻1000	⁻10	88	⁻5
⁻31	199	4	38	5	99	500	⁻25
⁻298	⁻8	500	22	⁻19	⁻46	⁻19	⁻42

2 **Example**
'The answer is 3. What was the question?'
It could have been: $1 + 2$ or $^-4 + 7$ or $^-1 + 4$ or … .

Here are some answers. Write down three different questions for each answer.

(a) 5 (b) 0 (c) ⁻2 (d) ⁻5 (e) 100

3 **Example**
Being more imaginative! 'The answer is 3. What was the question?'
It could have been: $1\cdot5 + 1\cdot5$ or $^-2\cdot5 + 5\cdot5$ or $6\cdot6 + {}^-3\cdot6$.

Give an imaginative question for each of these answers.

(a) 1 (b) 10 (c) ⁻3 (d) ⁻7 (e) 50

4 Complete the grid below.

x	⁻22	42	19		⁻13	⁻241	⁻84	100
y	⁻35			62				
$x + y$		⁻11	⁻40	⁻4	⁻26	0	⁻42	⁻100

5 Write the equations for the following maths stories.

(a) I placed three negative ones on the maths table and then I placed ten more negative ones on the maths table. Finally I placed seven ones on the maths table. I looked at the maths table and saw negative six.

(b) I placed eight negative ones on the maths table. I placed seven more negative ones and then I placed fifteen ones on the maths table. I looked at the maths table and saw zero.

Number and Algebra

Challenging exercises

6 (a) In this figure, the sum of each line of four numbers is the same. Find all the missing numbers. What is the sum?

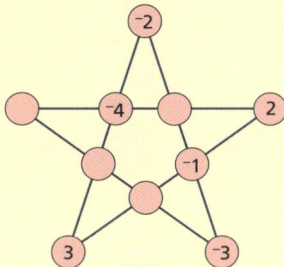

(b) Complete this figure so that the sum of the three numbers at the vertices of each small triangle is equal to ⁻5.

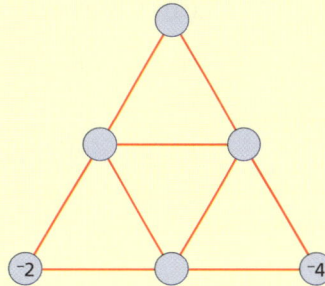

7 Complete this figure so that the sum of the three numbers at the vertices of each small triangle is equal to ⁻5.

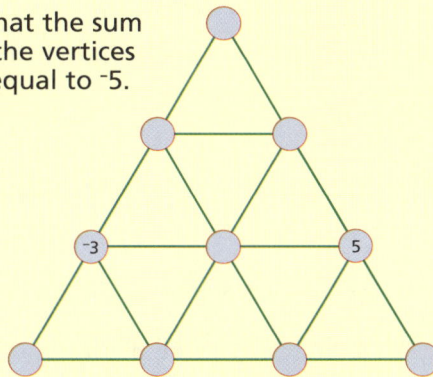

Problem-solving exercise

8 In a quiz four contestants were asked 20 questions. For every correct answer they were awarded 2 points, for every incorrect answer they were awarded ⁻1 point and for every pass they were awarded 0 points. Work out the final scores and say who won the quiz.

	Contestant A	Contestant B	Contestant C	Contestant D
Correct	11	9	8	9
Incorrect	6	2	0	1
Pass	3	9	12	10
Total points				

Homework

The answer is ⁻2. Write down five different questions that give this answer.

Negative numbers 3

Goals

By the end of this lesson you will be able to answer questions such as this:

👁 Complete the following equations.

(a) $7 - 12 =$ (b) $9 - 21 =$ (c) $64 - 74 =$ (d) $0 - 5 =$

(e) $^-5 - ^-5 =$ (f) $^-5 - ^-6 =$ (g) $^-14 - 33 =$ (h) $^-999 - ^-999 =$

Starter

1 Act out with cards.

(a) $3 + 2 = 5$ (b) $^-3 + 2 = ^-1$ (c) $3 + ^-2 = 1$

(d) $^-3 + ^-2 = ^-5$ (e) $^-1 + 1 = 0$ (f) $1 + ^-1 = 0$

(g) $^-1 + ^-2 + ^-3 + 1 + 5 = 0$

Demonstration 1

Get ready to take away.

Think about: $^-3 - ^-2 = ^-1$

Take away $^-2$.

Start by putting $^-3$ on the maths table.

-1 -1 -1

You can now see $^-1$ on the table.
So: $^-3 - ^-2 = ^-1$

-1

-1 + $+1$ = 0

$^-1 + 1 = 0$

$0 - 1 = ^-1$

$0 - ^-1 = 1$

Whenever you see zero you can visualise:

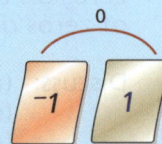

0

-1 1

Letts **I See Maths** Year 7

► Demonstration 2

Think about: $^-3 - 2 = 5$

Get ready to take away.

Start by putting $^-3$ on the maths table.

$\boxed{^-1}$ $\boxed{^-1}$ $\boxed{^-1}$

Take away 2. It is not possible to take away 2.

$\boxed{^-1}$ $\boxed{1}$ $\boxed{^-1}$ $\boxed{1}$

So, visualise zero, and another zero.

Now take away 2.

Look at the maths table.

$\boxed{^-1}$ $\boxed{^-1}$ $\boxed{^-1}$ $\boxed{^-1}$ $\boxed{^-1}$

You can now see $^-5$ on the table.

So: $^-3 - 2 = {}^-5$

► Worked example

Exercise bank ☞

1 Complete these equations.

(a) $8 - 13 = {}^-5$

(b) $8 - {}^-13 = 21$

(c) $^-8 - 13 = {}^-21$

(d) $^-8 - {}^-13 = 5$

► Plenary

👁 There is nothing on the maths table. There is zero on the maths table. There are lots of zeros on the maths table. There is still nothing on the maths table! Visualise lots and lots of zeros on the maths table to help you do the questions in the Goals.

👁 Discuss:
(a) $^-\cdot14 - {}^-\cdot1 - {}^-\cdot04 = 0$
(c) $^-\cdot14 - {}^-\cdot1 = {}^-\cdot04$
(e) $3 + {}^-2 = 1$ and $3 - 2 = 1$
  Adding $^-2$ has the same value as taking away 2.

(b) $1 + {}^-\cdot4 - {}^-\cdot1 = \cdot7$
(d) $^-\cdot14 - {}^-\cdot04 = {}^-\cdot1$
(f) $3 + 2 = 5$ and $3 - {}^-2 = 5$
  Adding 2 has the same value as taking away $^-2$.

Negative numbers 3

Essential exercises

1 Complete the equations below.

(a) -7 – -3 =   (b) -17 – -13 =   (c) -9 – -5 =   (d) -15 – -8 =

(e) -30 – -20 =   (f) -35 – -34 =   (g) -50 – -50 =   (h) -100 – -40 =

(i) -9 – -4 – -5 =   (j) -11 – -3 – -6 =   (k) -20 – -12 – -4 =   (l) -70 – -50 – -20 =

2 Complete the equations below.

(a) 7 – 8 =   (b) 3 – 6 =   (c) 7 – 10 =   (d) 5 – 9 =

(e) 3 – -4 =   (f) 5 – -9 =   (g) 6 – -4 =   (h) 10 – -3 =

(i) 14 – -20 =   (j) 3 – -7 =   (k) -6 – -9 =   (l) -12 – -15 =

3 The answer to a question is -1. The question could have been 1 – 2 or -3 – -2 or … . Here are some answers. Write down three different questions for each answer.

(a) -2   (b) 3   (c) 5   (d) -6   (e) 10

4 Complete the grid below.

x	10	15	3		-7	20		
y	20			-4			-5	-8
$x - y$		-15	6	0	1	40	10	-2

5 Complete the equations below.

(a) 3 + -4 – 6 =   (b) -2 + -5 – -3 =   (c) 9 + -5 – 7 =

(d) -2 – -2 – 2 =   (e) 0 – -4 =   (f) -1 + 3 – 2 =

Letts I See Maths Year 7

Number and Algebra

Challenging exercises

6 Work out the value of x in each of the following equations.

(a) $x + 3 = 0$

(b) $^-2 + x = 7$

(c) $x - {}^-3 = 9$

(d) $4 - x = 11$

(e) $3 - x = {}^-6$

(f) $x + 5 = {}^-6$

7 Complete the pyramid below. For each adjacent pair of numbers subtract the right-hand number from the left-hand number to make the number in the box above them.

$a - b$

a b

2

-1   -2

3   0

Problem-solving exercises

8 The daytime maximum temperature in London on 14 February 2002 was 9°C. The night-time temperature dropped to a minimum of ⁻2°C. By how many degrees did the temperature fall?

9 A hospital was built on the side of a hill. The main entrance was on the higher side of the hill. This floor was called zero in the lift. The lift went up to Floor 5 and down to Floor ⁻4. How many floors were there in the hospital?

Homework

Look up weather charts to find differences in temperatures around the world. Plan a trip around the world, stopping off at five different countries. Work out the difference in temperatures between the countries as you travel.

Factors and divisibility

Goals

By the end of this lesson you will be able to answer questions such as these:

👁 Write down all the integer factors of: 80, 12, 13, 10.

👁 Which of the following numbers are divisible by 9? 225 2709 2214 182 734

Starter

1 Look at: **375**

What is this digit?
How much is there here?

What is this digit?
How much is there here?

What is this digit?
How much is there here?

300
70
5

2 Now discuss: **37·5**

Demonstration 1

1 Multiplication pairs for the number 8

Think of cards.

$2 \times 4 = 8$ |2| |2| |2| |2|

Four twos make eight.

Visualise. 4 |2| make eight.

$4 \times 2 = 8$ |4| |4|

Two fours make eight.

2 |4| make 8.

Think of different cards.

$1 \times 8 = 8$ |1| |1| |1| |1| |1| |1| |1| |1|

Eight ones make eight.

8 |1| make eight.

$8 \times 1 = 8$ |8|

One eight makes eight.

1 |8| makes eight.

2 Factors of 8

$2 \times 4 = 8$ Think of |2| so 2 is a factor.

Think of |4| so 4 is a factor.

$1 \times 8 = 8$ Think of |1| so 1 is a factor.

Think of |8| so 8 is a factor.

Letts I See Maths Year 7

Number and Algebra

Demonstration 2

Think about: $17 \times 11 = 187$

Visualise. 17 or 11   17 $\times 11 = 187$ $17 \times$ 11 $= 187$

17 is a factor of 187.   11 is a factor of 187.

Look at: $17 \times 11 = 187$

How much is there here? **187**

Look at 187 and wonder how many 17 you can see. **11**   We say: 187 is divisible by 11

Look at 187 and wonder how many 11 you can see. **17**   We say: 187 is divisible by 17

Key words   divisible   factor   multiplication pairs

Worked examples

Exercise bank 👉

1. Write down all the multiplication pairs for 12.
$12 = 12 \times 1 = 6 \times 2 = 4 \times 3$

2. Write down all the factors of 18.
1, 2, 3, 6, 9, 18

3. Is 230 divisible by 5?
Yes because it ends in 0 or 5.

Plenary

- What is a factor? What is meant by 'divisible by'?

- Inspect the numbers in the Goals and answer the questions.

- Think about $1 \times 2 \times 3 \times 5 = 30$ to visualise 30.
Talk about the factors of thirty by talking about 'cards'.
Talk about '30 is divisible by … '.

Letts **I See Maths** Year 7

Factors and divisibility

Essential exercises

1 Write down all the multiplication pairs for the following numbers.

    (a) 8   (b) 10   (c) 20   (d) 36   (e) 100

2 Use the multiplication pairs for the following numbers to help you write down all their factors.

    (a) 15   (b) 24   (c) 30   (d) 55   (e) 75

3 '2 is a factor of 6.'   '6 is divisible by 2.'

    (a) How do you know that a number is divisible by 2?

    (b) Which of the following numbers are divisible by 2?

        (i) 56   (ii) 300   (iii) 183   (iv) 1050   (v) 2465

4 '5 is a factor of 20.'   '20 is divisible by 5.'

    (a) How do you know that a number is divisible by 5?

    (b) Which of the following numbers are divisible by 5?

        (i) 600   (ii) 75   (iii) 654   (iv) 9010   (v) 5052

    (c) Investigate rules for divisibility by 3 and 9.

5 True or false?

    (a) For a number to be divisible by 4, the last two digits are divisible by 4.

    (b) For a number to be divisible by 6, it has to be divisible by 2 and 3.

    (c) For a number to be divisible by 8, half of the number is divisible by 4.

Number and Algebra

Letts **I See Maths** Year 7

Factors and divisibility

Challenging exercises

6 True, sometimes true or never true?

'The sum of four even numbers is divisible by four.'

Explain and give reasons for your answer.

7 (a) Find at least one number with twelve factors.

(b) Which numbers, less than 100, have exactly three factors?

8 Find the highest common factors (HCF) of the following sets of numbers.

(a) { 24, 36 }　　　　　(b) { 56, 63 }　　　　　(c) { 210, 525, 735 }

Problem-solving exercises

9 Use factors to help you reduce each of the following fractions to its simplest form.

(a) $\frac{42}{66}$　　(b) $\frac{56}{70}$　　(c) $\frac{105}{120}$　　(d) $\frac{450}{630}$　　(e) $\frac{48}{64}$

10 Use factors to help you calculate these mentally.

Example　　$35 \times 12 = 35 \times 2 \times 6 = 70 \times 6 = 420$

(a) 43×20　　(b) 45×14　　(c) 75×16　　(d) 25×8

Homework

In the following diagrams, write a number in each circle so that the number in each square is the product of the two numbers on either side of it.

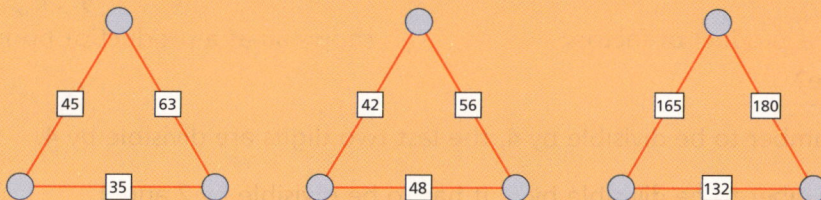

Triangle 1: 45, 63, 35
Triangle 2: 42, 56, 48
Triangle 3: 165, 180, 132

Letts **I See Maths** Year 7

Number and Algebra

67

Prime numbers

Goals

By the end of this lesson you will be able to answer questions such as these:

👁 Which numbers between 1 and 20 are prime numbers?

👁 Is 91 a prime number?

Starter

1 A number that is divisible only by 'one' and by 'itself' is called a prime number. Which of these are prime numbers?

2   3   4   5   6   7   8   9   10   11   12   13   14   15   16

Demonstration 1

1 Think about:

$$2 \times 5 \times 6 = 60$$ and $$2 \times 5 \times 2 \times 3 = 60$$

2 is a factor
5 is a factor
6 is a factor

The way these are written show

2 is a factor
5 is a factor
2 is a factor
3 is a factor

These are not all prime numbers.

These are all prime numbers.

$2 \times 5 \times 6 = 60$
shows 60 as a product of factors.

$2 \times 5 \times 2 \times 3 = 60$
shows 60 as a product of prime factors.

2 Think about: $287 = 17 \times 11$
17 is prime and 11 is prime.
$287 = 17 \times 11$ shows 287 expressed as a product of prime factors.

Letts I See Maths Year 7

Demonstration 2

1 Think of 60, and then write products with the same value.

60 is even.
One factor is 2.

60
2 × 30

30 is even.
One factor is 2.

2 × 2 × 15

15 is not even, but it is divisible by 3.   2 × 2 × 3 × 5

Same value:
different appearance

All these factors are prime.

60 = 2 × 2 × 3 × 5

2 The only way to express 5 as a product of factors is 5 = 1 × 5.
There are no proper factors of 5, so 5 is a prime number.

Key words   prime   prime factor

Worked examples

Exercise bank

1 Write these numbers as products of their prime factors.
(a) $21 = 7 \times 3$
(b) $84 = 2 \times 42 = 2 \times 2 \times 21 = 2 \times 2 \times 3 \times 7$

2 Are the following prime numbers?
(a) $52 = 2 \times 2 \times 13$ – not a prime number.
(b) $23 = 1 \times 23$ – is a prime number.

Plenary

👁 What is a prime number? How can you check if a number is prime? Inspect the numbers in the Goals and check whether they are prime numbers.

👁 Look at $1 \times 2 \times 2 \times 2 \times 5 \times 6 \times 7 \times 10 = 16\,800$.
Discuss the factors of 16 800.

👁 Put x on the maths table 6 times. We have $6x$.

Look at $6x$.

Visualise x ⟶ x is a factor.   Visualise 6 ⟶ 6 is a factor.

Prime numbers

Essential exercises

1 Find all the prime numbers between 1 and 100 using the sieve of Eratosthenes.

Instructions

On a 1–100 number square:

(i) Shade number 1.

(ii) Leave 2 blank and shade multiples of 2.

(iii) Leave 3 blank and shade multiples of 3.

(iv) Leave 5 blank and shade multiples of 5.

(v) Leave 7 blank and shade multiples of 7.

(vi) Leave 11 blank and shade multiples of 11.

(vii) Leave 13 blank and shade multiples of 13.

1	2	3	4	5	6	7	8	9	10
11	12	13	14	15	16	17	18	19	20
21	22	23	24	25	26	27	28	29	30
31	32	33	34	35	36	37	38	39	40
41	42	43	44	45	46	47	48	49	50
51	52	53	54	55	56	57	58	59	60
61	62	63	64	65	66	67	68	69	70
71	72	73	74	75	76	77	78	79	80
81	82	83	84	85	86	87	88	89	90
91	92	93	94	95	96	97	98	99	100

2 (a) Why is the number 1 *not* a prime number?

(b) Write down a prime number that is also even.

(c) Why is the number 87 *not* a prime number?

(d) How many prime numbers are there between 1 and 100?

(e) What is the next prime number after 97?

3 Work out which of the following numbers are prime numbers. Show your working.

(a) 101　　　(b) 197　　　(c) 201　　　(d) 221

4 Every number can be written as a product of prime numbers.

Example　　$12 = 2 \times 2 \times 3$

Write the following numbers as products of prime numbers.

(a) 18　　　(b) 25　　　(c) 36　　　(d) 50
(e) 72　　　(f) 81　　　(g) 44　　　(h) 100

Number and Algebra

Challenging exercises

5 Divide by prime numbers, in ascending order, to find all the prime factors of a non-prime number. Then write the number as a product of its prime factors.

> **Example**
>
> Write 12 as the product of its prime factors.
>
> $$2)\overline{12}$$
> $$2)\ \overline{\ 6}$$
> $$\overline{\ \ \ \ 3}$$
>
> $12 = 2 \times 2 \times 3$

(a) 420 (b) 1050 (c) 330 (d) 260

6 Write numbers as products of their prime factors to help work out the highest common factor (HCF).

> **Example**
>
> Find the HCF of 60 and 120.
>
> $60 = 2 \times 2 \times 3 \times 5$
> $210 = 2 \times 3 \times 5 \times 7$
> $HCF = 2 \times 3 \times 5 = 30$

(a) 252 and 330 (b) 525 and 455 (c) 392 and 504 (d) 1001 and 78

Problem-solving exercises

7 What is the probability of getting a prime number when you roll a die?

8 What is the probability of getting a prime number when you randomly select a number from the 1–100 number square?

9 Amy's birthday is in July. What is the probability that the date of her birthday is a prime number?

Homework

Roll a die 100 times and keep a tally of the results.

(a) How many times did you get a prime number?
(b) Write this as a fraction of the total 100.
(c) Is the result what you expected?

Order of operations

Goals

By the end of this lesson you will be able to answer questions such as this:

👁 Calculate the expressions below.

(a) $2 + 3 \times 4$ (b) $5 \times 4 + 3 \times 2$ (c) $(4 + 7) \times 2$
(d) $5 + 40 \div 8$ (e) $17 - 48 \div 4$ (f) $90 \div 10 - 5$

Starter

1 Think of the factors of 6. Think of the factors of 15. Which factors are common to both 6 and 15?

2 Think of the factors of 5. Think of the factors of 7. Which factors are common to both 5 and 7?

3 What are the common factors of 9 and 12?

Demonstration 1

Think about:
$2 \times 3 + 1 = 7$

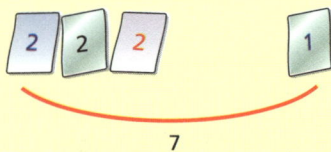

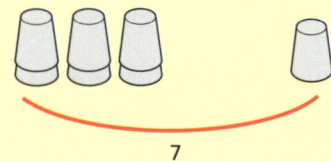

$2 \times 3 + 1 \times 4 = 10$

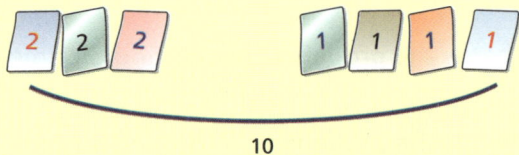

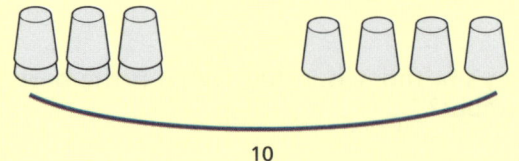

6 and 1 is 7.

6 and 4 is 10.

Think about:
$2 \times 3 - 1 = 5$
6 take away 1 is 5.

$2 \times 3 - 1 \times 4 = 2$
6 take away 4 is 2.

Discuss: $2 \times 3 + ^-1 = 5$

Number and Algebra

Letts I See Maths Year 7

Demonstration 2

1 Think about:
$2 \times (3 + 1) = 8$

Put 2 cups on the maths table.
Do the same thing lots of times.
Do it 3 times and also once more.
Do it 4 times altogether.
That makes 8.

Think about:
$(2 \times 3 - 1) \times 4 = 20$

Put 2 cups on the maths table.
Do the same thing 3 times.
Think 6. Take away 1 cup. That is 5 cups.
Do the same thing (5 cups) lots of times.
Do it 4 times.
That makes 20.

2 When you see $8 \div 2$ think of it as the vulgar fraction $\frac{8}{2}$. (The value of this is 4.)
Now think about: $10 + 8 \div 2 = 14$
Put 10 on the table; get ready to get some more. How much more? $\frac{8}{2}$ That is 4.
So: $10 + 8 \div 2 = 14$

Worked examples

Exercise bank 👉

1 Calculate these expressions.
(a) $4 + 6 \times 3 = 4 + 18 = 22$
(b) $31 - 2 \times 7 + 3 = 31 - 14 + 3 = 20$
(c) $4 \times 5 - 6 \div 3 = 20 - 2 = 18$

2 Insert brackets in the expressions to make the equations correct.
(a) $8 + 3 \times 6 + 1 = 29$ $8 + 3 \times (6 + 1) = 29$
(b) $10 + 2 \times 8 - 2 = 72$ $(10 + 2) \times (8 - 2) = 72$

Plenary

👁 Discuss the convention: 'In the absence of brackets, multiplication and division have precedence over addition and subtraction.'

👁 Inspect the questions in the Goals. Check for brackets first then answer the questions.

👁 Discuss: $3 + 2 = 5$

$\frac{12}{4} + \frac{6}{3} = 5$

$12 \div 4 + 6 \div 3 = 5$

👁 Discuss: $12 \div 2 + 1 = 7$ and $12 \div (2 + 1) = 4$

👁 Look at $7x$.   Think of $\boxed{x}$ ⟶ x is a factor. What is the other factor? **7**

Think of $\boxed{7}$ ⟶   7 is a factor. What is the other factor? x

Order of operations

Essential exercises

1 Calculate the expressions below.

(a) $6 \times 7 + 8$ (b) $3 + 7 \times 5$ (c) $25 + 4 \times 3$

(d) $46 - 6 \times 7$ (e) $9 \times 6 - 50$ (f) $3 \times 2 + 5 \times 4$

(g) $6 \times 5 + 4 \times 3$ (h) $4 \times 7 - 2 \times 5$ (i) $2 \times 7 + 3 - 4 \times 2$

2 One of the expressions below is equal to 30. Which one?

(a) $1 + 2 + 3 \times 4 \times 5$ (b) $1 + 2 \times 3 + 4 \times 5$

(c) $1 + 2 \times 3 \times 4 + 5$ (d) $1 \times 2 + 3 + 4 \times 5$

3 Put brackets in the expressions below to make the equations correct.

(a) $2 + 5 \times 4 = 28$ (b) $14 - 8 \times 2 = 12$ (c) $3 \times 2 + 4 + 5 \times 5 = 51$

(d) $6 + 3 \times 8 - 7 = 9$ (e) $1 + 7 \times 9 - 2 = 70$ (f) $1 + 7 \times 9 - 2 = 56$

(g) $1 + 7 \times 9 - 2 = 62$ (h) $7 + 3 \times 2{\cdot}5 = 25$ (i) $19 - 9 \times 3{\cdot}4 = 34$

4 Calculate the expressions below.

(a) $3 + 40 \div 8$ (b) $15 - 63 \div 9$ (c) $9 \div 3 + 50 \div 10$

(d) $96 \div 2 - 12 \div 4$ (e) $66 \div 6 - 4 \times 2$ (f) $56 \div 7 - 14 \div 2 - 1$

5 Four fours

Calculate the expressions below.

(a) $4 + 4 + 4 + 4$ (b) $4 - 4 + 4 \times 4$ (c) $4 + 4 \div 4 + 4$

(d) $44 + 4 \div 4$ (e) $(4 + 4) \div (4 + 4)$ (f) $4 \div 4 + 4 \div 4$

(g) Can you make all the whole numbers from 0 to 30 using four fours, the four operations $+$, $-$, $\times$ and $\div$, and brackets?

Number and Algebra

Challenging exercises

6 The teacher asked her class to work out $3 \times 5 + 3 - 2 \times 7 + 1$ and received the following responses.

(a) $3 \times 5 + 3 - 2 \times 7 + 1 = 3 \times 8 - 14 + 1 = 24 - 14 + 1 = 11$
(b) $3 \times 5 + 3 - 2 \times 7 + 1 = 3 \times 8 - 2 \times 8 = 24 - 16 = 8$
(c) $3 \times 5 + 3 - 2 \times 7 + 1 = 15 + 3 - 14 + 1 = 5$
(d) $3 \times 5 + 3 - 2 \times 7 + 1 = 15 + 1 \times 7 + 1 = 15 + 7 + 1 = 23$
(e) $3 \times 5 + 3 - 2 \times 7 + 1 = 15 + 1 \times 8 = 15 + 8 = 23$

Which one of these is correct, without inserting brackets?
Insert brackets in the rest to make them correct.

7 Calculate the expressions below when $p = 5 \cdot 4$.

(a) $p \times 5 + 3 \times p$ (b) $p + 5 \times 3 + p$

8 Calculate the expressions below when $q = 5 \cdot 1$.

(a) $3 + q \times q + 3$ (b) $3 \times q + q \times 3$
(c) $6 + (q + 5) \times 4 + q$ (d) $7 \times (q + 4) + 8 \times q$

Problem-solving exercises

9 I took a taxi for 20 minutes. This is how the tariff was calculated: a fixed charge of £3 plus 40 pence for every two minutes. How much did I pay?

10 For my party I ordered 30 sausage rolls, 25 chicken legs, 45 sandwiches and 50 cream cakes. Work out how much I paid if:

sausage rolls cost 75 pence for five
chicken legs cost 60 pence each
sandwiches cost £6 for five
cream cakes cost 89 pence for two.

Homework

Find the numbers.

Rules You *must* use the numbers 1, 2, 3 and 4 (but not more than once in any calculation).
You can use any of the operations +, −, ×, ÷.
You can use brackets.
Can you make all the numbers from 0 to 30?

Examples $1 + 2 + 3 + 4 = 10$ $12 + 3 - 4 = 11$ $1 \times 23 - 4 = 19$

Goals

By the end of this lesson you will be able to answer questions such as this:

👁 Work out the value of the number x in each of the following equations.

(a) $x + 6 = 12$ (b) $7 - x = 3$ (c) $x - 99 = 1$

(d) $\frac{2}{5} + x = \frac{9}{5}$ (e) $x + \frac{4}{9} = \frac{15}{9}$ (f) $x - \frac{2}{11} = \frac{7}{11}$

Starter

1 Act out these with cards.

(a) $x + 2$ (b) $2x + 3$ (c) $5 + 2x$ (d) $3x + 2$ (e) $3x + {}^{-}2$

2 Discuss: $11 - 2 = 11 + {}^{-}2$

Demonstration 1

Think about the equation $x + 8 = 12$.

Put x on the maths table. Get ready to get some more. **8**

How much is on the maths table? **12**

You know it is 12 because the equation says so.

Visualise the maths table.

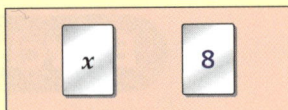

How much is there here? **12**

So $x = 4$

Look again at the equation $x + 8 = 12$.

So $x = 4$ because $4 + 8 = 12$. ———————— How much is there here? **12**

Look at the equation $5 - x = 3$.

So $x = 2$ because $5 - 2 = 3$. ———————— How much is there here? **3**

Demonstration 2

1 Think of $x + 8 = 12$.

Put $x + 8$ on this maths table.

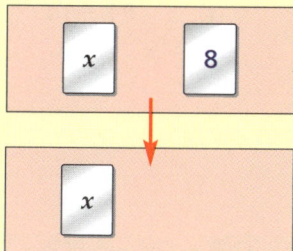

Use the twin maths tables.

Put 12 on this maths table.

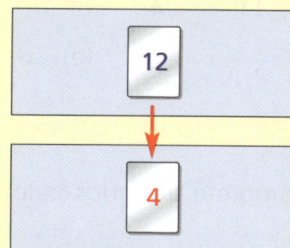

| x | 8 |

x

Get ready to take some away.
Take away 8.

$12 - 8 = 4$
$x = 4$

| 12 |

| 4 |

2 Think of $x - 2 = 11$.

Put $x - 2$ on this maths table.

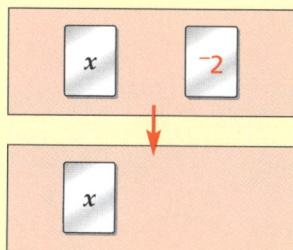

| x | $^-2$ |

x

Get ready to take some away.
Take away $^-$2.

$11 - {}^-2 = 13$
$x = 13$

Put 11 on this maths table.

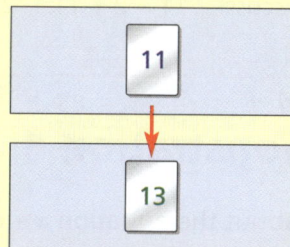

| 11 |

| 13 |

Key word   value

Worked example

Exercise bank 👉

1 Work out the value of x in each of the following equations.

(a) $x + 14 = 35$
$21 + 14 = 35$
$x = 21$

(b) $16 - x = 9$
$16 - 7 = 9$
$x = 7$

(c) $x + \frac{2}{3} = \frac{8}{3}$
$\frac{6}{3} + \frac{2}{3} = \frac{8}{3}$
$x = \frac{6}{3} = 2$

(d) $x - \frac{10}{23} = \frac{17}{23}$
$\frac{27}{23} - \frac{10}{23} = \frac{17}{23}$
$x = \frac{27}{23}$

Plenary

👁 When we are asked to solve an equation like this: $x + 4 = 7$, we have to work out the value of the number x. Solve the equations in the Goals.

👁 Discuss: $x - 1·3 = 2·4$

Letts **I See Maths Year 7**

Essential exercises

1 Work out the value of x in each of the following equations.

(a) $x + 8 = 19$ (b) $23 + x = 42$ (c) $x - 5 = 7$

(d) $11 - x = 4$ (e) $35 + x = 77$ (f) $x - 81 = 14$

2 Complete the grids below.

(a)

x	56	34		320	473			2007
y	27		47			199	86	
$x + y$		95	83	560	631	304	720	4504

(b)

x	85	77			201	364		
y	42		23	17			99	176
$x - y$		35	44	87	105	246	201	238

(c)

x	10·5		4·1				39·7	80·3
y	8·5	5·7		6·6	18·4	96·4		
$x + y$		10·9	7·4	13·2	20·0	100·5	56·4	94·2

(d)

x	9·6	10·9	19·6			17·5	15·0	
y	4·3			6·4	3·2			42·3
$x - y$		7·5	7·2	11·5	9·8	10·0	3·6	21·4

3 Work out the value of x in each of the following equations.

(a) $\frac{3}{5} + x = \frac{7}{5}$ (b) $x + \frac{5}{7} = \frac{16}{7}$ (c) $\frac{7}{9} - x = \frac{2}{9}$

(d) $x - \frac{5}{8} = \frac{4}{8}$ (e) $\frac{29}{87} + x = \frac{37}{87}$ (f) $x - \frac{2}{91} = \frac{8}{91}$

Challenging exercises

4 Write down the equation for each of the following sentences and work out the value of x.

(a) Start with a number x. Add 7·3. The answer is 9·2.
(b) Start with a number x. Subtract negative four. The answer is 5.
(c) Start with the number negative four. Subtract a number x. The answer is negative six.
(d) Start with the number 9·5. Add the number x. The answer is 11·7.

5 $x + y = 10$. Write down all the pairs of positive whole numbers (x, y) to satisfy this equation.

6 $x + y = 5$. Write down ten different pairs of numbers (x, y) to satisfy this equation. (x and y can be whole numbers, fractions, decimal fractions or negative numbers.)

Problem-solving exercises

7 (a) The perimeter of a rectangle is 18 cm. One side is 3 cm. What is the length of the other side?

(b) The perimeter of a pentagon is 34 cm. The sum of four sides is 29 cm. What is the length of the fifth side?

8 Work out the lengths of the lines labelled x cm.

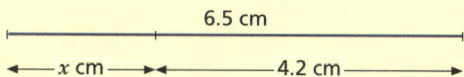

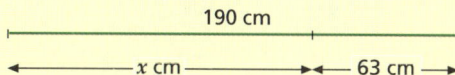

Homework

Calculate the perimeter of each of these shapes.

(a)

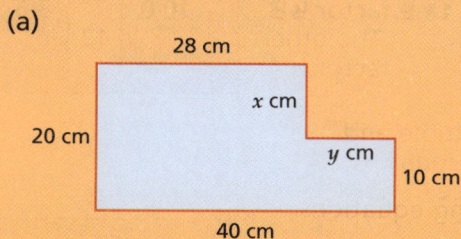

(b)

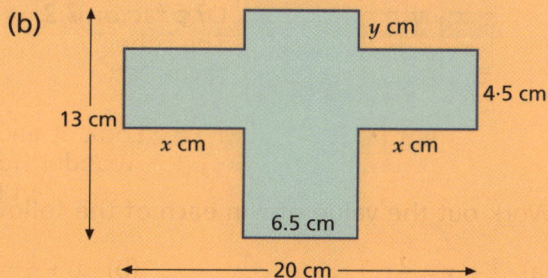

Number and Algebra

Algebra 2

▶ Goals

By the end of this lesson you will be able to answer questions such as this:

👁 Work out the value of the number x in each of the following equations.

(a) $5x = 25$ (b) $9x = 63$ (c) $7x = 28$

(d) $\frac{x}{3} = 4$ (e) $\frac{x}{9} = 1$ (f) $\frac{x}{2} = 102$

▶ Starter

1 Act out with cards: $x \times 3 = 3x$. Imagine $3 \times x = 3x$.

Discuss: x is a factor. The other factor is 3.
3 is a factor. The other factor is x.

2 Act out with cards: $x \times 7 = 7x$. Imagine $7 \times x = 7x$.

Discuss: x is a factor. The other factor is 7.
7 is a factor. The other factor is x.

▶ Demonstration 1

Think about $3x = 12$.

Use the twin maths tables.

Put $3x$ on this table.

Put 12 on this table.

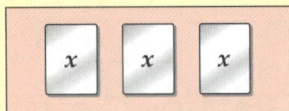

One factor is 3.
The other factor is x.

One factor is 3.
The other factor is 4.

Look at each table and wonder how many 3s can I see?

$x = 4$

Number and Algebra

Letts **I See Maths Year 7**

Demonstration 2

Think about $\frac{x}{4} = 3$.

Put $\frac{x}{4}$ on this table.

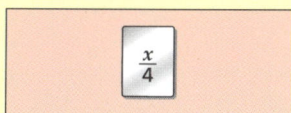

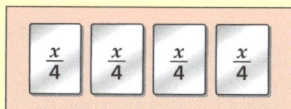

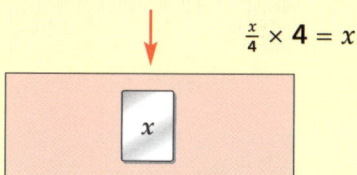

Use the twin maths tables.

Put 3 on this table.

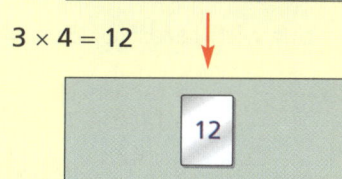

$$\frac{x}{4}$$

$$3$$

Do the same thing lots of times: do it 4 times altogether.

| $\frac{x}{4}$ | $\frac{x}{4}$ | $\frac{x}{4}$ | $\frac{x}{4}$ |

| 3 | 3 | 3 | 3 |

$$\frac{x}{4} \times 4 = x$$

$$3 \times 4 = 12$$

$$x$$

$$12$$

$$x = 12$$

| **Key word** | factor |

Worked example

Exercise bank 👉

1. Work out the value of x in each of the following equations.

(a) $3x = 15$
   $3x = 3 \times 5$
   $x = 5$

(b) $4x = 28$
   $4x = 4 \times 7$
   $x = 7$

(c) $\frac{x}{2} = 10$
   $2 \times \frac{x}{2} = 2 \times 10$
   $x = 20$

(d) $\frac{x}{7} = 9$
   $7 \times \frac{x}{7} = 7 \times 9$
   $x = 63$

Plenary

👁 Discuss the difference between the equations in Algebra 1 and on these pages.

👁 Solve the equations in the Goals.

👁 Discuss: $\frac{x}{7} = 5 \cdot 1$

Letts **I See Maths** Year 7

Algebra 2

Essential exercises

1 Work out the value of x in each of the following equations.

(a) $2x = 12$ (b) $3x = 33$ (c) $9x = 45$

(d) $6x = 42$ (e) $8x = 56$ (f) $7x = 49$

2 Complete the grids below.

(a)

x	8	6		5		9		11
y	7		3		7		6	
$x \times y$		24	27	40	49	81	48	55

(b)

x	42	45		44	54			36
y	6		8			7	14	
$x \div y$		5	4	4	9	7	0	6

(c)

x	70	30	500			90	23	
y	9			250	8			700
$x \times y$		120	1500	1000	640	810	460	0

(d)

x	100	400	66			6400	150	2800
y	25			30	7	80	30	70
$x \div y$		80	6	40	50			

3 Work out the value of x in each of the following equations.

(a) $\frac{x}{4} = 3$ (b) $\frac{x}{20} = 5$ (c) $\frac{x}{2} = 7$

(d) $\frac{x}{3} = 3$ (e) $\frac{x}{4} = 8$ (f) $\frac{x}{25} = 1$

Number and Algebra

Letts **I See Maths** Year 7

Challenging exercises

4 Write down the equations for the following sentences and work out the value of x for each equation.

(a) Start with a number x. Multiply by 9. The answer is 13·5.

(b) Start with a number x. Multiply by 10. The answer is 1·7.

(c) Start with a number x. Multiply by 8. The answer is 9·6.

(d) Start with a number x. Multiply by 5. The answer is 17·5.

5 $xy = 24$. Write down all the pairs of positive whole numbers (x, y) to satisfy this equation.

6 $xy = 4$. Write down ten different pairs of numbers (x, y) to satisfy this equation. (x and y can be whole numbers, fractions, decimal fractions or negative numbers.)

Problem-solving exercise

7 (a) The area of a rectangle is 63 cm². One side is 9 cm. What is the length of the other side?

(b) The area of a triangle is 65 cm². The base is 10 cm. What is the length of its perpendicular height?

(c) The volume of a cuboid is 120 cm³. Its base area is 10 cm². What is its height?

Homework

Work out the answers to the following questions.

(a) The cost of 12 pizzas is £54. What is the cost of one pizza?

(b) David saves the same amount of money each week. After eighteen weeks he has saved £112·50. How much did he save each week?

(c) Carole cycled from home to school and back every day for three weeks. Altogether she cycled 105 miles. How far is it from Carole's home to her school?

Goals

By the end of this lesson you will be able to answer questions such as this:

👁 Work out the value of the number x in each of the following equations.

(a) $4x + 3 = 11$ (b) $5x - 3 = 17$ (c) $4x + 5 = 15$

(d) $50 - 6x = 14$ (e) $\frac{x}{6} + 7 = 9$ (f) $\frac{x}{9} - 7 = 20$

Starter

1 Discuss the following:

(a) Think of 18. One factor is 3. The other factor is 6.

(b) Think of 19. One factor is 3. The other factor is $\frac{19}{3}$.

(c) Think of 17·2. One factor is 3. The other factor is $\frac{17·2}{3}$.

(d) $5 - 2 = 5 + {}^-2$

Demonstration 1

Think about $3x + 7 = 19$.

Put $3x + 7$ on this table.

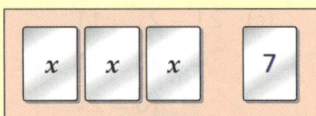

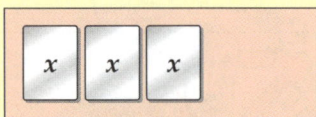

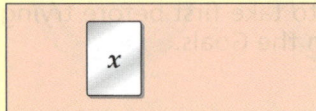

Use the twin maths tables.

Put 19 on this table.

| x | x | x | 7 |

| 19 |

Get ready to take away.
Take away 7.

| x | x | x |

| 12 |

One factor is 3.
The other factor is x.

One factor is 3.
The other factor is 4.

| x |

| 4 |

$x = 4$

Number and Algebra

Demonstration 2

Think about $9x - 2 = 16$.

Put $9x - 2$ on this table.

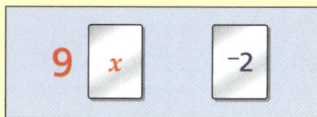

$9x - 2$ has the same value as $9x + {}^-2$.

Put 16 on this table.

| 9 | x | $^-2$ |

| 16 |

Get ready to take away. Take away $^-2$.

| 9 | x |

One factor is 9. The other factor is x.

One factor is 9. The other factor is 2.

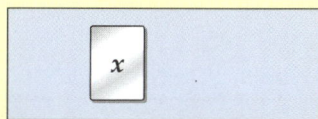

| 18 |

| x |

| 2 |

$x = 2$

Worked example

Exercise bank

1 Work out the value of x in each of these equations.

(a) $2x + 5 = 11$
$2x = 6$
$2x = 2 \times 3$
$x = 3$

(b) $4x - 7 = 5$
$4x = 12$
$4x = 4 \times 3$
$x = 3$

(c) $21 - 2x = 11$
$21 = 11 + 2x$
$10 = 2x$
$x = 5$

Plenary

◉ In Algebra 1 and Algebra 2 you solved single-step problems (easy!). Now you can solve multi-step problems. Always stop and think about which step to take first before trying to solve the problem. Now work in pairs to solve the equations in the Goals.

◉ Discuss: $5x - 2 = 7 \cdot 6$

Letts I See Maths Year 7

Essential exercises

1 Work out the value of x in each of the following equations.

(a) $2x + 9 = 19$ (b) $3x + 10 = 37$

(c) $7x - 6 = 50$ (d) $9x - 12 = 60$

(e) $4x + 25 = 105$ (f) $6x - 20 = 160$

2 Complete the grid below.

x	3	2		5		10		15
y	4		6		3		0	
$2x$								
$x + 3y$		17	25			28		
$4x - y$			11	25			36	59

3 Complete the grid below.

x	4		1		8		0	
y	5	8		6		4		9
$5y$								
$4y - x$			27	22				25
$3x + y$		17			27	34	7	

4 Work out the value of x in each of the following equations.

(a) $19 + 5x = 64$ (b) $23 + 8x = 55$

(c) $71 + 7x = 148$ (d) $204 + 9x = 285$

(e) $68 + 4x = 132$ (f) $3 \cdot 5 + 7x = 21$

5 Work out the value of x in each of the following equations.

(a) $\frac{x}{2} + 5 = 9$ (b) $\frac{x}{5} + 3 = 10$

(c) $\frac{x}{8} - 2 = 1$ (d) $\frac{x}{7} - 4 = 3$

(e) $\frac{x}{10} + 8 = 17$ (f) $\frac{x}{15} - 4 = 0$

Challenging exercises

6 Write down the equations for the following sentences and work out the value of x for each equation.

(a) Start with a number x. Multiply by 4. Add 30. The answer is 86.

(b) Start with a number x. Divide it by 4. Subtract 2. The answer is 1·2.

(c) Start with a number x. Multiply it by 6. Take it away from 20. The answer is 5·6.

(d) Start with a number x. Multiply it by 9. Take away 15. The answer is ⁻60.

7 $3x + 2y = 12$. Write down all the pairs of positive whole numbers (x, y) to satisfy this equation.

8 $2x + 5y = 10$. Write down ten different pairs of numbers (x, y) to satisfy this equation. (x and y can be whole numbers, fractions, decimal fractions or negative numbers.)

Problem-solving exercises

9 The monthly bill for a mobile phone is calculated by adding a £25 standing charge to the number of minutes of calls times 24 pence. Work out the bills for the following minutes of calls.

(a) 72 minutes   (b) 250 minutes   (c) 96 minutes

10 After deductions Mr Jones earns £19 500 per year. How much is left after paying £90 a week in rent for 52 weeks?

11 Mrs Roberts has a daily paper that costs 35p. Her two children both have a magazine once a week. One magazine costs £1·00, the other £1·40. If the delivery charge is £4·75 a month, how much did she pay the newsagent altogether in February?

Homework

Rule: 'Multiply by 3 and add 1.'

Begin with the number 1. Apply the rule. Apply the rule to the answer. How many times do you have to apply the rule to get to the first number greater than 1000?

Formulae

Goals

By the end of this lesson you will be able to answer questions such as these:

👁 Write down the formulae for working out the volume and surface area of a cuboid with length l, width w and height h.

👁 The formula for working out the number of white tiles needed for a particular tiling pattern is $2n + 6$, where n is the number of red tiles. How many white tiles are needed when $n = 4$?

Starter

1 If $m = 2 \times 7 + 2 \times 5$, what is the value of m?

2 If $m = \frac{10}{2}$, what is the value of m?

3 If $m = 1\cdot5 \times 4$, what is the value of m?

4 If $m = 0 \times 7 + 0 \times 5$, what is the value of m?

Demonstration 1

1 **Explicit information**
$P = 2l + 2w$
l and w are measured in cm, P is measured in cm.

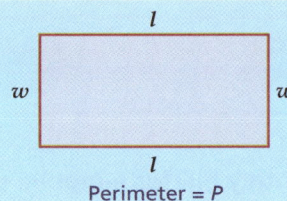

Perimeter = P

Implicit information
Put l cm on the maths table. Do the same thing twice altogether.
Get ready to get some more. Put w cm on the maths table. Do the same thing twice altogether.
I can see $2l + 2w$ cm.
So: $P = 2l + 2w$

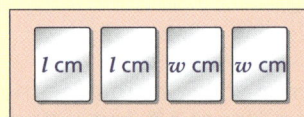

l cm l cm w cm w cm

2 **Explicit information**
$A = lw$
l and w are measured in cm, A is measured in cm².

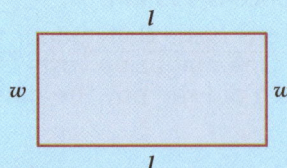

Implicit information
Put w cm² on the maths table. Do the same thing lots of times. Do it l times.
I can see w cm² $\times l$.
I can see lw cm².
So: $A = lw$

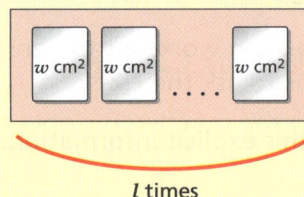

w cm² w cm²   . . . . w cm²

l times

Letts I See Maths Year 7

Demonstration 2

3 **Explicit information**
The area of a rectangle is $A = lw$.

Implicit information
When l cm = 6 cm and w cm = 1 cm,
the area of this rectangle is 6 cm².

6 cm

1 cm

When l cm = 5 cm and w cm = $1\frac{1}{2}$ cm,
the area of this rectangle is $7\frac{1}{2}$ cm².

$1\frac{1}{2}$ cm

5 cm

4 **Explicit information**
Speed (s) and distance (d) and
time (t) are connected by the formula $s = \dfrac{d}{t}$.

Implicit information
If d is measured in kilometres and t in hours, speed is measured in km/hour.
If d is measured in metres and t in seconds, speed is measured in metres/second.
If s is measured in miles per day, distance is measured in miles and time is measured in days.

Key words   explicit   formula   implicit

Worked examples

Exercise bank

1 Find the area and perimeter of a rectangle with width 3 cm and length 8 cm.
$P = 2l \times 2w$ $A = lw$
P cm = $2 \times 3 + 2 \times 8 = 22$ cm A cm² = $3 \times 8 = 24$ cm²

2 Write down the formula for the distance (d km) travelled by a car in t hours at a speed of
s km/hour. Use this formula to find the distance travelled in 3 hours at 45 km/h.
$s = \dfrac{d}{t}$, so: $d = s \times t = 3 \times 45 = 135$
The distance is 135 km.

Plenary

- Look for a number pattern. Make a conjecture. Test it. Work out a formula for the pattern. Test it again. Use the formula to solve problems.

- See if you can work out the answers to the questions in the Goals. Make up your own questions to ask the class.

- Discuss this explicit information: $d = \dfrac{m}{v}$, where m is measured in grams and v is measured in cm³.

Letts I See Maths Year 7

Number and Algebra

Formulae

Essential exercises

1 **Area and perimeter of a rectangle**

Let the length of the rectangle be l.
Let the width of the rectangle be w.

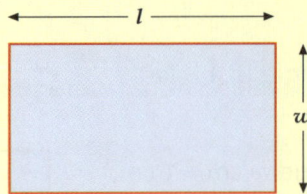

(a) Write down the formula for the perimeter P of the rectangle.

(b) Write down the formula for the area A of the rectangle.

(c) Calculate the perimeters and areas of the following rectangles.

    (i) l cm = 8 cm, w cm = 6 m   (ii) l cm = 14 cm, w cm = 5 cm

    (iii) l cm = 24 cm, w cm= 18 cm   (iv) l cm = 16 cm, w cm= 2·5 cm

2 **Area of a triangle**

Let the base of the triangle be b.
Let the perpendicular height of the triangle be h.

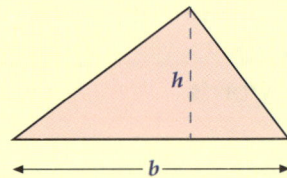

(a) Write down the formula for the area A of the triangle.

(b) Calculate the areas of the following triangles.

    (i) b cm = 12 cm, h = 7 cm   (ii) b cm = 20 cm, h cm = 15 cm

    (iii) b cm = 6 cm, h = 4·5 cm   (iv) b cm = 7 cm, h cm = 7 cm

3 **Surface area and volume of a cuboid**

Let the length of the cuboid be l.
Let the width of the cuboid be w.
Let the height of the cuboid be h.

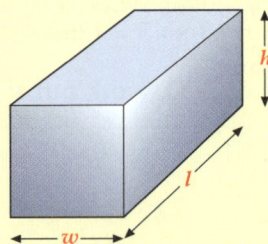

(a) Write down the formula for the surface area SA of the cuboid.

(b) Write down the formula for the volume V of the cuboid.

(c) Calculate the surface areas and volumes of the following cuboids.

    (i) w cm = 3 cm, l cm = 4 cm, h cm = 5 cm   (ii) w cm = 10 cm, l cm = 20 cm, h cm = 10 cm

    (iii) w cm = 6 cm, l cm = 8 cm, h cm = 7 cm   (iv) w cm = 2·5 cm, l cm = 10 cm, h cm = 16 cm

Number and Algebra

Letts **I See Maths** Year 7

Challenging exercises

4 When a vehicle is travelling at an average speed (s m.p.h.) over a distance (d miles) for a time (t hours) then:

$$d = st \qquad \text{(distance = speed} \times \text{time)}$$

Calculate the missing numbers in the table below.

s	50	63	65			55		450
t	3	4		$2\frac{1}{2}$	$1\frac{1}{4}$		$4\frac{1}{2}$	$6\frac{1}{2}$
d			325	150	35	275	1350	

5 Calculate the expression $3t + 4u$ when:

(a) $t = 2$, $u = 4$ (b) $t = 0$, $u = 7$

(c) $t = 1$, $u = 9$ (d) $t = 25$, $u = 42$

(e) $t = 0.5$, $u = 1.5$ (f) $t = 1.2$, $u = 2.3$.

Problem-solving exercise

6 A timber yard has a formula to work out the cost of a length of wood.

Let the fixed charge per length of wood be £x.
Let the cost per 10 cm of wood be £y.
Let the number of 10 cm be n.
Total cost = £$(x + ny)$

(a) If x is 2 and $y = 0.40$, work out the total cost for the following lengths.
  (i) 240 cm (ii) 4 m (iii) 6·2 m

(b) If x is 5 and $y = 0.50$, work out the total cost for the following lengths.
  (i) 160 cm (ii) 90 cm (iii) 2·80 m

Homework

A recipe for roasting beef says to cook any joint weighing over 1 kg for 20 minutes plus 40 minutes per kilogram.

(a) Write a formula for this recipe.

(b) Work out the cooking times for the following joints of beef.
  (i) 2 kg (ii) 1·5 kg (iii) 2·25 kg

Number and Algebra

Approximations

Goals

By the end of this lesson you will be able to answer questions such as this:

👁 Use rounding to find approximate answers to the following calculations.

(a) 5932×3099

(b) $5 \cdot 67 \times 7 \cdot 81$

(c) 29% of 187

(d) $4 \cdot 2 + 6 \cdot 1 \times 8 \cdot 9$

(e) $68 \times (52 + 49)$

(f) $5 \cdot 7 \times 8 \cdot 2 + 7 \cdot 4 \times 3 \cdot 8$

Starter

1 Think about 2·7 cups. Is the value of this closer to 2 cups or to 3 cups?

2 Think about 2·3 cards.  Is the value of this closer to 2 or to 3?

3 What is the closest whole number to each of these?

(a) 9·6

(b) 2·1

(c) 3·01

(d) 2·96

(e) 4728·2

Demonstration 1

Think of 28.  Which is the closer value?

Round 28 to the nearest '10'. **30**

Think of 2·8.  Round 2·8 to the nearest whole number. **3**

Letts **I See Maths Year 7**

Number and Algebra

► Demonstration 2

Some calculations are too hard to do mentally, but we can get an approximate idea of the answer by 'rounding'.

1 Think about 3097 × 183.

$$3000 \times 200 \qquad \text{3 thousand times 2 hundred is 6 thousand hundreds.}$$

So: $3097 \times 183 \approx 6\,000\,00$

You could round it to 3100 × 180 but that still looks hard!

2 Think about 2·19 × 5·6.

$$2 \times 6$$

So: $2\cdot19 \times 5\cdot6 \approx 12$

3 Think about 3·9 × 5·2 + 2·3 × 4·1.

$$4 \times 5 + 2 \times 4$$

So: $3\cdot9 \times 5\cdot2 + 2\cdot3 \times 4\cdot1 \approx 28$

Key words   approximate   rounding

► Worked examples

Exercise bank

1 Round these numbers to (i) the nearest 10 and (ii) the nearest 100.

(a) 127
  (i) 130   (ii) 100

(b) 468
  (i) 470   (ii) 500

2 Use rounding to find approximate answers to the following calculations.

(a) $27 \times 12 \approx 30 \times 10$
  $= 300$

(b) $4102 \times 99 \approx 4000 \times 100$
  $= 4\,000\,00$

(c) $2\cdot8 + \dfrac{2\cdot1 \times 3\cdot2}{0\cdot9 \times 1\cdot8} \approx 3 + \dfrac{2 \times 3}{1 \times 2}$
  $= 3 + 3 = 6$

► Plenary

👁 Discuss different ways of rounding numbers to help you get approximate answers to calculations. Use rounding to answer the questions in the Goals.

👁 Discuss: $1 \div \frac{1}{3} = 3$ and $1 \times \frac{1}{3} = \frac{1}{3}$

Letts **I See Maths Year 7**

Number and Algebra

Approximations

Essential exercises

1 Use rounding to find approximate answers to the following calculations.

(a) 3721×12

(b) $1 \cdot 87 \times 2 \cdot 63$

(c) $9641 - 5737$

(d) $6825 \div 73$

(e) 19% of 78

(f) $3 \cdot 22 + 0 \cdot 85$

(g) $5928 \div 29$

(h) 5683×989

(i) 24% of 88

2 Use rounding to find approximate answers to the following calculations.

(a) $2 \cdot 3 + 3 \cdot 1 \times 4 \cdot 7$

(b) $5 \cdot 2 \times 2 \cdot 7 + 6 \cdot 4 \times 8 \cdot 3$

(c) $(4 \cdot 7 + 3 \cdot 2) \times 6 \cdot 1$

(d) $9 \cdot 2 - 4 \cdot 3 \times 1 \cdot 9$

(e) $76 \times (23 + 39) + 48$

(f) $19 - 68 \div 6 \cdot 9$

(g) $57 + 18\%$ of 79

(h) $2 \cdot 9 \times 2 \cdot 9 \times 2 \cdot 9$

(i) $4 \cdot 6 + 5 \cdot 4 \times 3 \cdot 14$

3 Use a calculator to work out the answers to the following calculations.

(a) $77 - 5 \times 15$

(b) $37 \times 19 + 42 \times 14$

(c) $8 \cdot 2 + 4 \times \frac{3}{5}$

(d) $\frac{65 \times 24}{22 \times 15}$

(e) $3 \cdot 6 + \frac{52 \times 7 \cdot 2}{4 \cdot 8 \times 13}$

(f) $364 \div \frac{2}{7}$

(g) $43 + 6 \times 17 \times 99$

(h) $45 + 17\%$ of $\cdot 350$

(i) $144 \div \left(15 - \frac{4 \times 12}{16}\right)$

4 Without using a calculator, insert the signs < (less than), > (greater than) or = (equal to) in the following statements to make them correct.

(a) 329×46 [_____] 329

(b) $401 \times 0 \cdot 89$ [_____] 401

(c) 96×13 [_____] 24×52

(d) $\frac{7}{5} \times \frac{3}{5}$ [_____] $\frac{7}{5}$

(e) $630 \div 9$ [_____] 630

(f) $421 \div 0 \cdot 3$ [_____] 421

(g) $1 \div \frac{1}{2}$ [_____] 1

(h) $1 \times \frac{1}{2}$ [_____] 1

Letts I See Maths **Year 7**

Number and Algebra

Challenging exercises

5 Use rounding to find approximate answers to the following calculations.

(a) $8 \cdot 7^2$ (b) $4 \cdot 2 + 3 \cdot 9^2$ (c) $\sqrt{48}$

(d) $3 \cdot 2^3$ (e) $\sqrt{77}$ (f) $\sqrt[4]{15.8}$

6 In the questions below, use a calculator to help you calculate:

(i) $p - q - r - s$ (ii) $p - q - (r - s)$ (iii) $p - (q - r - s)$ (iv) $p - (q - (r - s))$

when

(a) $p = ^-1,$ $q = 1,$ $r = 3,$ $s = ^-2,$

(b) $p = ^-3,$ $q = ^-7,$ $r = ^-1,$ $s = ^-4,$

(c) $p = 4 \cdot 2,$ $q = 0,$ $r = ^-5 \cdot 2,$ $s = 6 \cdot 5,$

(d) $p = 3 \cdot 7,$ $q = ^-6 \cdot 2,$ $r = ^-4 \cdot 5,$ $s = 8 \cdot 3.$

7 Let p and q be any real number.
Is it always, sometimes or never true that $pq > p$?

Problem-solving exercise

8 Use rounding to find approximate answers to the following calculations.

(a) Work out the area of a rectangle with length 19 cm and width 42 cm.

(b) Work out the area of a triangle with base 9·5 cm and perpendicular height 7·8 cm.

(c) Work out the volume of a cuboid with length 4·9 cm, width 2·3 cm and height 5·8 cm.

Homework

A game for two or more players
Player A: Enter a number between 0 and 10 in your calculator.
Player B: Multiply Player A's number by a number to try to make the answer 100.

Players take it in turns to multiply until the calculator reads 100 exactly or 100 with some figures after the decimal point. The first player to reach this number is the winner.

▶ Goals

By the end of this lesson you will be able to answer questions such as these:

👁 Generate the next five consecutive terms of the following number sequences:

The first term is one. The term-to-term rule is 'add four'.
The first term is two. The term-to-term rule is 'add five and multiply by two'.

👁 The position-to-term rule is $4n - 3$. Generate the first three terms.

▶ Starter

1 Look at these lists of numbers. Point to each number and say:
(i) its value (ii) its position in the list.

(a) 4   7   3 $\frac{1}{2}$ 2 – 1   4   ⁻1

(b)

(c) nth number

▶ Demonstration 1

This is a list of numbers: 5   1·7   2   ⁻1   3   217   6

There is implicit information here. You know there is not a rule for calculating the next number.

This is the first number.
There are seven numbers in the list.

This is a sequence of numbers: 3   7   11   15   19   23   27

There is implicit information here. You know there is a rule for calculating the next number (even if you do not know the rule).

This is the first term.

One way of describing the rule is to state the relationship between consecutive terms. This is called the 'term-to-term rule'.

Talk about:
In the number sequence above the first number is 3. The term-to-term rule is 'add 4'.

Number and Algebra

Demonstration 2

This is a number sequence.

3	7	11	15	19	23	27
1st term	2nd term	3rd term	4th term	5th term	6th term	7th term

The position-to-term rule is:

nth term $= 4n - 1$

The value of the nth term is related to its position.

Think about the 5th term (in other words, term number 5). Its value is 19.

$4n - 1 = ?$
$4 \times 5 - 1 = 19$

Key words   consecutive   list   position-to-term   rule
sequence   term   term-to-term

Worked examples

Exercise bank

1 The term-to-term rule for a sequence is 'multiply by 2 and add 1'.
   The first term is 4. Find the next three consecutive terms.

   2nd term $= 2 \times 4 + 1 = 9$, 3rd term $= 2 \times 9 + 1 = 19$, 4th term $= 2 \times 19 + 1 = 39$

2 The position-to-term rule for a sequence is $3n - 2$.
   Find the 2nd and the 10th terms.

   2nd term $= 3 \times 2 - 2 = 4$
   10th term $= 3 \times 10 - 2 = 28$

Plenary

👁 What is the meaning of the word 'consecutive'?
    What is the meaning of the word 'sequence'?
    Go back and do the questions in the Goals.

👁 Talk about this:

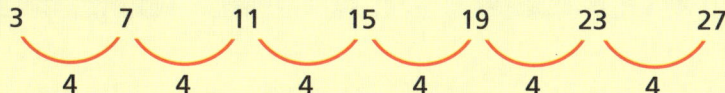

3   7   11   15   19   23   27
   4   4   4   4   4   4

nth term $= 4n - 1$

Letts **I See Maths** Year 7

Number and Algebra

Number sequences

Essential exercises

1 Generate the next ten consecutive terms of the following number sequences.

	1st term	Term-to-term rule
(a)	1	Add 3
(b)	10	Subtract 2
(c)	2	Multiply by 2
(d)	600	Divide by 2

	1st term	Term-to-term rule
(e)	0·5	Add 1·5
(f)	-4	Add 0·5
(g)	-2	Multiply by 3
(h)	0	Subtract -1

2 Generate the next five consecutive terms of the following number sequences.

	1st term	Term-to-term rule
(a)	1	Multiply by 2 and add 3
(b)	1	Add 3 and multiply by 2
(c)	$\frac{1}{2}$	Multiply by 2 and take away 4
(d)	1	Add 1, then add 2, then add 3, then …
(e)	25	Multiply by 4 and add 25

3 Generate the next three consecutive terms of the following number sequences using the position-to-term rule given.

	Position-to-term rule	Sequence
(a)	$2n + 1$	3, 5, 7, …
(b)	$3n - 2$	1, 4, 7, …
(c)	n^2	1, 4, 9, …
(d)	$\frac{n(n + 1)}{2}$	1, 3, 6, …

4 The numbers in the sequence in question 3(d) are called the 'triangular numbers'. What do you notice when you add consecutive terms of this sequence?

Challenging exercises

5 An arithmetic sequence is generated by starting with a number a, then adding a constant number d to the previous term.

> **Example** If $a = 5$ and $d = 2$, the sequence is 5, 7, 9, ...

Generate the following arithmetic sequences.

(a) $a = 2$, $d = 4$ (b) $a = 7$, $d = {}^-2$ (c) $a = 1$, $d = 0\cdot5$

6 The nth term of a sequence is $\frac{n(n+1)}{2} - 1$.

Write down the:
(a) 3rd term (b) 5th term (c) 10th term (d) 200th term.

7 (a) Find the sum of the first ten consecutive whole numbers.
(b) Find the sum of the first one hundred consecutive whole numbers.
(c) Find the sum of the first n consecutive whole numbers.

Problem-solving exercises

8 **Growing matchstick squares**

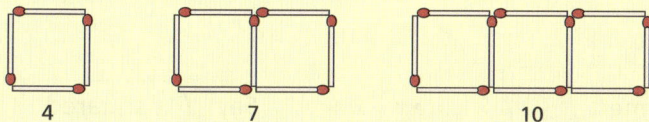

4   7   10

(a) How many matchsticks do you need to make five squares?

(b) How many matchsticks do you need to make ten squares?

(c) How many matchsticks do you need to make n squares?

(d) Explain how you achieved your answer to (c).

9 A chess board is made out of an eight-by-eight square. How many squares can you see?

Homework

You have packets of 1p, 2p and 3p stamps. In how many ways can you make the amounts 1p, 2p, 3p, 4p, 5p, 6p, ...?

> **Example** I can make 1p in one way, 2p in two ways (2p or 1p + 1p), 3p in three ways (3p, 1p + 1p + 1p, 1p + 2p) and so on.

Integers, powers and roots

► Goals

By the end of this lesson you will be able to answer questions such as these:

- 👁 What is six squared?
- 👁 What are the square roots of eighty-one?
- 👁 What is negative three squared?
- 👁 What is four point three squared?
- 👁 What are the square roots of one hundred and sixty-nine?

► Starter

1 Talk about each of these, using the words: 'digit', 'value', 'integer'.

(a) 5   (b) 27   (c) 5·4   (d) ·381

2 Talk about putting these cards on the maths table lots of times.

(a) 3 × 4   (b) 3 × 3   (c) 3 × $2·7$ (d) $2·7$ × 2.7

(e) x × 6   (f) x × x (g) y × x (h) y × y

► Demonstration 1

1 Put x on the maths table x times: x × $x = xx = x^2$ Say: (x squared)

Put $3·5$ on the maths table 3·5 times: $3·5 \times 3·5 = 3·5^2$ Say: (3·5 squared)

2 $$2·1 \times 2·1 = 2·1^2 = 4·41$$

What is the value of this?
4·41

What is the value of this?
4·41

What is the value of this?
4·41

They all have the same value (but a different appearance).

Look at 4·41. What number multiplied by itself gives the value 4·41?
2·1

When we want to ask this question about 4·41 we write $\sqrt{4·41}$ and say:

the square root of 4·41 is 2·1

Letts I See Maths Year 7

Demonstration 2

Think about:

$$\sqrt{xy} = \sqrt{x}\sqrt{y}$$

$$\sqrt{100} = \sqrt{4 \times 25} = \sqrt{4}\sqrt{25} = 2 \times 5 = 10$$

These are factors of 100.

$$\sqrt{10} = \sqrt{2 \times 5} = \sqrt{2}\sqrt{5}$$

$$\sqrt{400} = \sqrt{4 \times 100} = \sqrt{4}\sqrt{100} = 2 \times 10 = 20$$

One name for numbers like $\sqrt{2}$, $\sqrt{x}$ and $\sqrt{2 \cdot 7}$ is surds.

Talk about:

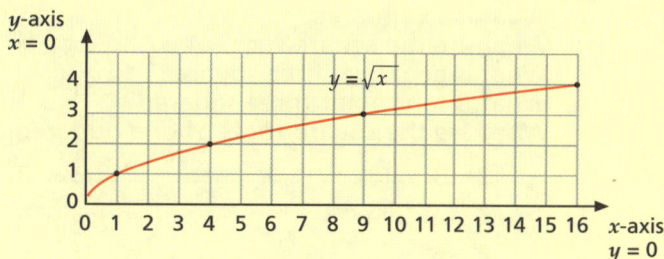

Key words   square   square root   surd

Worked examples

Exercise bank

1. Work out the following squares.

   (a) $14^2 = 14 \times 14 = 196$

   (b) $1 \cdot 4^2 = 1 \cdot 4 \times 1 \cdot 4 = 1 \cdot 96 = 2 \cdot 0$ (to 1 d.p.)

2. Use factors to find the square roots.

   (a) $\sqrt{441} = \sqrt{49 \times 9} = \sqrt{49} \times \sqrt{9} = 7 \times 3 = 21$

   (b) $\sqrt{484} = \sqrt{121 \times 4} = \sqrt{121} \times \sqrt{4} = 11 \times 2 = 22$

Plenary

👁 What is a square number?
What is the square root of a number?
See if you can answer the questions in the Goals.

👁 Think about: Put $\sqrt{2}$ on the maths table 5 times. $\sqrt{2} \times 5 = 5\sqrt{2}$

👁 Think about: Put $\sqrt{2}$ on the maths table $\sqrt{2}$ times. $\sqrt{2} \times \sqrt{2} = 2$

👁 Think about: Put $\sqrt{x}$ on the maths table m times. $\sqrt{x} \times m = m\sqrt{x}$

Number and Algebra

Integers, powers and roots

Essential exercises

1 Complete the table below.

0×0	$= 0^2$	$= 0$	0×0	$= 0^2$	$= 0$	$\sqrt{0}$	$=$	0
1×1	$= 1^2$	$= 1$	$^-1 \times ^-1$	$= (^-1)^2$	$= 1$	$\sqrt{1}$	$=$	1 or $^-1$
2×2	$=$	$=$	$^-2 \times ^-2$	$=$	$=$	$\sqrt{4}$	$=$	2 or $^-2$
3×3	$=$	$=$	$^-3 \times ^-3$	$=$	$=$		$=$	
4×4	$=$	$=$	$^-4 \times ^-4$	$=$	$=$		$=$	
5×5	$=$	$=$	$^-5 \times ^-5$	$=$	$=$		$=$	
6×6	$=$	$=$	$^-6 \times ^-6$	$=$	$=$		$=$	
7×7	$=$	$=$	$^-7 \times ^-7$	$=$	$=$		$=$	
8×8	$=$	$=$	$^-8 \times ^-8$	$=$	$=$		$=$	
9×9	$=$	$=$	$^-9 \times ^-9$	$=$	$=$		$=$	
10×10	$=$	$=$	$^-10 \times ^-10$	$=$	$=$		$=$	

2 Use a calculator to work out the following and write your answers to one decimal place.

(a) $3 \cdot 2^2$

(b) $5 \cdot 8^2$

(c) $\sqrt{40}$

(d) 23^2

(e) $\sqrt{56}$

(f) $(^-4 \cdot 5)^2$

(g) $\sqrt{92}$

(h) $\sqrt{212}$

(i) 83^2

3 Use factors to help you with the following questions.

Example $\sqrt{225} = \sqrt{25 \times 9} = \sqrt{25}\sqrt{9} = 5 \times 3 = 15$

(a) $\sqrt{1600}$

(b) $\sqrt{324}$

(c) $\sqrt{900}$

(d) $\sqrt{196}$

(e) $\sqrt{729}$

(f) $\sqrt{2304}$

4 Can every square number up to 12×12 be expressed as the sum of two prime numbers?

Example $36 = 5 + 31$

Challenging exercises

5 **Powers**

> **Examples**
>
> $2 \times 2 \times 2 = 2^3 = 8$ $\qquad$ $5 \times 5 \times 5 \times 5 = 5^4 = 625$ $\qquad$ $^-2 \times {^-2} \times {^-2} \times {^-2} \times {^-2} = (^-2)^5 = {^-32}$

Work out the following.

(a) 3^3 $\qquad$ (b) 4^5 $\qquad$ (c) 10^6

(d) $(^-3)^3$ $\qquad$ (e) $(0.2)^3$ $\qquad$ (f) $(^-2)^8$

(g) $\left(\frac{1}{10}\right)^4$ $\qquad$ (h) $(^-1)^{13}$ $\qquad$ (i) $(^-1)^{24}$

6 $\sqrt{20}$ can be written as $\sqrt{4 \times 5} = \sqrt{4}\sqrt{5} = 2\sqrt{5}$.

Find similar ways of simplifying the following expressions.

(a) $\sqrt{45}$ $\qquad$ (b) $\sqrt{12}$ $\qquad$ (c) $\sqrt{48}$

(d) $\sqrt{75}$ $\qquad$ (e) $\sqrt{72}$ $\qquad$ (f) $\sqrt{98}$

Problem-solving exercises

7 Work out the areas of squares with these side lengths.

(a) 3 cm $\qquad$ (b) 5 cm $\qquad$ (c) 10 cm $\qquad$ (d) 4·5 cm $\qquad$ (e) 7·2 cm

8 Work out the volumes of cubes with these edge lengths.

(a) 2 cm $\qquad$ (b) 4 cm $\qquad$ (c) 2·2 cm $\qquad$ (d) 5 cm $\qquad$ (e) 8·5 cm

9 $5^2 = 3^2 + 4^2$ and $13^2 = 5^2 + 12^2$

Can you find any more triples where the square of one number equals the sum of the squares of the other two?

Homework

$5^2 - 3^2 = (5 - 3) \times (5 + 3)$

Investigate the difference of two square numbers.
Can you make a statement about $a^2 - b^2$?

Letts **I See Maths** Year 7

Number and Algebra

Functions and graphs 1

Goals

By the end of this lesson you will be able to answer questions such as this:

👁 Sketch the graphs of the following.

(a) $y = x + 4$ (b) $y = x + 27$ (c) $y = x - 2$ (d) $y = x + 0.5$

Starter

1 Discuss why all these line segments are parallel.

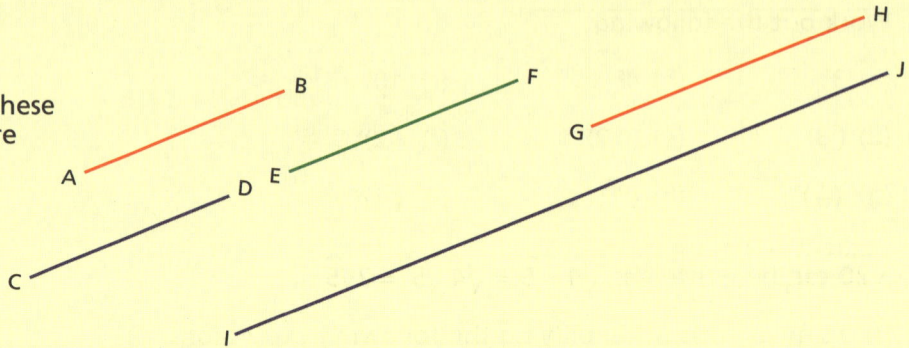

Demonstration 1

Talk about this:

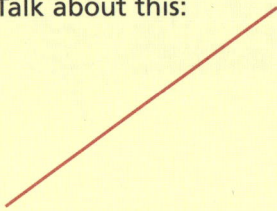

This line segment consists of an infinite number of points.

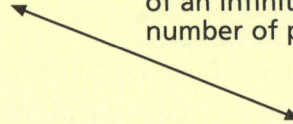

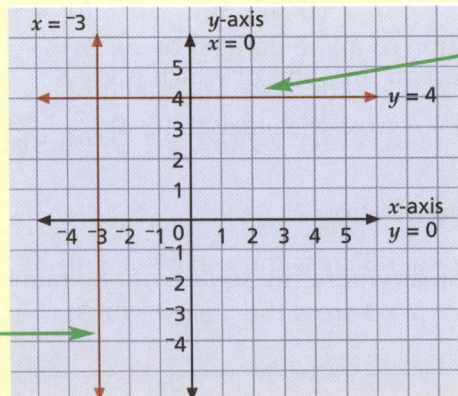

This line consists of an infinite number of points.

$(0, 4)$, $(1, 4)$, $(1.5, 4)$ and $(^-1, 4)$ are a few of the points on the line $y = 4$.

$(^-3, 0)$, $(^-3, 4)$ and $(^-3, ^-2)$ are a few of the points on the line $x = ^-3$.

$y = 0$ and $y = 4$ are parallel. $x = 0$ and $x = ^-3$ are parallel.

$x = 0$ and $y = 0$ are perpendicular. $x = 0$ and $y = 4$ are perpendicular.

Letts I See Maths Year 7

Demonstration 2

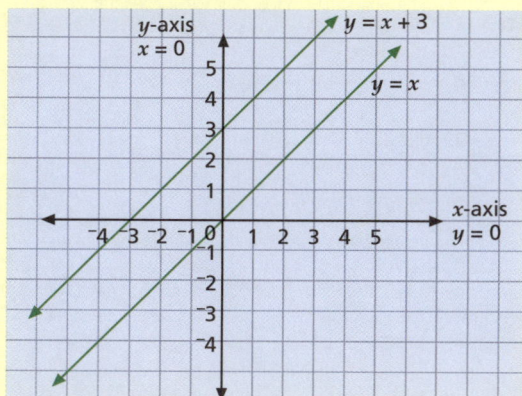

(3, 3), (⁻2, ⁻2), (1·7, 1·7) are some of the points on the line $y = x$.

$y = x$ and $y = x + 3$ are parallel.

The gradient of $y = x$ is 1.
The gradient of $y = x + 3$ is 1.

Key words axis gradient infinite parallel perpendicular

Worked examples

Exercise bank

1 Look at the graph in Demonstration 1.

(a) Write down the equation of a line parallel to $y = 4$.
There are many answers to this, one of which is $y = ⁻2$.

(b) Write down the equation of a line parallel to $x = ⁻3$.
There are many answers to this, one of which is $x = 2$.

(c) Where does the line $y = 4$ cross the y-axis?   (0, 4)

2 Look at the graph in Demonstration 2.

(a) Where does the line $y = x + 3$ cross the x-axis?   (⁻3, 0)

(b) Where does the line $y = x + 3$ cross the y-axis?   (0, 3)

Plenary

👁 What does the instruction 'sketch' ask you to do?
Inspect the equations in the Goals and visualise the graphs before sketching them.

👁 Discuss: Sketch the line $y = x − 3$.

Functions and graphs 1

Essential exercise

1 Linear graphs

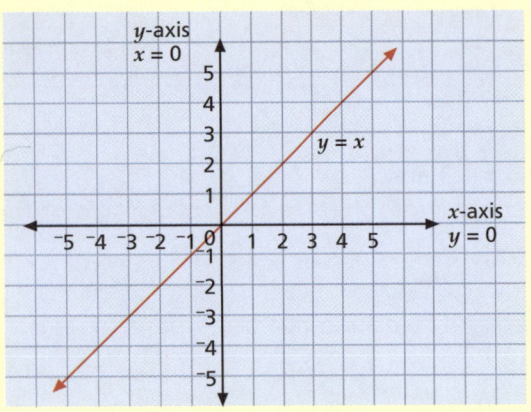

$y = ax + b$

This is the graph of the equation $y = x$.

(a) Where does the graph of $y = x$ cut the x- and y-axes?

(b) At what angle is the graph of $y = x$ to the x-axis?

(c) Which of the following points are on the line $y = x$?

(i) (-2, -2)   (ii) (7, 7)   (iii) (3, -3)   (iv) (2, 1)   (v) (17, 17)

(d) What is the equation of the x-axis?

(e) What is the equation of the y-axis?

(f) Write down an equation of a line parallel to the x-axis.

(g) What is the gradient of the line $y = x$?

(h) Which of the following equations have graphs parallel to the graph of $y = x$?

(i) $y = x + 2$ (ii) $y = 3x$ (iii) $y = x + 5$

(iv) $y = x - 7$ (v) $y = x - 20$ (vi) $y = x + 150$

(i) The graph of the equation $y = x + 17$ is parallel to the graph of $y = x$. Where does it cut the y-axis?

(j) What is the equation of the graph that is perpendicular to $y = x$ and that passes through the origin?

(k) What is the equation of the graph that is parallel to $y = x$ and that is a translation of $y = x$ by 4 units in the y direction?

Number and Algebra

Challenging exercises

2 On a square grid, sketch the graphs of the following equations, marking any points that you know.

(a) $y = x + 6$ (b) $y = x + \frac{1}{2}$ (c) $y = x - 2$

3 The equation $y = {}^-x + 5$ can also be written as $x + y = 5$.

(a) Write down three pairs of numbers (x, y) to satisfy this equation.

(b) On a square grid, plot the three pairs of numbers and join them with a straight line to give the graph of $x + y = 5$.

4 Draw the graphs of the following equations accurately by working out three pairs of numbers (x, y) satisfying the equations.

(a) $x + y = 10$ (b) $x + y = 15$ (c) $x + y = {}^-2$

Problem-solving exercise

5 This is a graph showing the volume of lemonade left in a bottle against the amount drunk.

(a) Describe what the graph is showing.

(b) How much lemonade has been drunk when the bottle has 0·25 litres left?

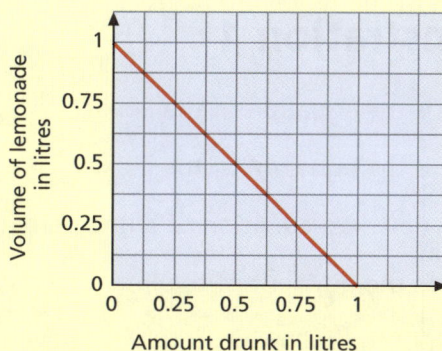

Homework

Write a paragraph about the graphs of the equations $y = x$ and $y = x + 2$ using the following words.

origin	axes	parallel	gradient
graph	axis	equation	linear

Functions and graphs 2

Goals

By the end of this lesson you will be able to answer questions such as this:

◉ Sketch the graphs of the following.

(a) $y = 2x$ (b) $y = 5x$ (c) $y = 3x + 2$ (d) $y = 2x - 0.5$

Starter

1 Visualise movements:

(i) from A to B

(ii) from A to C

(iii) from B to C.

For each movement, say:

> The change in y is … .
> The change in x is … .

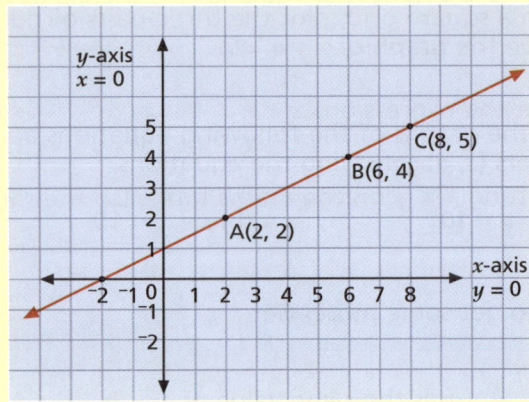

Demonstration 1

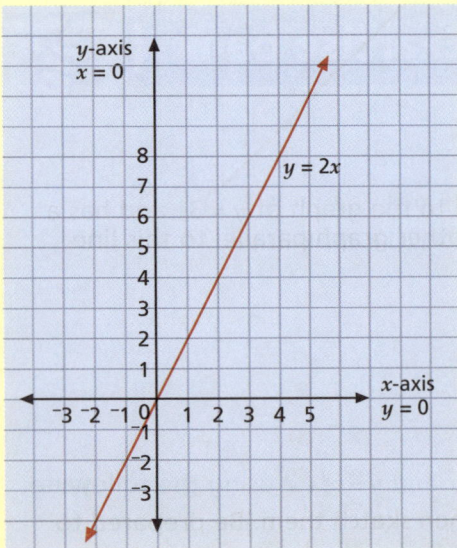

Look at the graph $y = 2x$.

For any movement on this line, 'the change in y' compared to 'the change in x' has the value 2.

Look at the line $y = 2x$.
The gradient is 2.

The gradient is a measure of 'steepness'.

Visualise: $y = 2x + 1$

$y = 2x + 2$

$y = 2x + 3$

$y = 2x - 1$

$y = 2x - 2$

For each line, the gradient is 2.

Letts **I See Maths Year 7**

▶ Demonstration 2

$$y = ax + b \text{ is an equation for every straight line.}$$

The gradient is a.   The line cuts the y-axis at $y = b$.

Look at $y = 5x + 2$.

Say: ⟨ The gradient is 5. The line cuts the y-axis at $y = 2$. ⟩

Think about the expression $ax + b$.

Start by putting $\boxed{x}$ on the maths table. Do the same thing lots of times. Do it a times.

Get ready to get some more. Get $\boxed{b}$

$\boxed{x}$ × a + $\boxed{b}$ has the same value as $ax + b$.

▶ Worked example

Exercise bank 👉

1 Describe fully the graph of $y = 3x + 5$.

The graph of this equation is a straight line. It is parallel to the graph of $y = 3x$ and has a gradient of 3. The intercept on the y-axis is at (0, 5). Another graph parallel to this line could have the equation $y = 3x - 4$.

▶ Plenary

◉ Visualise the graphs of the equations in the Goals and then sketch them. Be prepared to explain how you knew what to sketch.

◉ Talk about: The general equation of a straight line is $y = ax + b$.

Letts **I See Maths Year 7**

Number and Algebra

Functions and graphs 2

Essential exercise

1 **Linear graphs**

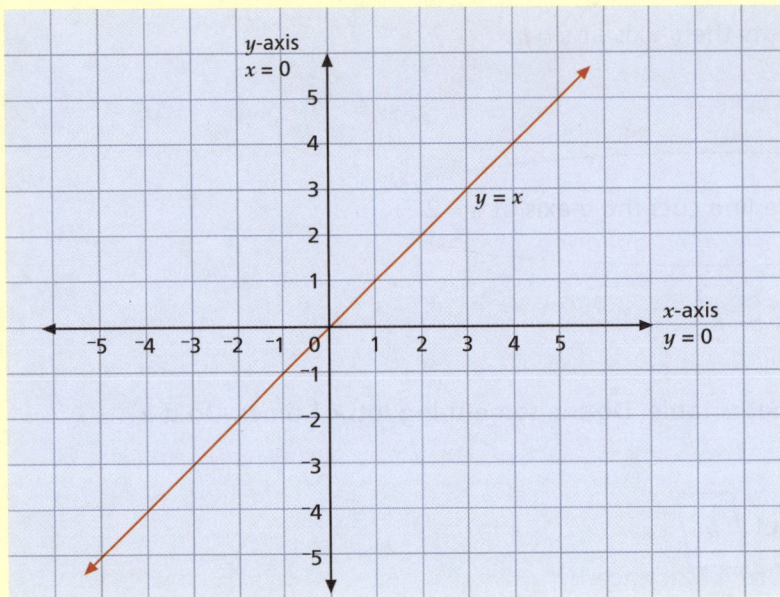

$$y = ax + b$$

This is the graph of the equation $y = x$.

(a) What is the gradient of the graph of $y = x$?

(b) Copy the graph of the equation $y = x$.

(c) Sketch the graph of the equation $y = 2x$.

(d) Does the graph of the equation $y = 2x$ pass through the origin?

(e) What is the gradient of the graph of $y = 2x$?

(f) Describe the graphs of the following equations.

    (i) $y = 3x$ (ii) $y = 10x$ (iii) $y = 0\cdot5x$

(g) Visualise the graph of the equation $y = 3x$.

    Visualise the graphs of the equations $y = 3x + 1$, $y = 3x + 2$, $y = 3x + 3$, ...

    Describe what you 'see' in your imagination.

(h) (i) Sketch the graph of the equation $y = 2x + 4$.

    (ii) Explain how you knew what to draw.

Letts **I See Maths Year 7**

Challenging exercises

2 Use a graphics calculator or graph package on the computer to investigate the graphs of the following equations.

(a) $y = x^2$ (b) $y = x^2 + 1$ (c) $y = x^2 + 5$

(d) $y = x^2 + 0.5$ (e) $y = x^2 - 3$ (f) $y = x^2 - 4$

(g) $y = 2x^2$ (h) $y = 0.5x^2$ (i) $y = x^2 + x - 1$

3 The graphs in question 2 are called quadratic graphs.

The general equation of a quadratic graph is $y = ax^2 + bx + c$.

Write a paragraph describing quadratic graphs.

Problem-solving exercises

4 On 18 February 2002, 1 euro = 62 pence.
Draw a graph to convert euros to pounds sterling.

5 To convert temperature in degrees Fahrenheit to degrees Celsius, subtract 32 and multiply by $\frac{5}{9}$. Draw a graph to convert degrees Fahrenheit to degrees Celsius.

Homework

Find out how to convert from miles to kilometres. Draw a conversion graph for this.

In an athletics competition, the following four races took place: 800 metres, 1500 metres, 3000 metres, 10 000 metres.
Use your conversion graph to estimate these distances in miles.

Review of Number and Algebra 1

1 Complete the following equations.

(a) $\frac{6}{10} + \frac{2}{10} =$

$\cdot6 + \cdot2 =$

(b) $\frac{4}{10} + \frac{5}{10} =$

$\cdot4 + \cdot5 =$

(c) $\frac{8}{10} + \frac{15}{10} =$

$\cdot8 + 1\cdot5 =$

(d) $\frac{23}{100} + \frac{41}{100} =$

$\cdot23 + \cdot41 =$

(e) $\frac{65}{100} + \frac{34}{100} =$

$\cdot65 + \cdot34 =$

(f) $\frac{114}{100} + \frac{125}{100} =$

$1\cdot14 + 1\cdot25 =$

2 Complete the following equations.

(a) $\frac{5}{6} = \frac{}{30}$

(b) $\frac{3}{7} = \frac{}{49}$

(c) $\frac{3}{5} = \frac{}{100}$

3 Write the following vulgar fractions as mixed numbers.

(a) $\frac{23}{4}$

(b) $\frac{73}{10}$

(c) $\frac{19}{5}$

4 Reduce the following fractions to their simplest forms.

(a) $\frac{21}{35}$

(b) $\frac{48}{80}$

(c) $\frac{10}{15}$

5 Complete the following equations.

(a) $\frac{3}{5} + \frac{7}{5} + \frac{9}{5} =$

(b) $\frac{8}{7} + \frac{3}{7} - \frac{4}{7} =$

(c) $\frac{1}{6} + \frac{2}{5} =$

(d) $\frac{3}{7} - \frac{1}{3} =$

6 Use the multiplication tables to help you complete the following equations.

(a) $\frac{2}{5} \times 4 =$

(b) $\frac{5}{6} \times 8 =$

(c) $\frac{3}{10} \times 5 =$

7 Visualise the following and answer the questions.

(a) Look at $\frac{8}{5}$. How many $\frac{1}{5}$ can you see?

(b) Look at $\frac{8}{5}$. How many $\frac{4}{5}$ can you see?

Letts **I See Maths** Year 7

8 Write each of the following numbers as a percentage.

(a) $\frac{3}{4}$
(b) 0·7
(c) 0·04
(d) $\frac{3}{20}$
(e) 1·17

9 Work out the following.

(a) $\frac{3}{5}$ of 25
(b) $\frac{2}{3}$ of 300
(c) $\frac{3}{8}$ of 48
(d) $\frac{1}{6}$ of 60

10 Work out the following.

(a) 5% of 80
(b) 25% of 10
(c) 10% of 65
(d) 1% of 624

11 Complete the following equations.

(a) $^-2 + {}^-4 =$
(b) $^-5 + 5 =$
(c) $6 + {}^-4 =$
(d) $^-3 + {}^-3 + 5 =$

(e) $^-7 - {}^-7 =$
(f) $^-6 - {}^-4 =$
(g) $^-1 + {}^-3 - {}^-4 =$
(h) $^-89 + 89 =$

12 Complete the following equations.

(a) $3 - 9 =$
(b) $^-5 - {}^-6 =$
(c) $0 - 4 =$
(d) $5 - {}^-2 =$

13 Use the multiplication pairs for each of the following numbers to help you write down all its factors.

(a) 12
(b) 18
(c) 27
(d) 35

14 (a) How do you know that a number is divisible by 9?

(b) Which of the following numbers is not divisible by 9?

(i) 126
(ii) 207
(iii) 326
(iv) 1008

15 Find the highest commmon factor (HCF) for each of the following sets of numbers.

(a) {60, 126}
(b) {90, 135, 693}

Review of Number and Algebra 2

1 Which of the following numbers are prime numbers?

(a) 7   (b) 9   (c) 19   (d) 91

2 Write each of the following numbers as a product of prime numbers.

(a) 15   (b) 26   (c) 49   (d) 27

3 Calculate the expressions below.

(a) $2 + 7 \times 6$ (b) $3 \times 4 + 2 \times 5$ (c) $2 \times 7 - 3 \times 4$

(d) $4 + 12 \div 6$ (e) $6 + \frac{10}{5}$ (f) $9 - \frac{15}{3}$

4 Put brackets in the expressions below to make the equations correct.

(a) $3 + 2 \times 9 = 45$ (b) $17 - 9 \times 2 = 16$ (c) $4 \times 2 + 5 - 3 \times 6 + 2 = 4$

5 Work out the values of the number x in the following equations.

(a) $x + 21 = 53$ (b) $46 + x = 84$ (c) $x - 16 = 63$

(d) $\frac{9}{5} + x = \frac{18}{5}$ (e) $x + \frac{7}{9} = \frac{15}{9}$ (f) $x - \frac{3}{4} = \frac{5}{4}$

6 Work out the values of the number x in the following equations.

(a) $3x = 30$ (b) $9x = 81$ (c) $10x = 80$

(d) $\frac{x}{5} = 4$ (e) $\frac{x}{7} = 3$ (f) $\frac{x}{10} = 5$

7 Work out the values of the number x in the following equations.

(a) $15 + 4x = 23$ (b) $6x + 21 = 45$ (c) $9x - 7 = 20$

(d) $100 - 4x = 50$ (e) $\frac{x}{3} + 2 = 5$ (f) $\frac{x}{4} - 2 = 3$

Letts I See Maths Year 7

8 (a) Write down the formula for the area of a triangle with base length b and perpendicular height h.

(b) Calculate the areas of the following triangles.

(i) b cm = 10 cm, h cm= 6 cm (ii) b cm = 15 cm, h cm = 8 cm (iii) b cm = 7 cm, h cm = 9 cm

9 Use rounding to find approximate answers to the following calculations.

(a) 3099×2932 (b) $21{\cdot}9 \times 37{\cdot}8$ (c) $4926 \div 51$

10 Use a calculator to work out the answers to the following calculations.

(a) $324 - 14 \times 4$ (b) $47 \times 23 + 56 \times 79$ (c) $456 - \frac{19 \times 15}{5}$

11 Generate the next three consecutive terms for each of the following number sequences using the position-to-term rule given.

	Position-to-term rule	Sequence
(a)	$3n - 1$	$^-1, 2, 5, \dots$
(b)	$5n + 2$	$2, 7, 12, \dots$
(c)	$n^2 + 1$	$1, 2, 5, \dots$

12 Work out the values of the following.

(a) 9^2 (b) 14^2 (c) $\sqrt{121}$

13 Write down the equations of two graphs that are parallel to $y = 2x + 3$.

14 Write down the coordinates of the point where $y = 5x - 12$ cuts the y-axis.

15 Write down the equation of a straight-line graph with gradient equal to 2, which cuts the y-axis at (0, 5).

Lines and angles

Goals

When you have completed this lesson you will be able to:

👁 visualise two coincident lines – an object and an image

👁 visualise the object and the image after a turn

👁 recognise objects and images for acute angles, obtuse angles and reflex angles

👁 use a protractor to draw angles of 67°, 138°, 207°.

Starter

1 Act out each of the following with cups.

(a) $6 \div 6$ (b) $6 \div 1$ (c) $6 \div \frac{1}{2}$ (d) $6 \div \frac{1}{4}$ (e) $0 \div 6$ (f) $0 \div 1$

(g) $0 \div \frac{1}{2}$ (h) $0 \div \frac{1}{4}$ (i) $6 \div 0$ (j) $1 \div 0$ (k) $\frac{1}{2} \div 0$ (l) $\frac{1}{4} \div 0$

Demonstration 1

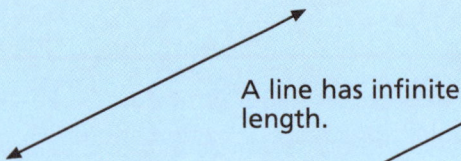

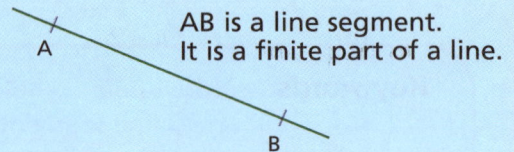

A line has infinite length.

AB is a line segment. It is a finite part of a line.

There are two coincident lines here.

object image

The image has turned through an acute angle.

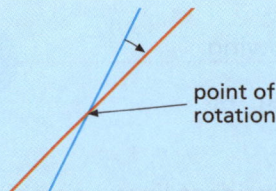

point of rotation

object

point of rotation

The image has turned through an obtuse angle.

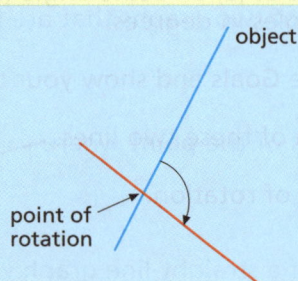

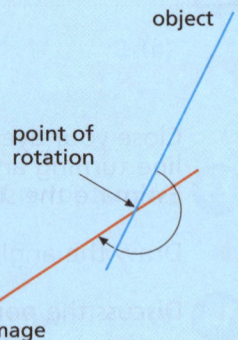

point of rotation

object

image

The image has turned through a reflex angle.

Demonstration 2

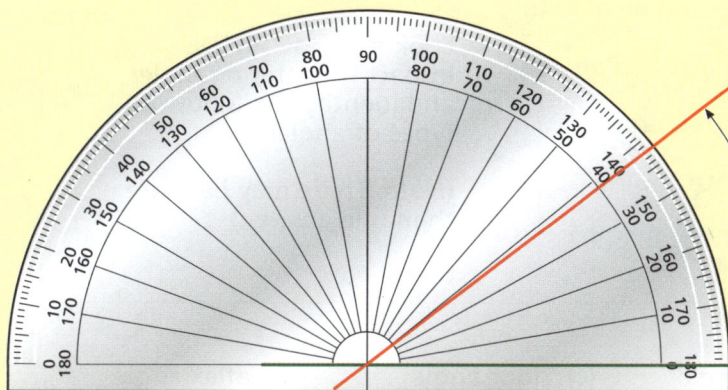

The image has turned through 38°.

A protractor is a scale that measures degrees of turn.

There are two coincident lines: the object and the image.

The picture shows two protractors.

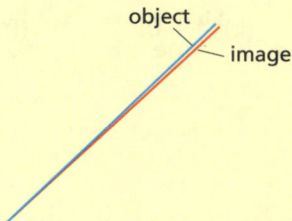

object

image

Look at these two lines. The image has turned through an angle of 1°.

Key words   acute angle   angle   coincident lines   degrees   image   infinite
line   line segment   object   obtuse angle   protractor   reflex angle
turn through

Exercise bank

Plenary

- 👁 Close your eyes. Visualise two coincident lines – an object and an image. Now imagine one line turning and make it stop at (a) an acute angle (b) an obtuse angle and (c) a reflex angle. Estimate the size of your angles in degrees.

- 👁 Draw the angles given in the Goals and show your teacher.

- 👁 Discuss the point of rotation of these two lines.

- 👁 Discuss measuring the angle of rotation.

object

image

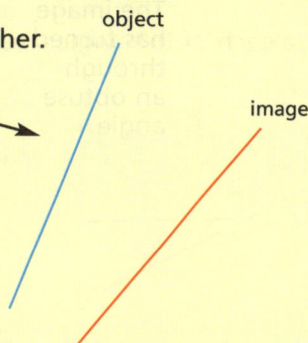

Letts **I See Maths** Year 7

Shape and Space

Lines and angles

Essential exercises

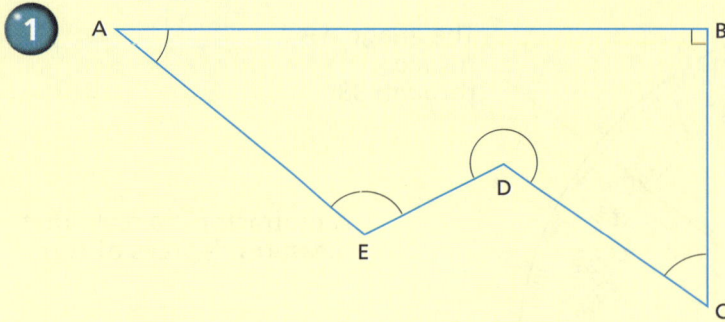

1

Look at shape ABCDE. Inspect the interior angles and identify the following types of angles.

(*Note*: There may be more than one answer.)

(a) acute angle   (b) obtuse angle   (c) right angle   (d) reflex angle

2 Copy and complete the following table by putting a tick in the correct box.

Angle	Acute angle	Obtuse angle	Right angle	Reflex angle	Straight line	Full turn
260°						
35°						
145°						
90°						
300°						
180°						
21°						
360°						
171°						
250°						

3 Draw a line segment AB, 8 cm in length. Use a protractor and ruler to construct an angle at B such that:

(a) $\hat{ABC} = 90°$ (b) $\hat{ABC} = 60°$ (c) $\hat{ABC} = 120°$.

4 Calculate each of the angles marked with a letter.

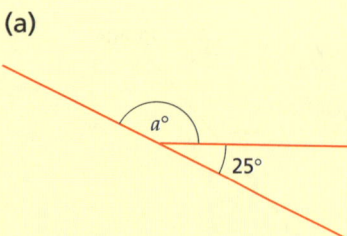

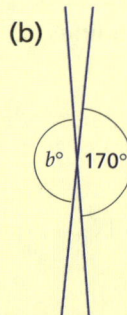

(a)

(b)

(c)

Shape and Space

Challenging exercises

5

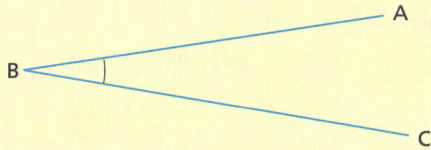

For each question below, first copy the angle ABC.

(a) Draw $A\hat{B}D$ such that $A\hat{B}C$ and $A\hat{B}D$ are complementary.

(b) Draw $A\hat{B}D$ such that $A\hat{B}C$ and $A\hat{B}D$ are supplementary.

(c) Draw $D\hat{B}E$ such that $A\hat{B}C$ and $D\hat{B}E$ are vertically opposite angles.

(d) Draw $C\hat{B}D$ such that $A\hat{B}C$ and $C\hat{B}D$ are adjacent and equal in size.

6 Draw a line segment AB, 6 cm in length. Draw a line BC at B, perpendicular to AB, such that BC = 8 cm. Join AC.

Measure the following accurately.

(a) the length of the line segment AC   (b) $A\hat{C}B$ (c) $B\hat{A}C$

7 Complete the phrases below using these words: 'complementary', 'supplementary' or 'vertically opposite'.

(a) The angles $a°$ and $b°$ are … .

(b) The angles $c°$ and $d°$ are … .

(c) The angles $d°$ and $e°$ are … .

(d) The angles $f°$ and $g°$ are … .

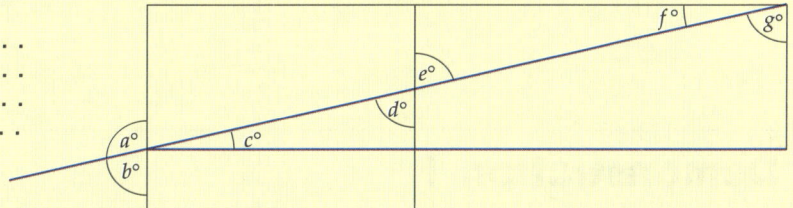

Problem-solving exercise

8 Shape ABCDEFG is drawn on the playground. Xavier stands at A and begins to walk around the shape. Describe Xavier's walk, explaining the angles he turns through until he returns to A again.

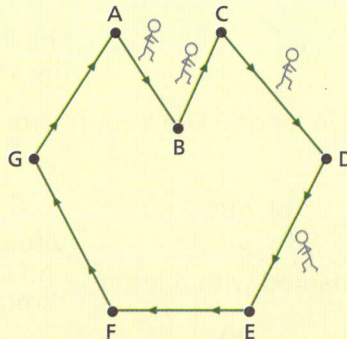

Homework

(a) Construct line segments AB and CD perpendicular to each other.

(b) Construct line segments EF and GH parallel to each other.

Letts **I See Maths Year 7**

Parallel lines

Goals

When you have completed this lesson you will be able to:

- visualise the image t after a turn of 87°

- calculate a, b, c, d on this diagram

- identify corresponding angles, vertically opposite angles, alternate angles and supplementary angles.

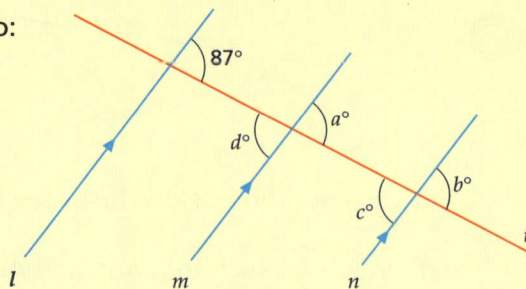

Starter

1 Discuss:

(a)
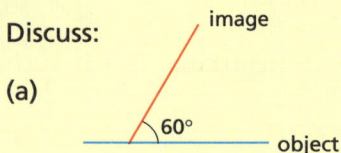

(b)
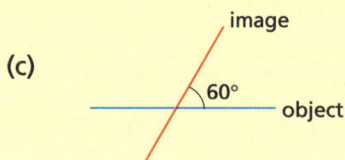

(c)
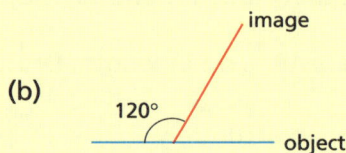

(d)
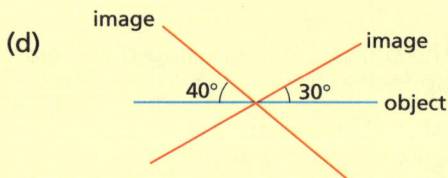

Demonstration 1

Figure 1

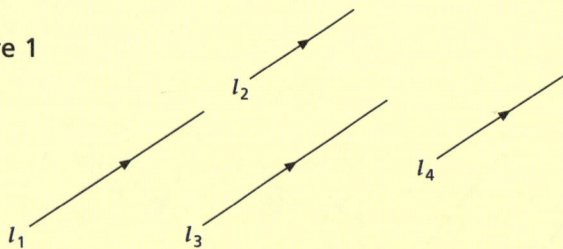

The lines l_1, l_2, l_3 and l_4 are parallel.

The lines l_1, l_2, l_3 and l_4 all point in the same direction.

Figure 2

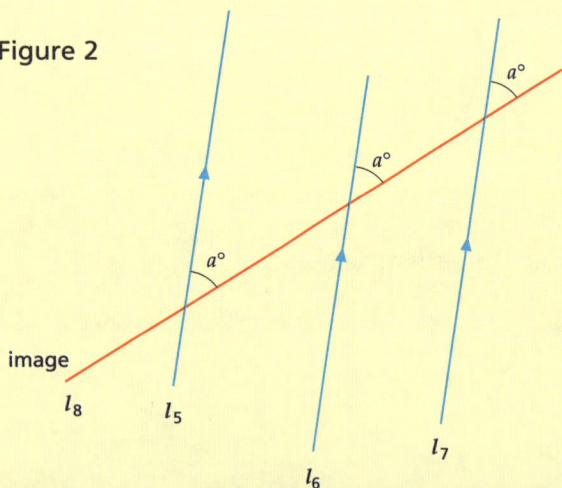

Visualise three parallel lines, l_5, l_6 and l_7, and visualise the image l_8 after a turn through $a°$.

Letts **I See Maths** Year 7

Demonstration 2

Figure 3

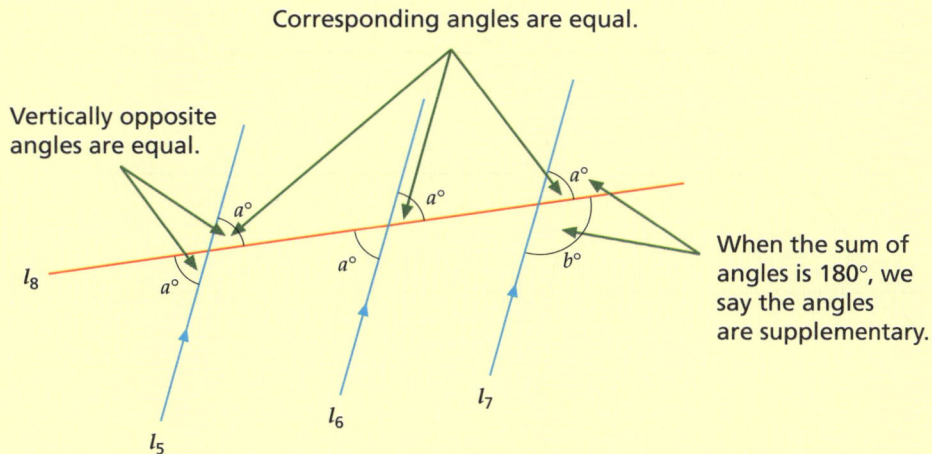

Corresponding angles are equal.

Vertically opposite angles are equal.

When the sum of angles is 180°, we say the angles are supplementary.

l_8 l_5 l_6 l_7

Key words   alternate angles   corresponding angles   parallel   supplementary angles   transversal   vertically opposite angles

Worked example

Exercise bank

1   Calculate the angles marked with letters.

$a° = 180° - 72°$ (supplementary angle)
    $= 108°$
$b° = 108°$ (vertically opposite to $a°$)
$c° = 72°$ (corresponding angle)

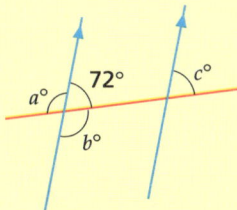

Plenary

- Go back to the Goals and calculate the angles marked with letters. Give reasons for your answers. Identify the three parallel lines and one transversal.

- In Figure 1, discuss l_1 and l_2.

- In Figure 2, discuss the point of rotation of l_8.

- In Figure 3, discuss all the supplementary angles.

Parallel lines

Essential exercises

1

(a) Using the labelled angles, write down the following:
    (i) three pairs of corresponding angles
    (ii) three pairs of alternate angles
    (iii) three pairs of vertically opposite angles
    (iv) three pairs of supplementary angles.

(b) If $c° = 60°$ and $g° = 108°$, work out all the angles a to l.

2

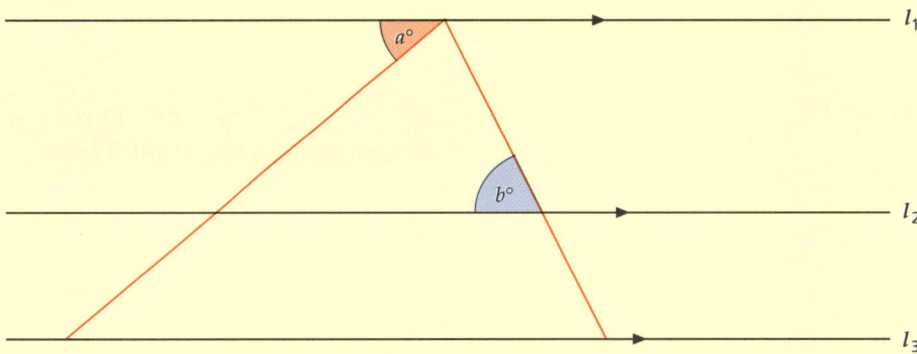

Copy the diagram above. Lines l_1, l_2 and l_3 are all parallel.
(a) Colour all the angles equal to angle a in red.
(b) Colour all the angles equal to angle b in blue.

3

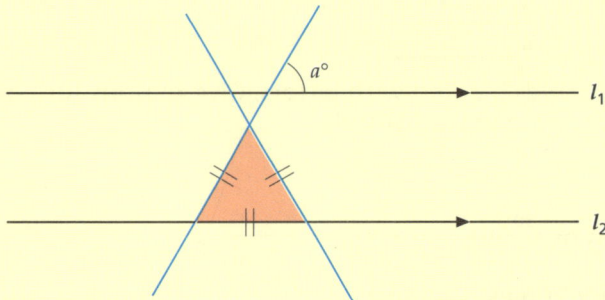

Lines l_1 and l_2 are parallel.

What is the value of the angle marked $a°$?

Parallel lines

Challenging exercises

4

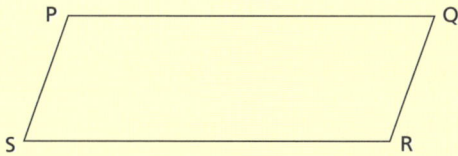

PQRS is a parallelogram.
Copy the diagram.
(a) Mark the lines that are parallel.
(b) Mark the lines that are equal.
(c) Mark the angles that are equal.
(d) Make a statement about the opposite angles of a parallelogram.

5

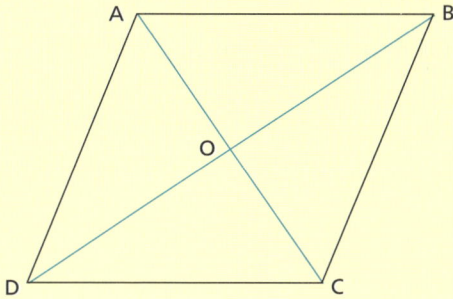

ABCD is a rhombus.
Copy the diagram.
(a) Mark the lines that are parallel.
(b) Mark the lines that are equal.
(c) Mark the angles that are equal.
(d) Work out the value of $A\hat{O}B$.

Problem-solving exercise

6

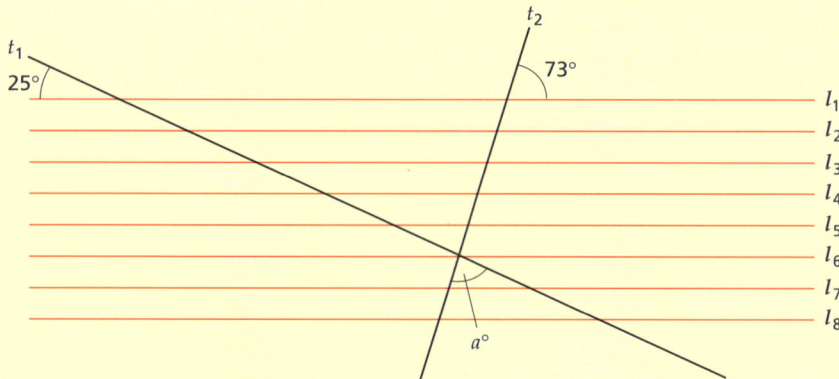

The lines l_1 to l_8 are all parallel; t_1 and t_2 are transversal lines.

Copy the diagram.
(a) Work out the size of the angle marked $a°$.
(b) Mark all the angles equal to 25° with the letter b.
(c) Mark all the angles equal to 73° with the letter c.

Homework

ABCD is an isosceles trapezium.

Inspect the isosceles trapezium ABCD. See if you can work out the angles marked $a°$, $b°$, $c°$ and $d°$ to discuss in your next lesson.

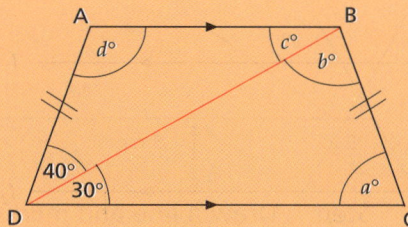

Construction of shapes

Goals

When you have completed this lesson you will be able to:

- 👁 sketch and construct △LMN, given that LM = 4·6 cm, MN = 5·2 cm, $\hat{LMN}$ = 43°

- 👁 sketch and construct △PQR, given that PQ = 5 cm, $\hat{QPR}$ = 32°, $\hat{PQR}$ = 105°

- 👁 sketch and construct △ABC, given that AB = 7·6 cm, BL = 4·8 cm, CA = 5·9 cm

- 👁 visualise why the three line segments 8 cm, 2 cm and 5 cm will not form a triangle.

Starter

1 Use a ruler and a pair of compasses to construct the following.

(a) a regular hexagon
(b) an equilateral triangle
(c) a square

Demonstration 1

Draw △PQR with PQ = 5 cm, QR = 3 cm and $\hat{PQR}$ = 67°.

Sketch

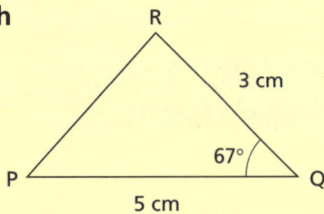

Construction

Step 4: Draw the line PR using a ruler.

Step 3: Draw the line segment QR = 3 cm with a pair of compasses (centre Q, radius 3 cm).

Step 2: Construct $\hat{PQR}$ = 67° using a protractor.

Step 1: Draw a line and mark a line segment PQ = 5 cm with a pair of compasses.

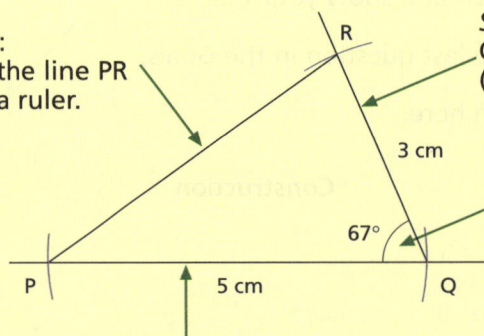

Demonstration 2

Draw ΔLMN with LM = 7·7 cm, MN = 5 cm and NL = 8·3 cm.

Sketch

N
8.3 cm
5 cm
L
7.7 cm
M

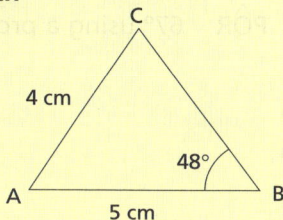

Construction

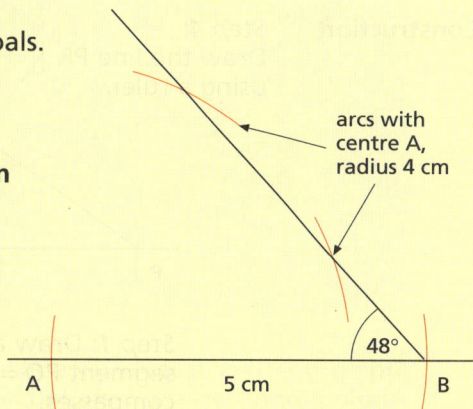

Step 3: With centre L and radius 8·3 cm, draw an arc.

Step 2: With centre M and radius 5 cm, draw an arc.

N

Step 4: Use a ruler to draw line segments MN and LN.

8.3 cm

5 cm

L

7.7 cm

M

Step 1: Draw a line and mark the line segment LM = 7·7 cm.

Key words   construct   draw $A\hat{B}C$ = 67°   draw an arc with centre A and radius 3 cm   draw line segment AB = 5 cm   included angle   included side   sketch

---

Exercise bank

Plenary

◉ Sketch the triangles in the Goals and show your teacher.

◉ Prepare an explanation for the last question in the Goals.

◉ Discuss the construction shown here.

Sketch

C
4 cm
48°
A
5 cm
B

Construction

arcs with centre A, radius 4 cm

48°
A
5 cm
B

Shape and Space

Construction of shapes

Exercise Bank Exercise Bank Exercise Bank Exercise Ban

Essential exercises

1 Use a ruler and protractor to construct triangles accurately, using the information given in the following table.

Triangle	Side 1	Included angle	Side 2
△ABC	CB = 5 cm	$A\hat{C}B = 40°$	CA = 4 cm
△DEF	DF = 6 cm	$E\hat{D}F = 100°$	DE = 5 cm
△GHI	HG = 3 cm	$I\hat{H}G = 90°$	HI = 4 cm

2 Use a ruler and protractor to construct triangles accurately, using the information given in the following table.

Triangle	Included side	Angle 1	Angle 2
△ABC	CB = 4·5 cm	$A\hat{B}C = 50°$	$A\hat{C}B = 50°$
△DEF	FE = 5 cm	$D\hat{E}F = 65°$	$D\hat{F}E = 45°$
△GHI	IH = 3·5 cm	$G\hat{H}I = 20°$	$G\hat{I}H = 120°$

3 Use a pair of compasses to construct triangles accurately, using the information given in the following table.

Triangle	Side 1	Side 2	Side 3
△ABC	AB = 4 cm	CB = 5 cm	CA = 7 cm
△DEF	DE = 5·5 cm	FE = 6·5 cm	FD = 8 cm
△GHI	GH = 6 cm	IH = 8 cm	IG = 10 cm

4 You have sticks of the following lengths: 6 cm, 6 cm, 8 cm, 10 cm, 2 cm, 3 cm. Work out which combinations will make triangles and name the triangles using side and angle properties. Copy and complete the table below.

Combination	Is the triangle possible?	Triangle name using side properties	Triangle name using angle properties
6, 6, 8			
6, 6, 10			
6, 6, 2			

Side properties: scalene, isosceles, equilateral
Angle properties: right-angled, acute-angled, obtuse-angled

Letts **I See Maths Year 7**

Construction of shapes

Challenging exercises

5 Construct a rhombus ABCD such that the length AB = 4 cm and $A\hat{B}C = 120°$.

6 Construct the two possible nets for a tetrahedron with side length 3 cm.

7 Use a pair of compasses to construct a regular hexagon with side length 5 cm.

8 Given that △ABC has one side equal to 6 cm, another side equal to 4 cm and an angle of 40°, how many different triangles can you make?

9 Construct a net for a square-based pyramid given that the side of the base is 4 cm and the sloping edge is 6·5 cm.

Problem-solving exercises

10 A twelve-metre ladder rests against a vertical wall with its foot four metres away from the wall. From the side view this is a right-angled triangle. Sketch the diagram and then construct a diagram to scale using a ruler, set square and a pair of compasses.

11 Draw the right-angled triangle ABC with $C\hat{A}B = 90°$, AB = 3 cm and CA = 4 cm. Mark the midpoint H of CB. Use a pair of compasses to draw a circle with centre H that passes through the points A, B and C.

Homework
Construct the shapes below and continue the pattern for each one.

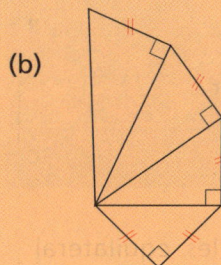

(a)

(b)

Letts **I See Maths** Year 7

Shape and Space

127

Visualising shapes

Goals

> When you have completed this lesson you will be able to:

👁 name and describe the three-dimensional shape on the right

👁 visualise and name the shape of each of its faces

👁 imagine cutting the shape in half from its vertex to the middle of its base

👁 describe the two shapes that are made.

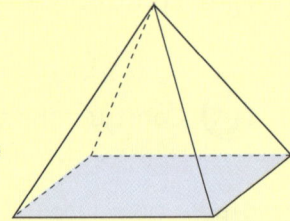

Starter

1 Name these shapes. Describe these shapes.

(a) 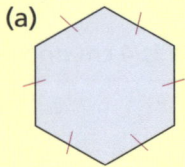 (b) 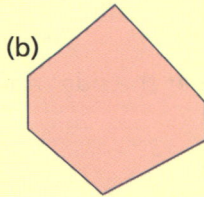 (c) 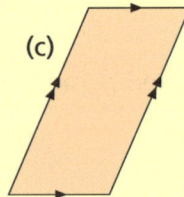 (d) 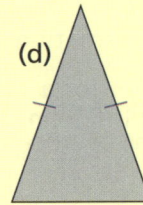 (e)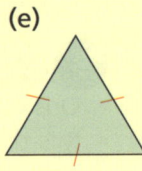

Demonstration 1

Naming the 3-D shape:

• triangular prism

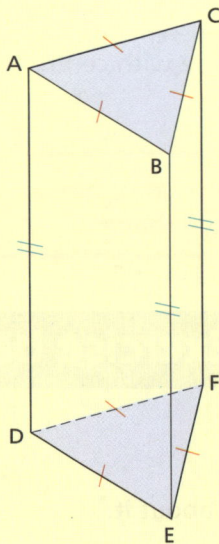

Reading explicit information:

• AC = AB = BC

• AD = BE = CF

Deducing implicit information:

• The two triangular faces are parallel.

• The three rectangular faces are congruent.

Looking at each face in turn and sketching it:

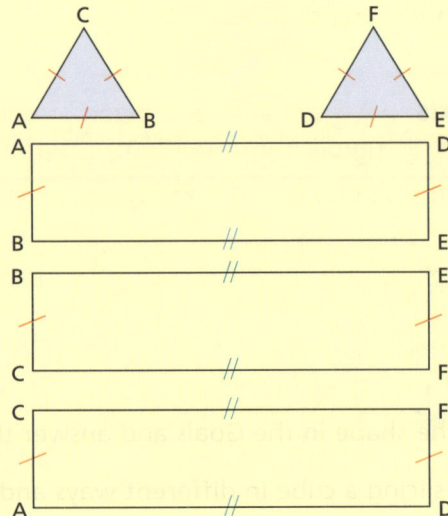

Letts **I See Maths** Year 7

Demonstration 2

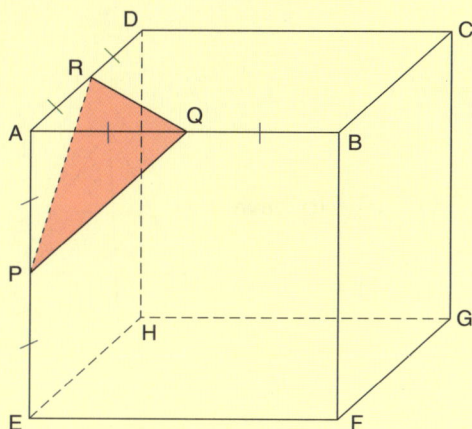

The cube ABCDEFGH is cut into two shapes along the face PQR.

Reading explicit information:

- P is the midpoint of AE.
- Q is the midpoint of AB.
- R is the midpoint of AD.

Deducing implicit information:

- The smaller shape is a pyramid with four faces.
- Three of its faces are right-angled triangles and one is an equilateral triangle.
- The larger shape has seven faces.
- Three faces are squares.
- Three faces are pentagons.
- One face is an equilateral triangle.

Key words   2-D shapes   3-D shapes   deducing   explicit information   implicit information   plane shapes   solid shapes

Exercise bank 👉

Plenary

👁 Inspect the shape in the Goals and answer the questions about it.

👁 Imagine slicing a cube in different ways and contemplate the results.

Shape and Space

Visualising shapes

Essential exercises

1 Describe each of the polyhedra below by stating:

   (i) the number of faces it has
   (ii) the name(s) of the shapes of its faces.

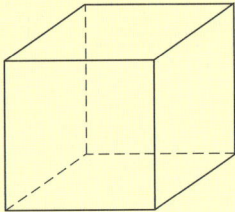

(a) cube

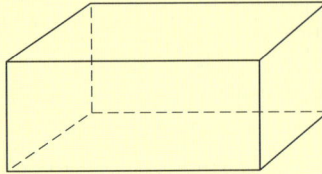

(b) cuboid

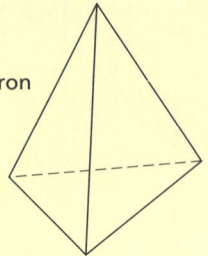

(c) tetrahedron

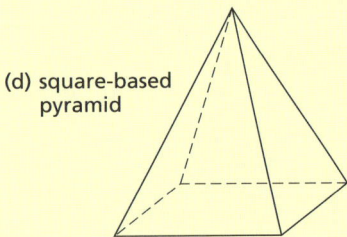

(d) square-based pyramid

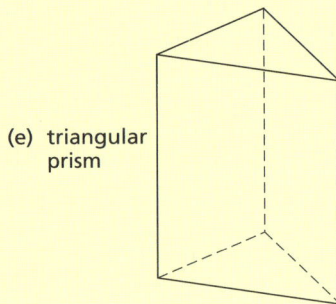

(e) triangular prism

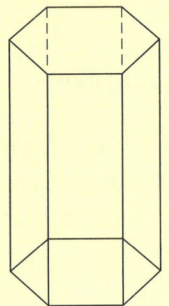

(f) hexagonal prism

2 A cube is cut into two equal pieces by cutting vertically along a diagonal of one of its faces, through the plane ABCD.

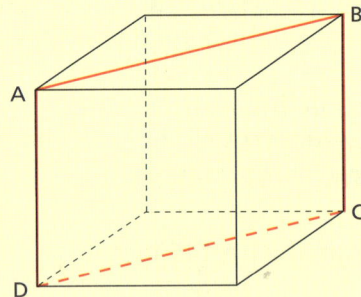

(a) What is the name of each piece?
(b) Describe the faces of one of the pieces.

3 A cone is cut into two equal pieces by cutting from its vertex to the diameter of its base.

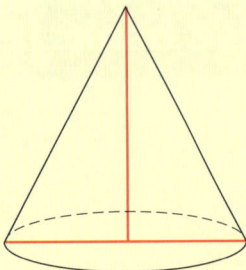

The diameter of the base is 6 cm.

The slant edge of the cone is 7 cm.

Sketch and name the shape of the face produced by the cut.

Letts **I See Maths Year 7**

Challenging exercises

4 A slice is taken from a cube in the following way. H1, H2 and H3 are the midpoints of three sides. A straight cut is made along the plane shown.

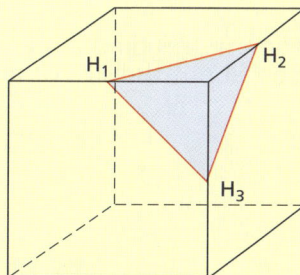

  (a) Describe in detail the shape of the slice that is removed.

  (b) Describe the faces of the shape that is left.

5 A, B, C, D and E, F, G, H are the midpoints of opposite faces of a cube.

Is the shape ABCDEFGH a cube? Explain.

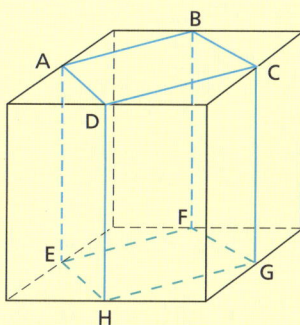

Problem-solving exercises

6 Imagine a prism with 501 faces.

  (a) How many edges will its base have?
  (b) How many vertices will the prism have?

7 Imagine a pyramid with 145 faces.

  (a) How many edges will its base have?
  (b) How many vertices will the pyramid have?

Homework

A cuboid is cut along the red lines as shown. A, E, F and G are midpoints of the lines.

Describe the three shapes you get after cutting.

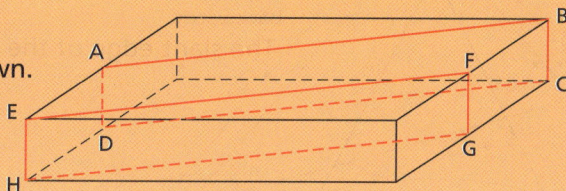

Angles in a triangle

Goals

When you have completed this lesson you will be able to:

👁 read the explicit information in this diagram and deduce implicit information about the size of all the angles.

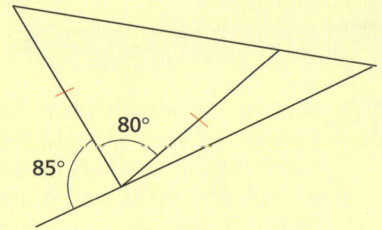

Starter

1 Discuss explicit and implicit information in this statement: 'A right-angled isosceles triangle has only one side equal to 6 cm.'

2 Discuss the image and object.

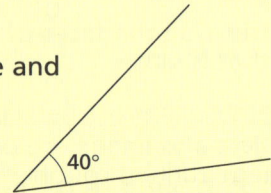

Demonstration 1

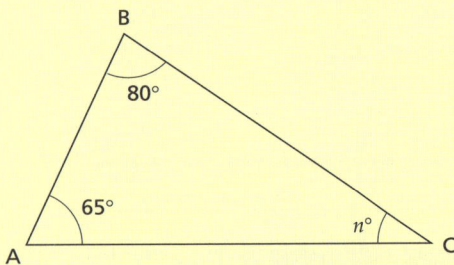

Explicit information

- ABC is a triangle.
- $\hat{ABC} = 80°$
- $\hat{BCA}$ is not known.
- $\hat{CAB} = 65°$

Implicit information

If you were walking, you would start at A facing B, walk forwards along AB, turn through 80° and walk backwards along BC, turn through $n°$ and walk forwards along CA, then turn through 65°. You now have your back towards B. You now have turned through 180°.

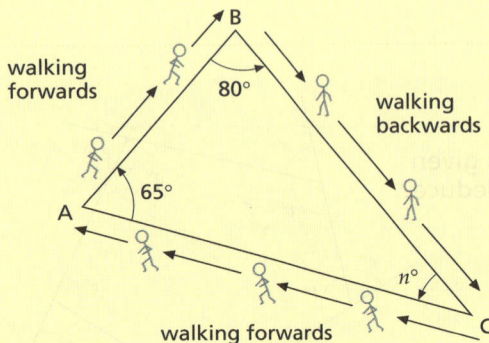

walking forwards

walking backwards

walking forwards

$$80° + n° + 65° = 180°$$
$$n° = 55°$$
$$\hat{BCA} = 55°$$

Shape and Space

Demonstration 2

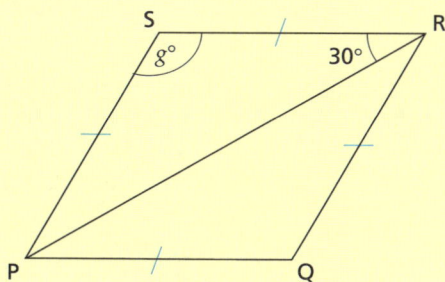

Explicit information

- SR = RQ = QP = PS
- SRQP is a rhombus.
- △PRS is isosceles.
- △PQR is isosceles.
- $S\hat{R}P = 30°$

Implicit information

- $S\hat{P}R = 30°$ as △PRS is isosceles.
- The object and image are parallel to the line segment PS.
  The image turns through $g°$ and 30° and 30°.
  It turns through a total of 180°.

$$g° + 30° + 30° = 180°$$
$$g° = 120°$$
$$P\hat{S}R = 120°$$

- △PRS is congruent to △PRQ.

| **Key words** | congruence | image | object | rhombus |

Worked example

Exercise bank 👉

1 Work out the angles labelled with letters.

$$a° + 50° + 45° = 180°$$
$$a° = 85°$$
$$b° + 85° = 180°$$
$$b° = 95°$$

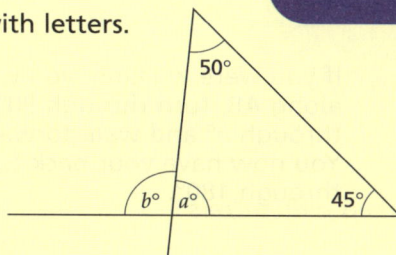

Plenary

👁 Inspect the diagram in the Goals. What informaton is given in the diagram? What further information can you deduce?

👁 Look at the diagram. Discuss:
$$p° + q° + r° + s° + t° =$$
$$a° + b° + c° + d° + e° =$$
$$a° + b° + c° + d° + e° + p° + q° + r° + s° + t° =$$

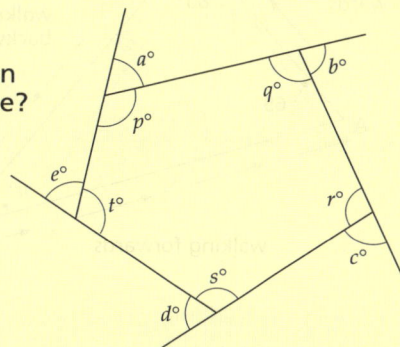

Shape and Space

Angles in a triangle

Essential exercises

1 Work out the angles labelled with letters.

(a)

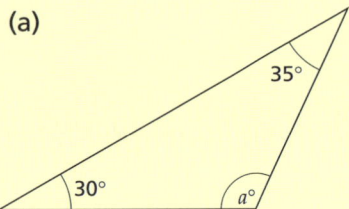

(b)

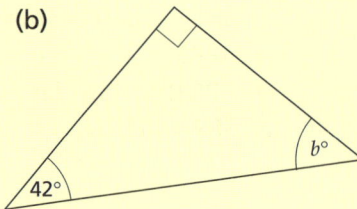

(c)

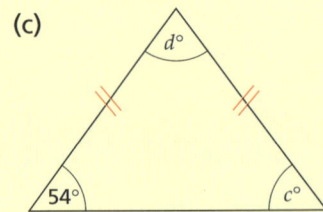

2 Work out the angles labelled with letters.

(a)

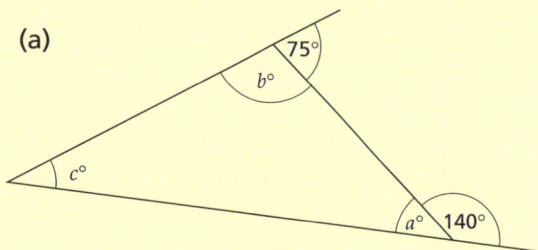

(b)

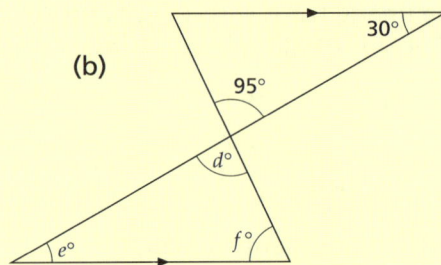

3 Work out the angles marked with letters.

(a)

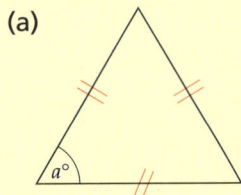

(b)

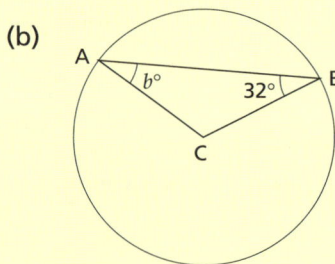

(c)

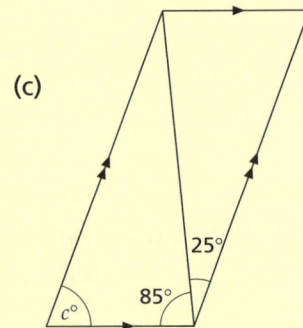

4 Work out the angles marked with letters.

(a)

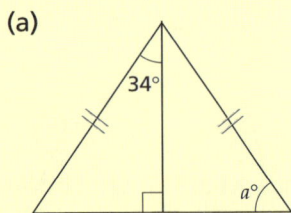

(b)

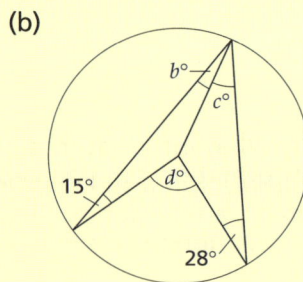

(c)

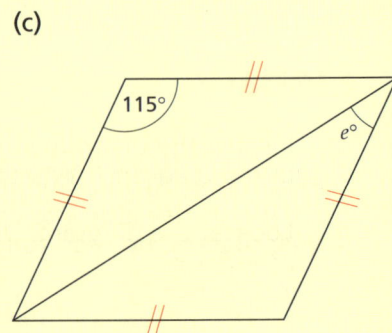

Shape and Space

Challenging exercises

5

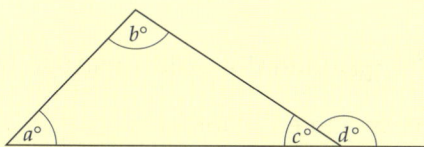

What is the connection between the exterior angle $d°$ and the two interior opposite angles, $a°$ and $b°$?

6 Use the sum of the interior angles of a triangle to prove that the sum of the interior angles of a quadrilateral is 360°.

7 By studying the sum of the interior angles of triangles, quadrilaterals, pentagons and so on, find a general formula for the sum of the interior angles of a polygon with n sides.

8 By studying the sum of the exterior angles of triangles, quadrilaterals, pentagons and so on, find a general formula for the sum of the exterior angles of a polygon with n sides.

Problem-solving exercises

9 Which of the following statements are true?

(a) A triangle can have two obtuse angles.

(b) A triangle can have three acute angles.

(c) A triangle can have a right angle and an obtuse angle.

(d) An equilateral triangle can have an angle of 70°.

(e) A triangle can have three obtuse exterior angles.

10 Draw any triangle on card and cut it out. Use it as a template to make a tessellation (a tiling pattern with no gaps). Explain why this will work for any triangle.

Homework

In question 10 you saw that any triangle will tessellate. Draw any quadrilateral on card and cut it out. Use it as a template to make a tessellation (a tiling pattern with no gaps). Can any quadrilateral be used to make a tessellation? Explain your answer.

Goals

When you have completed this lesson you will be able to:

- state the connection between the scale factors $\frac{50\,000}{1}$, $\frac{1}{50\,000}$ and the scale 1 : 50 000

- use the ideas of 'object' and 'image' in relation to maps and environments.

Starter

1 Think about:

(a)   object   image

$$\frac{2}{3} \text{ of } 6 = 4$$

The scale factor of the operation is $\frac{2}{3}$.

(b)   object   image

$$\frac{3}{2} \text{ of } 4 = 6$$

The scale factor of the operation is $\frac{3}{2}$.

Demonstration 1

Drawing of room (plan)

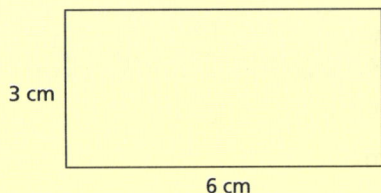

3 cm

6 cm

The real room

object $\xrightarrow{\quad\frac{211}{3}\quad}$ image

image $\xleftarrow{\quad\frac{3}{211}\quad}$ object

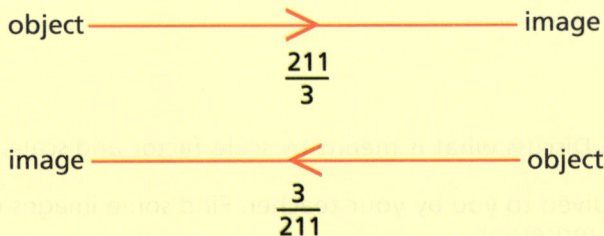

The scale of the plan is 3 : 211.

Demonstration 2

Map of Forest of Wayne

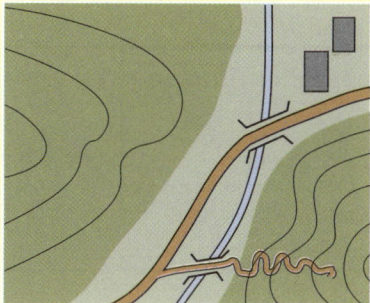

The real Forest of Wayne

object ———————————▶ image

Scale factor is $\dfrac{50\,000}{1}$.

image ◀——————————— object

Scale factor is $\dfrac{1}{50\,000}$.

The scale of the map is 1 : 50 000.

Key words   compare   scale   scale factor

Worked example

Exercise bank 👉

1 A map has a scale of 1 : 25 000.
So, 1 cm on the map represents an actual distance of 25 000 cm = 0·25 km.

(a) How many centimetres represent a distance of 4 km?
4 km are represented by 4 ÷ 0·25 = 16 cm

(b) How many kilometres are represented on the map by 10 cm?
10 cm represents 10 × 0·25 km = 2·5 km

Plenary

👁 Look at the Goals. Discuss what is meant by scale factor and scale.

👁 Inspect the maps given to you by your teacher. Find some images on the maps and discuss what objects they represent.

👁 A model plane has a scale of 3 : 18·5. Discuss.

Letts I See Maths **Year 7**

Shape and Space

Scales

1 Look at this plan of an apartment.

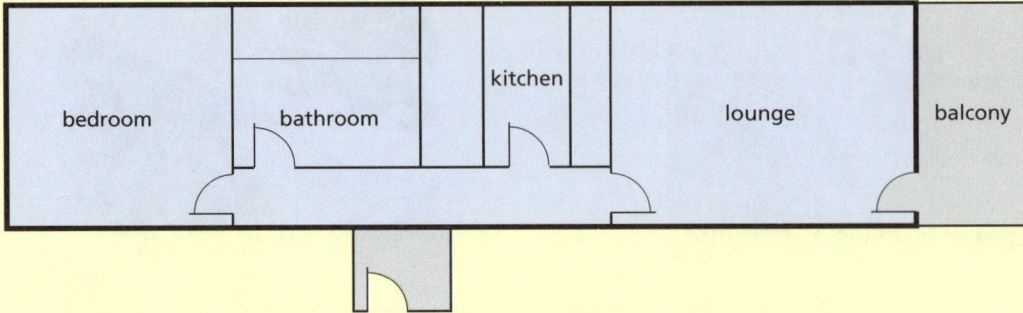

(a) The plan has been drawn to scale. The actual length of the lounge is 4 metres. What scale has been used?

(b) What are the actual measurements of the bedroom?

(c) The new occupants of the appartment have a plant stand with a length of 1·75 metres. Will it fit along the width of the balcony?

2 The Ordnance Survey Landranger Series of maps is drawn to the scale 1 : 50 000.

(a) What does 1 cm in length on the map represent in real life?

(b) How many centimetres on the map represent a distance of 1 km in real life?

(c) Sarah plans a walk using a Landranger map. The distance on the map is 5·5 cm. How far will she actually walk?

3 David plans a hexagonal paved feature for his garden. The scale of the plan is 1 : 200.

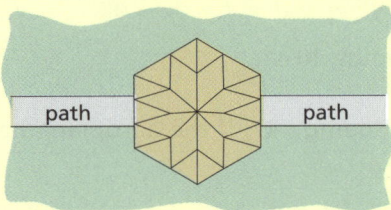

(a) What is the actual length of each side of the hexagon?

(b) What is the maximum width of the hexagon?

(c) What does each interior angle of the hexagon measure on the plan?

(d) What will each interior angle of the hexagon measure in the actual garden?

Challenging exercises

4 Ben found a one-inch Ordnance Survey map of Alnwick.

(a) What would be the scale on an equivalent metric map?

(b) Ben's ruler only measured in centimetres. The boat journey from Bamburgh to Farne Island measured 6 cm on the map. About how many miles is this?

(c) The train journey from Amble to Morpeth is 16 miles. How many centimetres would this be on the map?

5 Amy drove 17 miles in 20 minutes. What was her average speed?

6 A map is drawn with a scale of $1 : n$.

(a) A distance measures x cm on the map. What is this distance in real life?

(b) A distance in real life is y km. What will this distance measure on the map?

Problem-solving exercises

7 (a) The aeroplane, Concorde, has a length of 62·10 m. A model representing the aeroplane has a length of 414 mm. What is the scale of the model?

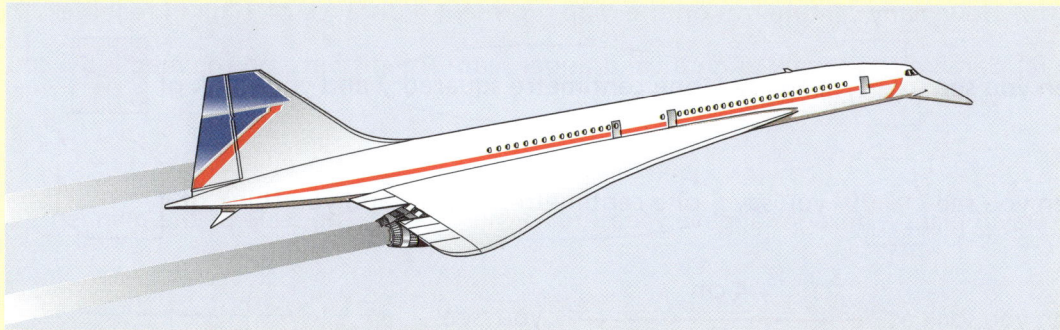

(b) What is the length of a model of the aeroplane, Boeing 747, if the aeroplane has a length of 71·25 m, using a scale of 1 : 125?

Homework

Use an Ordnance Survey map or a road map to plan a journey.

(a) Work out the distance on the map.

(b) Work out the distance in real life.

Shape and Space

Area and volume

▶ Goals

When you have completed this lesson you will be able to:

👁 visualise a cuboid 6 cm long, 3 cm wide and 4 cm deep, and calculate:
  – the area of an end as 3 cm² × 4
  – the volume of the cuboid as 3 cm³ × 4 × 6

👁 visualise a cuboid 6·2 cm long, 3·2 cm wide and 4·3 cm deep, and calculate:
  – the volume of the cuboid as 3·2 cm³ × 4·3 × 6·2.

▶ Starter

1 Work out these expressions.

(a) $3 \times 4 \times 6$ (b) $2 \times 17 \times 5$ (c) $2 \times 8\cdot7 \times 5$

(d) $(3 \times 4 \times 6) \div 2$ (e) $\frac{3 \times 4 \times 6}{2}$ (f) $\frac{1}{2}(3 \times 4 \times 6)$

▶ Demonstration 1

When you see | 1 cm | you say ⟨ one centimetre ⟩ and you think of the line segment ├———┤

When you see | 1 cm² | you say ⟨ one centimetre squared ⟩ and you think of ▢

When you see | 1 cm³ | you say ⟨ one centimetre cubed ⟩ and you think of ▢

When you look at ├——— 4 cm ———┤ you 'see' ├─┼─┼─┼─┤

and you say: ⟨ four centimetres ⟩

When you look at [rectangle 4 cm × 1 cm]   When you look at [cuboid 4 cm × 1]

you say: ⟨ four centimetres squared ⟩   you say: ⟨ four centimetres cubed ⟩

Demonstration 2

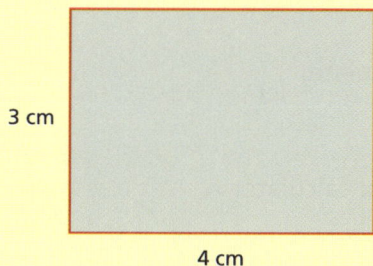

3 cm

4 cm

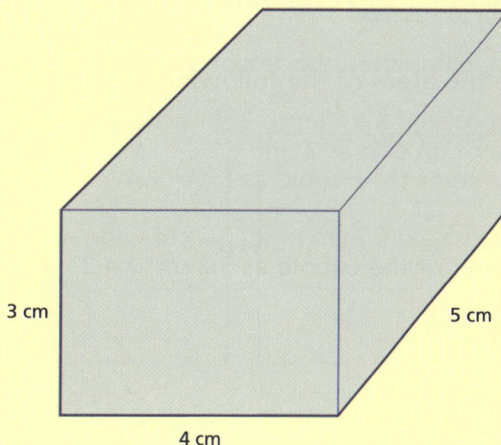

3 cm

5 cm

4 cm

Perimeter = 3 cm × 2 + 4 cm × 2
= 14 cm

Area = 3 cm² × 4 = 12 cm²

Volume = 3 cm³ × 4 × 5
= 60 cm³

Key words   area   cubed   length   perimeter   squared   volume

Worked example

Exercise bank 👉

1 Look at the shape on the right.

Find (a) area ABCD (b) the volume of the cuboid.

(a) Area = 2 cm² × 3 = 6 cm²

(b) Volume = 2 cm³ × 3 × 4·5 = 27 cm³

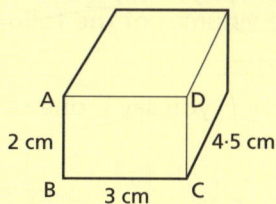

A   D

2 cm   4·5 cm

B   3 cm   C

Plenary

👁 Visualise the cuboids described in the Goals. Work out the answers to the questions and show your teacher.

👁 Discuss the volume of the shape on the right when PQCDAB is removed.

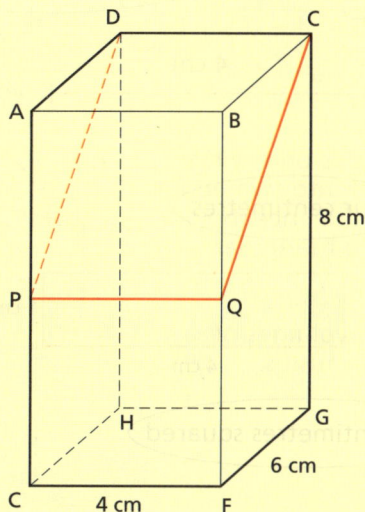

D   C

A   B

8 cm

P   Q

H   G

C   4 cm   F

6 cm

Shape and Space

Area and volume

Essential exercises

1 Calculate the areas of the following shapes.

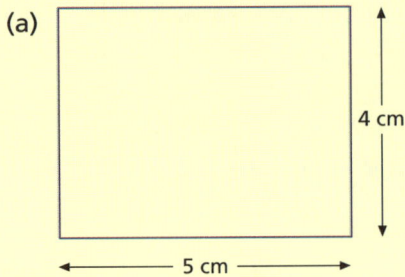

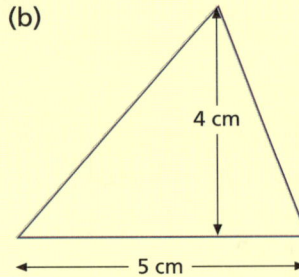

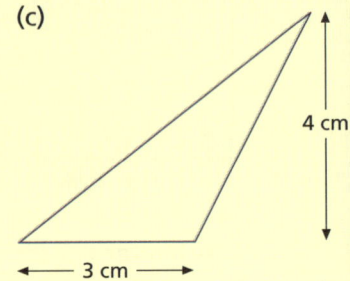

(a)

4 cm

5 cm

(b)

4 cm

5 cm

(c)

4 cm

3 cm

2 Calculate the areas of the following shapes.

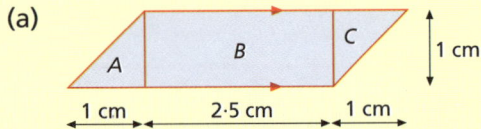

(a)

A   B   C

1 cm

1 cm   2·5 cm   1 cm

(b)

D

1 cm

4·5 cm

Area A =
Area B =
Area C =
Area $A + B + C$ =

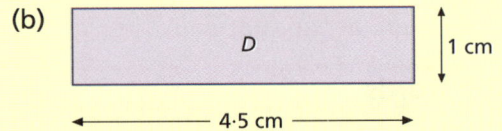

Area D =

3 Calculate the volumes of the following shapes.

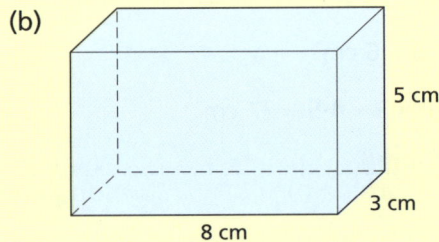

(a)

6 cm

3 cm

5 cm

(b)

5 cm

3 cm

8 cm

4 The two cuboids on the right have been cut into two equal pieces along the lines shown. Each piece is a triangular prism.

Work out the volumes of the triangular prisms.

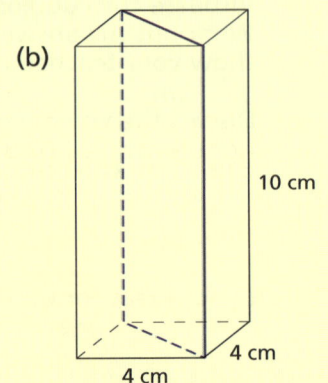

(a)

2 cm

4 cm

6 cm

(b)

10 cm

4 cm

4 cm

Challenging exercises

5 Calculate the areas of the following shapes.

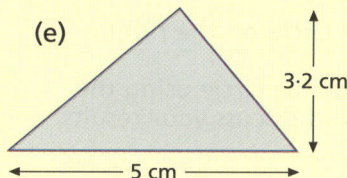

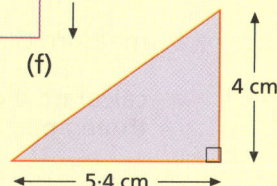

(a) 0·5 cm
0·5 cm

(b) 4 cm
0·5 cm

(c) 3·5 cm
2·5 cm

(d) 1 cm
1·5 cm

(e) 3·2 cm
5 cm

(f) 4 cm
5·4 cm

6 (a) Calculate the area of the net of a cuboid with dimensions 3 cm, 2 cm, 4 cm.

(b) Look at the shape on the right. Calculate:

(i) the surface area

(ii) the volume of the shape.

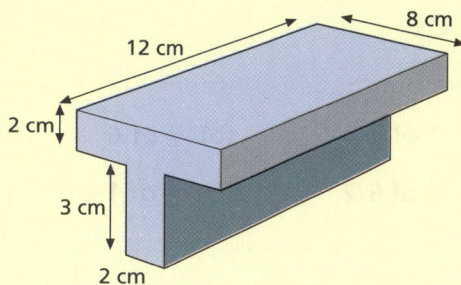

8 cm
12 cm
2 cm
3 cm
2 cm

Problem-solving exercise

7 On squared paper consider polygons, such as these below, whose vertices are at the intersection of the lines.

(a)   (b)   (c)   (d)

Complete the following table.

	Number of points inside (i)	Number of points on perimeter (p)	Area of polygon (A)
(a)	0	4	1
(b)	0	8	3
(c)			
(d)			

See if you can discover a relationship between A, i and p.

Homework

Test your ideas for question 7 on more shapes to bring to your next lesson.

Shape and Space

Goals

When you have completed this lesson you will be able to:

👁 state approximations for π to (a) the nearest whole number (b) to one decimal place (c) to two decimal places

👁 write down the approximation for π given in your calculator

👁 measure the diameter of the circle on the right

👁 calculate the circumference of the circle using the three approximations for π and discuss your results.

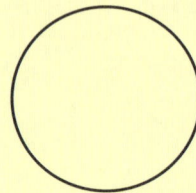

Starter

1 Work out these expressions.

(a) $\frac{2}{3}$ of 6 (b) $\frac{3}{2}$ of 6 (c) $\frac{1}{3}$ of 6 (d) $\frac{3}{1}$ of 6

(e) $\frac{2}{7}$ of 6·2 (f) $\frac{7}{3}$ of 1·7 (g) $\frac{1}{23}$ of 4·1 (h) $\frac{23}{1}$ of 4·1

Demonstration 1

Measuring diameter
These two line segments are parallel.

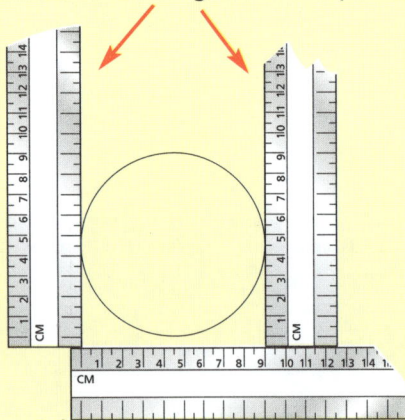

Measuring circumference

This string has the same value as the circumference.

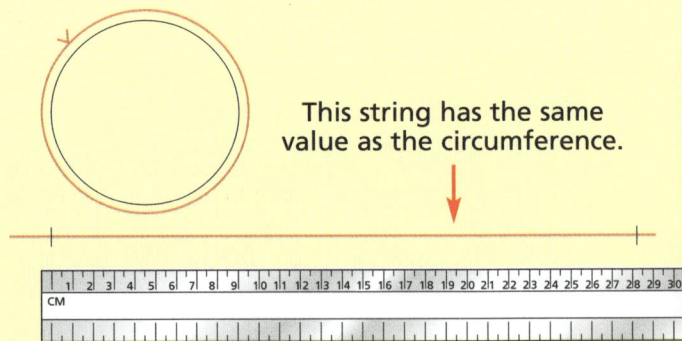

(the circumference C)

Compare this
to this

(the diameter d).

bigger

$C \approx \frac{3 \cdot 14}{1}$ of d

$C = \pi d$

Shape and Space

Demonstration 2

$\pi \approx 3\cdot 14159265358979328462643383279$

Graph of circumference against diameter of a circle

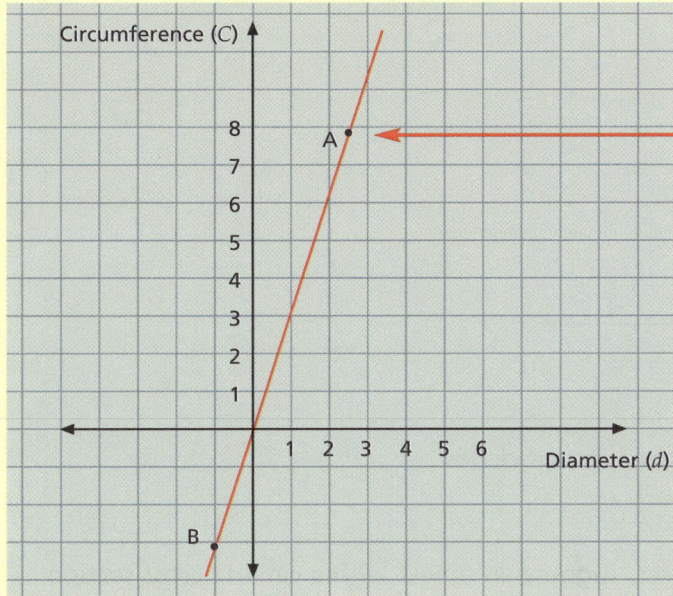

Point A is not a circle. It is not a picture of a circle. It is a hint about a circle that I am thinking of. Describe the circle.

Key words circumference   diameter π radius   scale factor

Worked example

Exercise bank

1 Calculate the circumference of this circle, to one decimal place. Use $\pi \approx 3\cdot 1$.

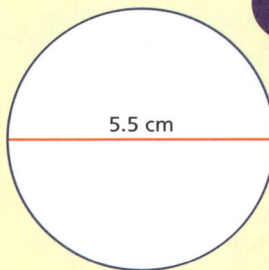

5.5 cm

C cm $= 5\cdot 5 \times \pi$ cm
C cm $\approx 17\cdot 27$ cm
       $= 17\cdot 3$ cm (to 1 d.p.)

Plenary

👁 Discuss the symbol π.

👁 Inspect the circle in the Goals and answer the questions.

👁 Discuss the circle at Point B in Demonstration 2.

Circles 1

Essential exercises

1 This graph shows the circumference (C) of a circle against the diameter (d).

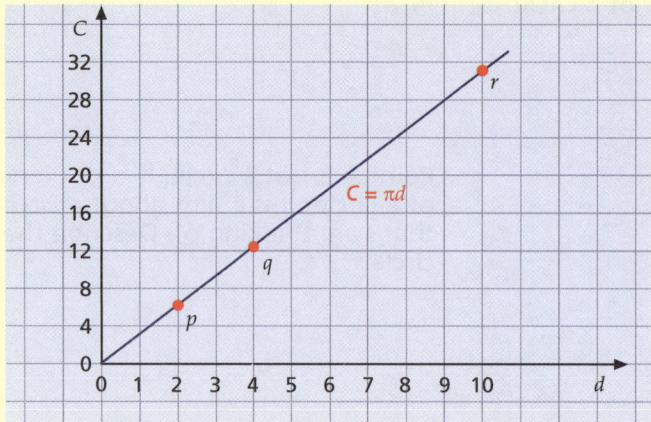

The points p, q and r on the line $C = \pi d$ are hints of circles.
For each point answer these questions.
(a) Write down the value of d.
(b) Write down the value of C.
(c) If d and C are measured in centimetres, suggest an object with a circular cross-section of this size.
(d) If d and C are measured in metres, suggest an object with a circular cross-section of this size.

2 In the grid below, work out the values of the circumference or diameter using the approximation $\pi \approx 3 \cdot 1$.

Diameter of circle (d)	2	5	10	6·5		
Circumference of circle (C)					21·7	37·2

3 Calculate the perimeters of the figures below.

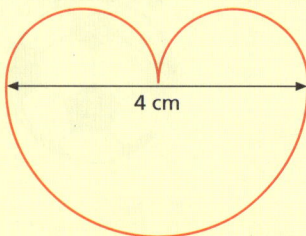

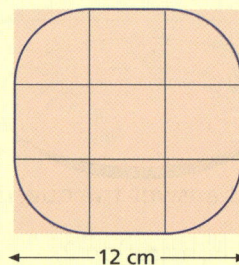

4 cm

12 cm

Letts I See Maths Year 7

Challenging exercises

4 Calculate the perimeters of the figures below.

(a)

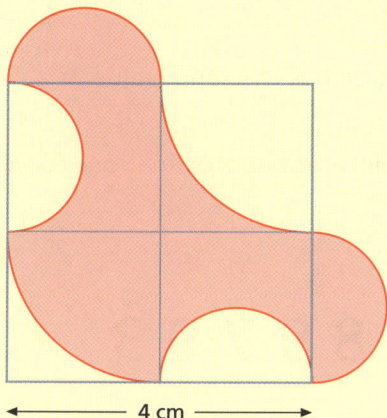

4 cm

(b)

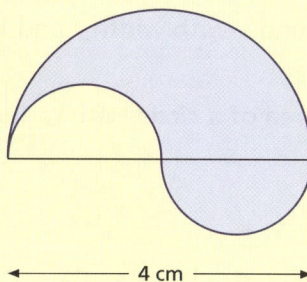

4 cm

5 The formula for calculating the circumference C of a circle with diameter d is $C = \pi d$.
The diameter is given by $d = 2r$, where r is the radius.
Rewrite the formula for the circumference using the radius r.

Problem-solving exercises

6 Jason's birthday cake has a diameter of 20 cm. His mum cuts a piece of ribbon to go around the cake. What length of ribbon should she cut?

7 The Designer Label company has been asked to make labels for tins of soup. The label overlaps by about 2 mm. The tins have a diameter of 7·5 cm. What should be the length of the label, to the nearest millimetre?

Homework

Find some circular objects in your home. Measure their diameters and calculate their circumferences using the approximation $\pi \approx 3$.

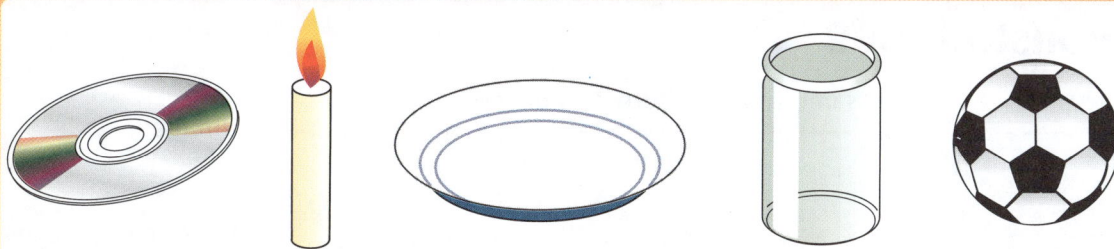

Shape and Space

Goals

When you have completed this lesson you will be able to:

👁 know the area of a circle is $A = \pi r^2$

👁 visualise a rectangle with width r and length πr: its area has the same value as a circle with radius r

👁 calculate the area of a circle with radius 3 cm using different approximations for π.

▶ Starter

$$\pi \approx 3{\cdot}1\ 4\ 1\ 5\ 9\ 2\ 6\ 5\ 3\ 5\ 8\ 9\ 7\ 9\ 3$$

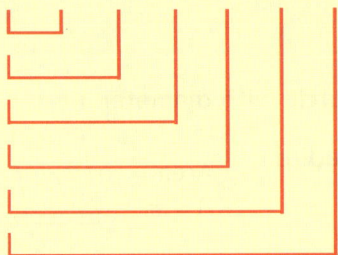

1 Look at each group of digits.

(a) How much is there here?

(b) 'Round off' each number.

2 Discuss:

(a) $C = \pi d$ and $C = 2\pi r$.

(b) $\frac{1}{2}\pi d$ or πr.

▶ Demonstration 1

The circle has radius r.

The area of the square ABCD is $4r^2$.

The area of the square PQRS is $2r^2$.

The area of the circle is less than $4r^2$ and greater than $2r^2$.

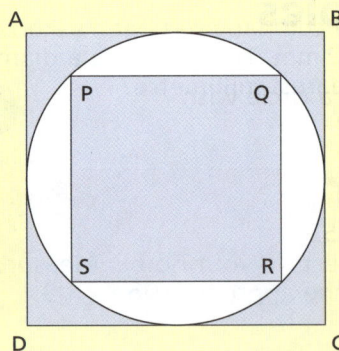

Demonstration 2

same value: different appearance

Object ───────────────────────────────────▶ Image

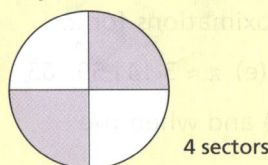

4 sectors

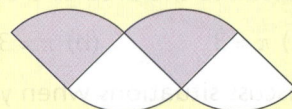

Letts **I See Maths** Year 7

Shape and Space

same value: different appearance

Object ─────────────────────────────────→ Image

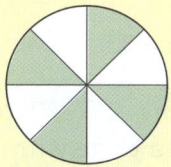

8 sectors

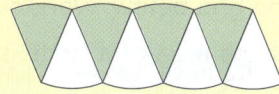

same value: different appearance

Object ─────────────────────────────────→ Image

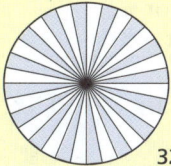

32 sectors

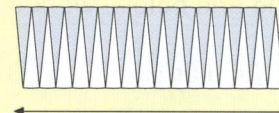

approximately r

approximately πr

same value: different appearance

Object ─────────────────────────────────→ Image

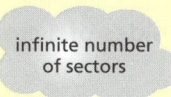

infinite number of sectors

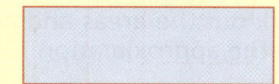

r

πr

Area $= \pi r$ r

$A = \pi r^2$

Key words   image   infinite   object

Worked examples

1 What is the area of a circle with diameter of 2·4 cm?

$d = 2 \cdot 4$, so $r = 1 \cdot 2$
$A = \pi r^2$
$A \approx 3 \cdot 14 \times 1 \cdot 2^2 = 4 \cdot 52$

Area $= 4 \cdot 52$ cm²

Exercise bank

2 What is the radius of a circle with area of 7 cm²?

$A = \pi r^2$, so $r = \sqrt{\dfrac{A}{\pi}}$

$r \approx \sqrt{\dfrac{7}{3 \cdot 14}} = 1 \cdot 49$

Radius $= 1 \cdot 49$ cm

Plenary

👁 Calculate the area of a circle with radius 3 cm using the following approximations for π.

(a) $\pi \approx 3$ (b) $\pi \approx 3 \cdot 1$ (c) $\pi \approx 3 \cdot 14$ (d) $\pi \approx 3 \cdot 142$ (e) $\pi \approx 3 \cdot 141\ 592\ 65$

👁 Discuss situations when you might need to use the approximation in (e) and when the approximation of 3 is sufficient.

Letts **I See Maths** Year 7

Shape and Space

Circles 2

Essential exercises

1 In the grid below, work out the areas of the circles using the approximation $\pi \approx 3$.

Radius (x)	1 cm	10 cm	5 cm	2 cm	4 cm	20 cm
Area (A)						

2 In the grid below, work out the areas of the circles using the approximation $\pi \approx 3.1$.

Radius (x)	3 cm	6 cm	10 cm	4 cm	100 cm	0·5 cm
Area (A)						

3 Work out the areas and perimeters of the following shapes. (Each square has sides of 1 cm.) Use the approximation $\pi \approx 3.14$.

(a) (b) (c) (d) (e) (f)

4 Work out the areas of the shaded parts in the figures below.

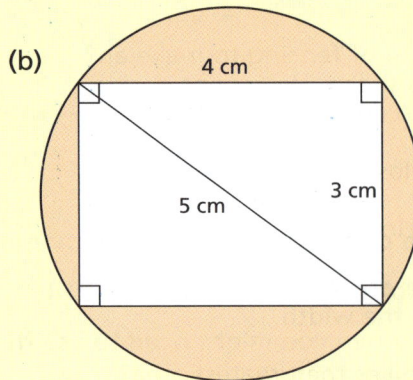

(a) 2 cm 2 cm

(b) 4 cm 5 cm 3 cm

Shape and Space

Circles 2

Challenging exercises

5

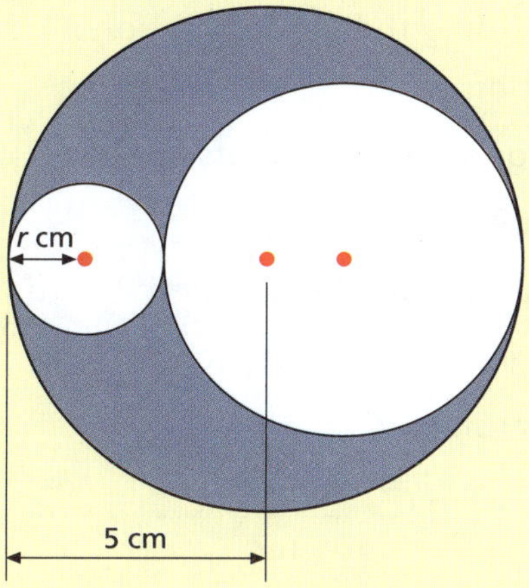

The outer circle has radius 5 cm.

The two inner circles just touch each other and just touch the outer circle.

The radius of one of the inner circles is r.

The area of the shaded part depends on the value of r. For what value of r is the area of the shaded part a maximum?

6 A round table with diameter 1·4 m can be pulled out to make a larger table like this one in the figure below.

(a) What length would the rectangle need to be to double the area of the table? (Use the approximation $\pi \approx 3{\cdot}14$.)

(b) What length would the rectangle need to be to double the perimeter?

Homework

Calculate the following:

(a) area of the yellow circle

(b) area of the dotted part

(c) area of the hatched part.

What do you notice?

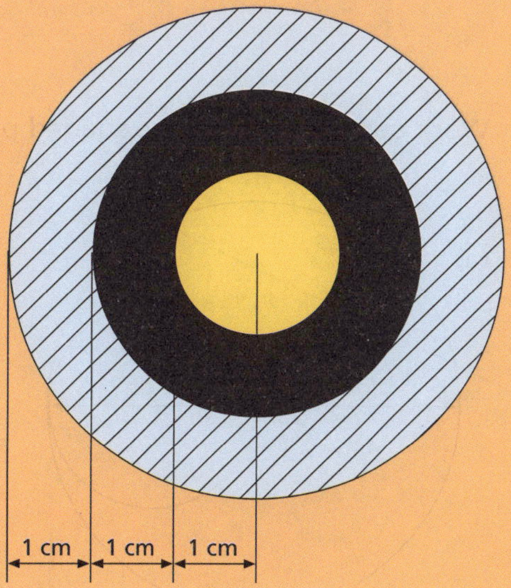

Problem-solving exercise

7 A farmer has 60 m of fencing to make an enclosure for his sheep. He cannot decide which of these to make:

(a) a square enclosure

(b) a circular enclosure

(c) a rectangular enclosure with the length twice the width.

Which of these gives the greatest area?

Letts **I See Maths** Year 7

Shape and Space

151

Goals

When you have completed this lesson you will be able to:

- 👁 accurately draw the image of an object after reflection
- 👁 accurately draw the axis of reflection (mirror line) for an object and its image
- 👁 accurately draw the image of an object after rotation
- 👁 construct the centre of rotation for an object and its image after rotation
- 👁 measure the angle of rotation for an object and its image after rotation
- 👁 accurately construct the image of an object after translation.

Starter

1. Draw the perpendicular bisector of a line segment.
2. Draw parallel lines using a ruler and set square.
3. Draw a rhombus and talk about the diagonals.

Demonstration 1

Reflection

The axis of reflection is the perpendicular bisector of any line segment joining a point object and its image.

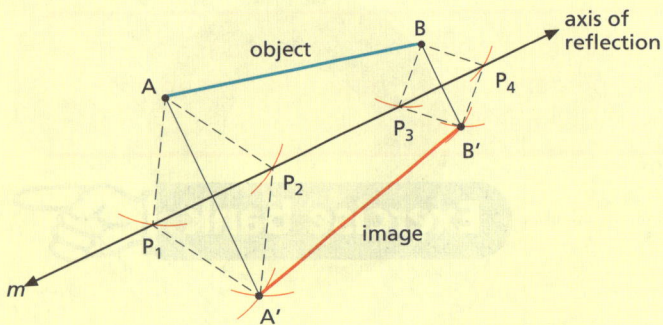

Object: line segment AB

Image: line segment A′B′

Axis of reflection: m
AA′ is a diagonal of rhombus $AP_1A′P_2$.
BB′ is a diagonal of rhombus $BP_3B′P_4$.
A′B′ is the reflection of AB in m.
AB is the reflection of A′B′ in m.

Discuss:
- objects
- images
- axes of reflection

Demonstration 2

Rotation

Visualise object PB and image PB'.

Visualise object PC and image PC'.

Visualise object PA and image PA'.

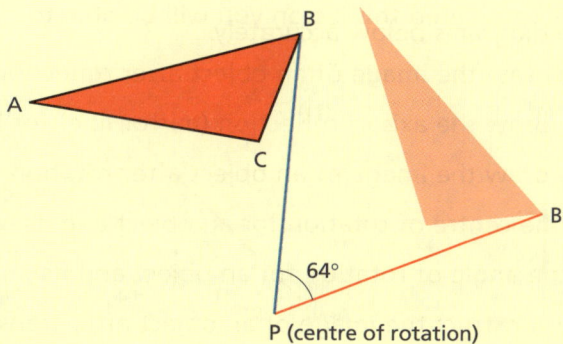

P (centre of rotation)

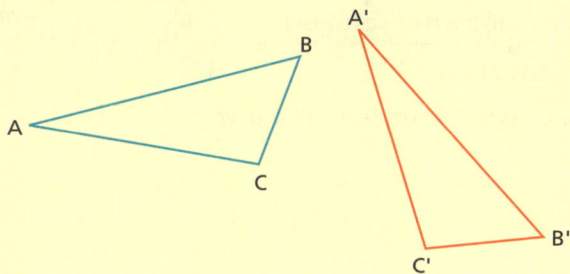

Visualise objects AB, BC and CA, and images A'B', B'C' and C'A'.

Translation

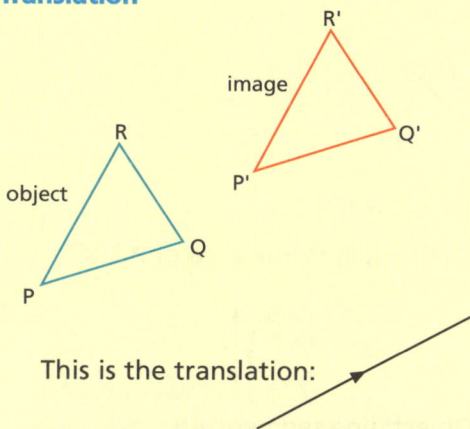

This is the translation:

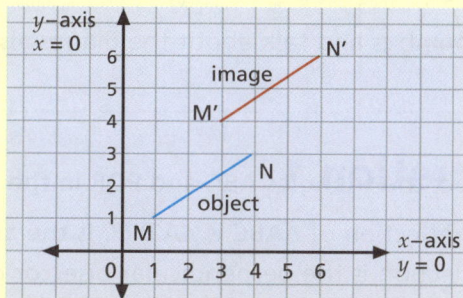

This is the translation: $\binom{2}{3}$

Key words   axes of reflection   axis of reflection   bisector   diagonals
mirror line   parallel lines   perdendicular   reflection   rhombus
rotation   rotational symmetry   translation   vector

Exercise bank

Plenary

👁 Describe the following transformations and explain what information you need for each one.

(a) a reflection   (b) a rotation   (c) a translation

👁 Discuss a rotation of 360°.

Shape and Space

Transformations

Essential exercises

1 Copy the diagrams below accurately.

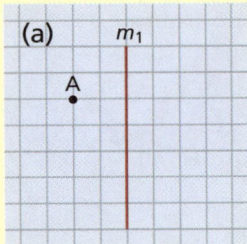

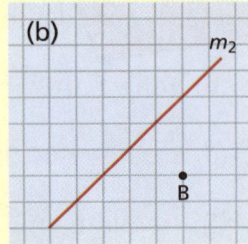

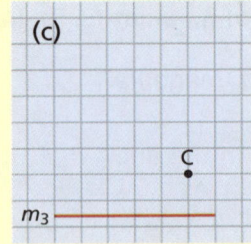

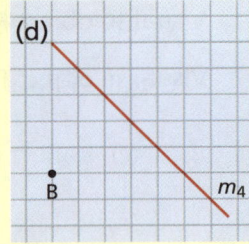

Reflect the points A, B, C and D in the mirror lines (axes of reflection) shown.

2 Copy the diagrams below accurately.

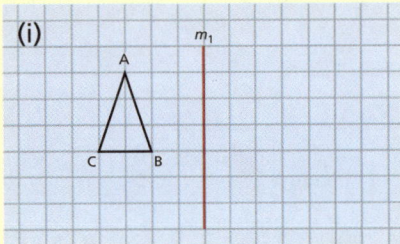

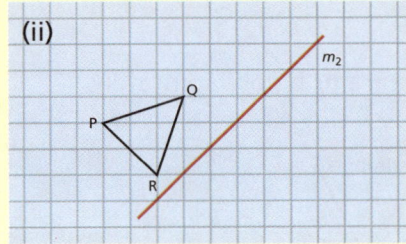

(a) Reflect the triangles ABC and PQR in the mirror lines shown.

(b) The reflection of △ABC is △A'B'C'. Is the area of △A'B'C' equal to the area of △ABC?

3 Copy the diagram on the right accurately.

(a) Rotate △ABC about (0, 0) through an angle of 90°.

(b) Rotate △ABC about (0, 0) through an angle of 180°.

(c) Rotate △ABC about (0, 0) through an angle of 270°.

(d) Rotate △ABC about (1, 0) through an angle of 180°.

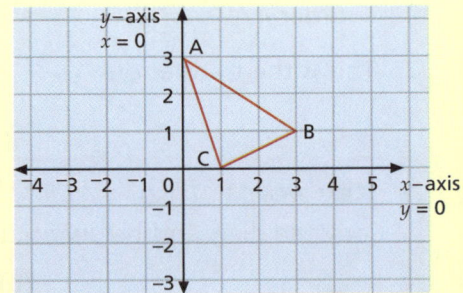

4 Copy the diagram on the right accurately.

(a) Translate △ABC two units to the right and one unit up. This is the translation $\binom{2}{1}$.

(b) Translate △ABC two units to the left and two units down. This is the translation $\binom{-2}{-2}$.

(c) After a translation, the vertices of △ABC are at (2, 1), (4, ⁻1) and (2, ⁻1). Describe the translation.

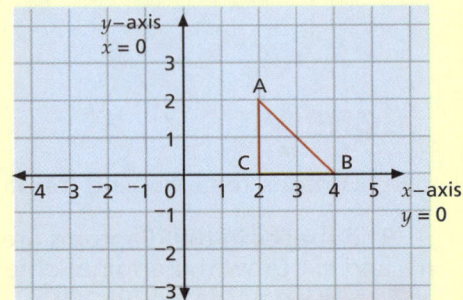

Shape and Space

Letts **I See Maths** Year 7

Transformations

Challenging exercise

5 Draw a grid for $-10 \le x \le 10$ and $-10 \le y \le 10$.

Plot the vertices of $\triangle ABC$ at (3, 3), (4, 2) and (2, 1) and join to make a triangle.

(a) Reflect $\triangle ABC$ in the line $x = 0$.

(b) Reflect $\triangle ABC$ in the line $y = x$.

(c) Reflect $\triangle ABC$ in the line $y = {}^-x$.

(d) Rotate $\triangle ABC$ 90° about (0, 0).

(e) Rotate $\triangle ABC$ 270° about (0, 0).

(f) Translate $\triangle ABC$ by $\binom{6}{5}$.

(g) Translate $\triangle ABC$ by $\binom{-8}{7}$.

(h) Translate $\triangle ABC$ by $\binom{0}{-6}$.

Problem-solving exercise

6 Copy the diagrams below accurately.

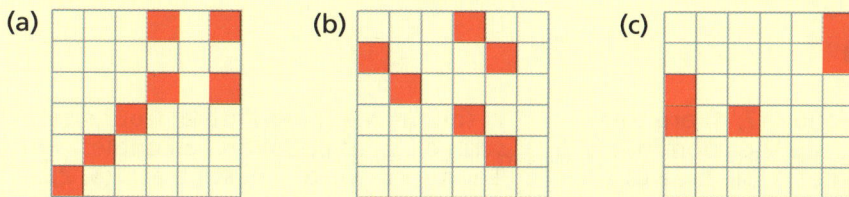

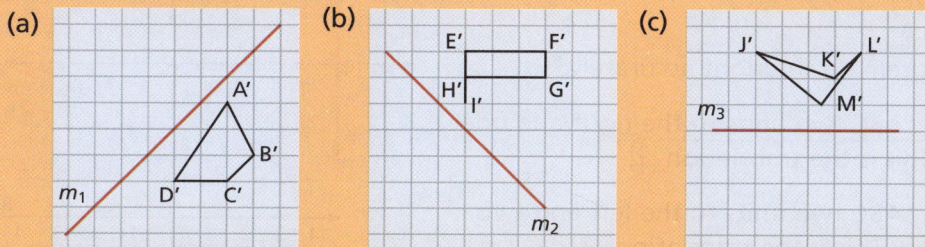

(a)

(b)

(c)

Complete each diagram by shading squares so that each grid has rotational symmetry of order 4.

Homework

Copy the diagrams below accurately.

(a)

(b)

(c)

The shapes in the diagrams are the images after reflection in the mirror lines m_1, m_2 and m_3. Draw the original objects.

Letts **I See Maths Year 7**

Shape and Space

Coordinates

Goals

When you have completed this lesson you will be able to:

- plot points (x, y) accurately on rectangular axes

- use information about geometrical shapes to identify coordinates

- answer questions such as this:
  The points (2, 2) and (5, 5) are opposite vertices of a square. What are the other two vertices of the square?

Starter

1 Plot the following points and label them with the letters given.

A(4, 3)	B(6, 2)	C(⁻5, 3)	D(⁻4, ⁻3)
E$(5, 2\frac{1}{2})$	F$(5, -2\frac{1}{2})$	G(0, ⁻4·5)	H(⁻5·5, 3·5)

Demonstration 1

The points A(3, 4), B(5, 6) and C(7, 4) are three vertices of a square. What are the coordinates of the fourth vertex D? What is the area of the square ABCD?

Draw axes and plot the points given.

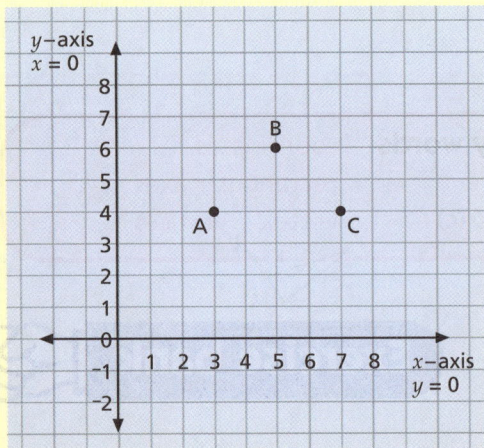

A square is a quadrilateral (four straight sides) with all sides equal and all angles right angles. The fourth vertex must be at D(5, 2).

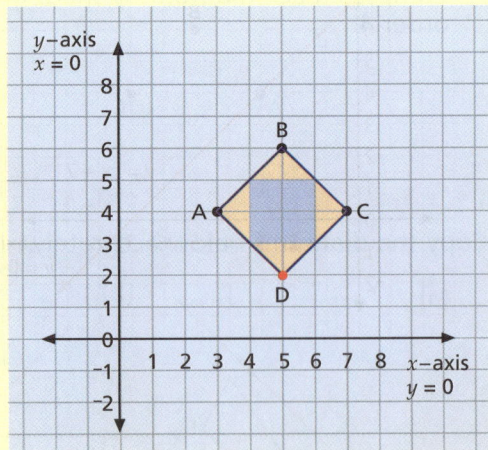

The square covers four whole small squares and eight small half-squares. This is a total of eight whole small squares.
The area is equal to eight square units.

Letts **I See Maths Year 7**

Demonstration 2

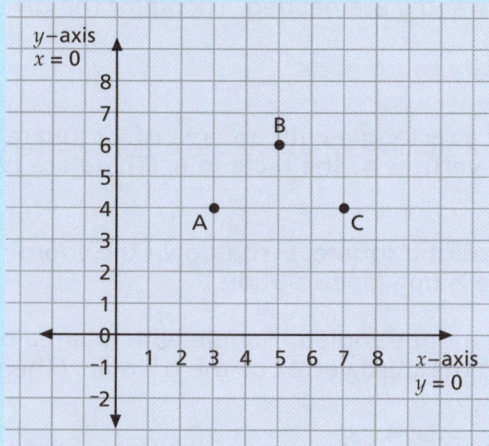

Suppose the points A, B and C are three vertices of a trapezium. Where might the fourth vertex E be?

A trapezium has two parallel sides.

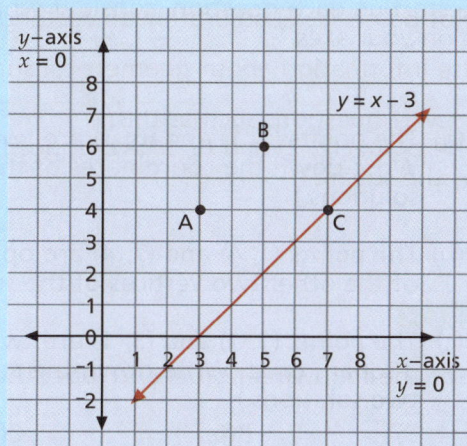

Suppose that AB is parallel to EC. Then E could be at (3, 0) or (4, 1) or (5, 2) or anywhere along the line shown.

The line has equation $y = x - 3$.

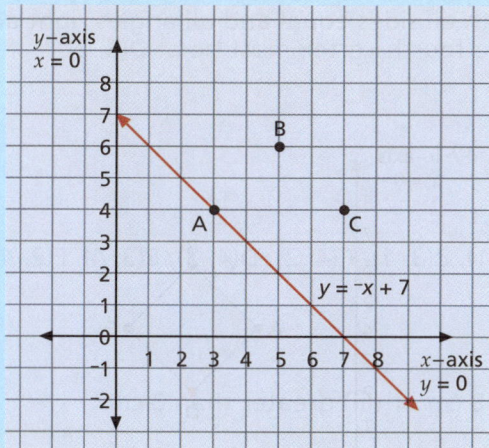

Suppose that BC is parallel to AE. Then E could be at (4, 3) or (5, 2) or (6, 1) or anywhere along the line shown.

The line has equation $y = ^-x + 7$.

Key words   coordinates
rectangular axes
vertex   vertices

Exercise bank

Plenary

◉ Go back to the Goals and find the fourth vertex of the square.

◉ Find the areas of the different trapezia in Demonstration 2.

Coordinates

Essential exercises

In all the exercises below, use a pencil and ruler to draw the x-axis ($y = 0$) and the y-axis ($x = 0$). Before starting each question, consider what values of x and y are needed. Then plot the given points on your axes.

1
  (a) The points (2, 1) and (6, 1) are two vertices of a rectangle with an area of 12 square units. Write down the coordinates of the other two vertices of the rectangle. (There are two solutions.)

  (b) The points (1, 4) and (7, 4) are opposite vertices of a square. Write down the coordinates of the other two vertices of the square. (There is only one solution.)

  (c) The points (1, 1) and (3, 1) are two vertices of a right-angled triangle with an area of 3 square units. Write down the coordinates of the third vertex of the triangle. (There are two solutions.)

  (d) The points (0, 2) and (4, 2) are two vertices of an isosceles triangle with an area of 8 square units. Write down the coordinates of the third vertex of the triangle. (There are two solutions.)

2
The points (1, 3), (⁻2, 2) and (⁻1, 4) are three vertices of a quadrilateral. Write down the coordinates of a fourth vertex such that the quadrilateral is the following:

  (a) a square

  (b) a kite

  (c) an arrowhead.

  (There is more than one solution to parts (b) and (c).)

3
On centimetre-square paper, plot the points A(2, 1), B(3, 1), C(4, 2), D(4, 3), E(3, 4), F(2, 4), G(1, 3) and H(1, 2), and join to form an octagon.

  (a) Calculate the area of the octagon.

  (b) Is the perimeter (i) less than 8 cm (ii) equal to 8 cm or (iii) greater than 8 cm? Explain your answer.

  (c) What is the equation of the line passing through AF?

4
On centimetre-square paper, plot the points A(2, 4), B(3, 5), C(6, 5) and D(7, 4).

  (a) Write down the coordinates of E and F such that ABCDEF is a hexagon that is symmetrical about $y = 4$.

  (b) Calculate the area of the hexagon.

Shape and Space

Letts **I See Maths** Year 7

Challenging exercises

5 A parallelogram is formed by joining the points of intersection of four lines. Three of the lines are $y = x$, $x = 2$ and $x = 4$. What is the equation of the fourth line if the parallelogram has an area of 4 square units? (There are two solutions.)

6 A parallelogram ABCD is formed by joining the points A(1, 5), B(5, 7), C(5, 3) and D(1, 1).

(a) Draw parallelogram ABCD.

(b) Plot M_1, the midpoint of AB, M_2, the midpoint of BC, M_3, the midpoint of CD and M_4, the midpoint of AD.

(c) Join $M_1M_2M_3M_4$ with straight lines. What shape is this?

Problem-solving exercises

7 **Four in a row**
Play this game with two players or two teams of players.

Aim: To get four crosses in a row (vertical, horizontal or diagonal). Players take turns putting crosses on the grid.

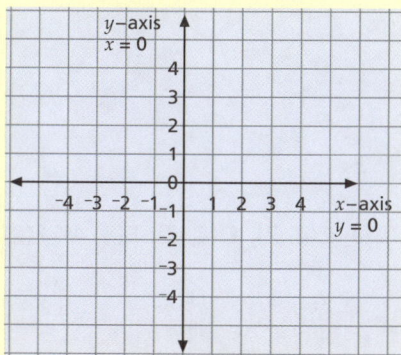

8 Triangle ABC with A(1, 0), B(3, 0) and C(3, 2) is transformed into triangle A′B′C′ with A′(0, 1), B′(0, 3) and C′(-2, 3).

Describe the transformation.

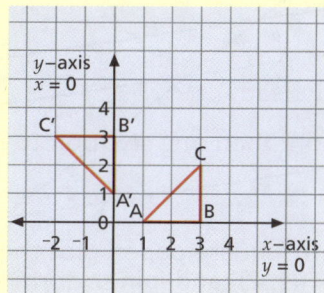

Homework

Write instructions giving the coordinates for the following shapes:

(a) a square with area 9 square units

(b) a triangle with area 6 square units

(c) a parallelogram with area 8 square units.

Letts **I See Maths** Year 7

Review of Shape and Space 1

1 Draw a line segment AB, 6 cm in length. Use a protractor and ruler to construct an angle at B such that:

(a) A$\overset{\wedge}{\text{B}}$C = 35°, BC = 5 cm

(b) A$\overset{\wedge}{\text{B}}$C = 135°, BC = 7 cm.

2 Calculate each of the angles marked with a letter in the diagrams below.

(a)

(b)

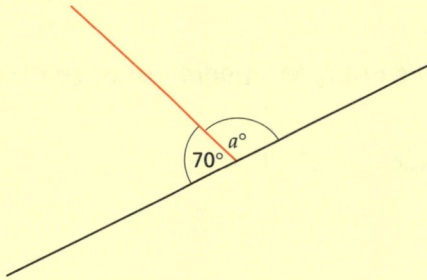
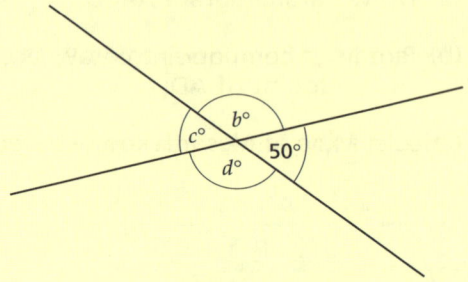

3 Calculate the angles marked with letters and give reasons for your answers.

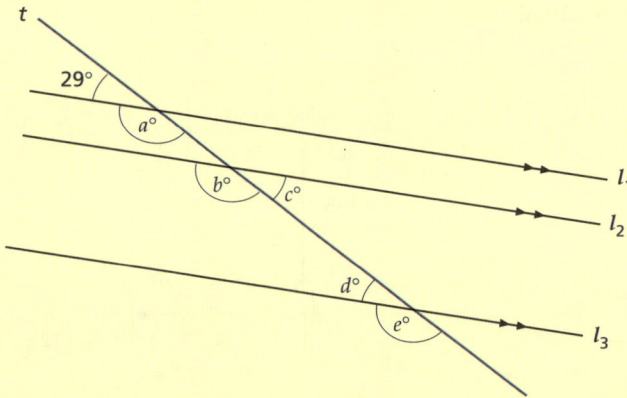

4 Name pairs of angles that are the following:

(a) vertically opposite

(b) supplementary

(c) alternate

(d) corresponding.

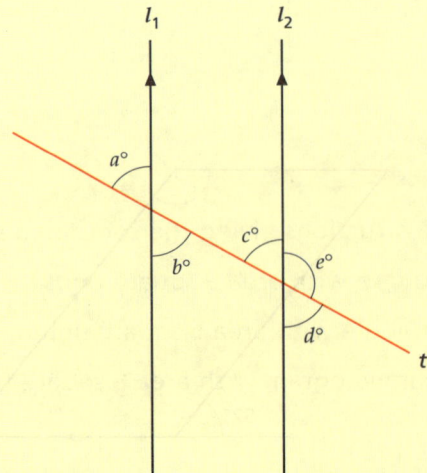

Letts **I See Maths Year 7**

5 You have four sticks of length 3 cm, 4 cm, 5 cm and 9 cm. How many different triangles can you make?

6 Use a pair of compasses to construct these triangles accurately .
(a) △ABC with AB = 5 cm, BC = 4 cm, AC = 3 cm
(b) △DEF with DE = 8 cm, EF = 7 cm, DF = 6 cm

7 Use a pair of compasses to draw, accurately, a hexagon with sides 4 cm.

8 Use a pair of compasses to draw, accurately, the net of a tetrahedron of edges 3 cm.

9 Calculate the angles marked with letters in the diagrams below.

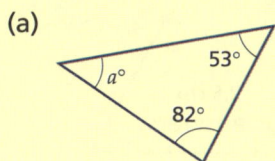

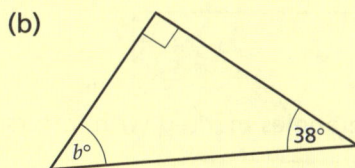

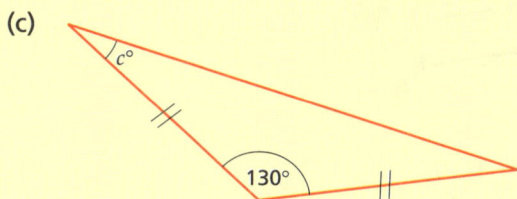

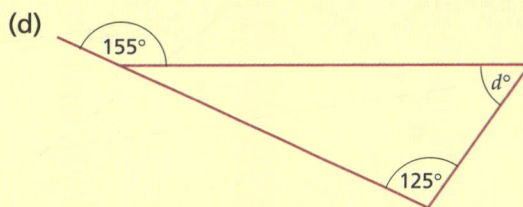

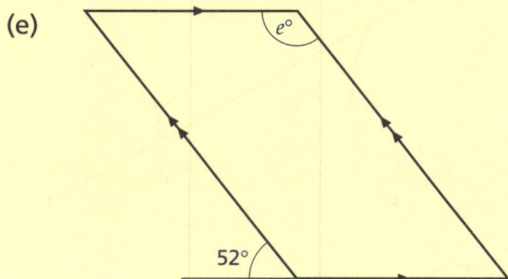

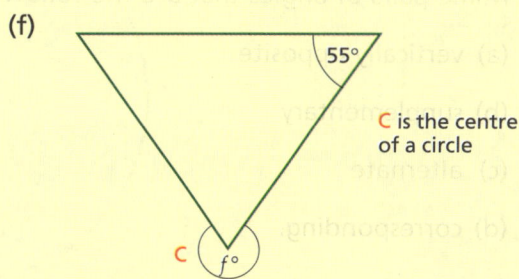

(a)

$a°$
$53°$
$82°$

(b)

$b°$
$38°$

(c)

$c°$
$130°$

(d)

$155°$
$d°$
$125°$

(e)

$e°$
$52°$

(f)

$55°$
C is the centre of a circle
C
$f°$

1 A model car made to the scale 1 : 50 has length 7 cm. What is the actual length of the real car?

2 An insect appears to be 2·5 cm long when magnified under a microscope with the scale 10 : 1. What is its actual length?

3 Calculate the areas of the following shapes.

(a)

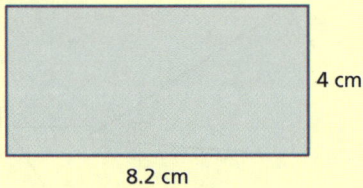

4 cm

8.2 cm

(b)

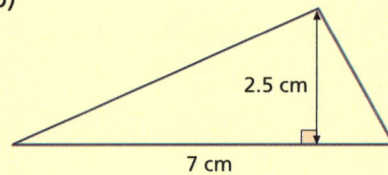

2.5 cm

7 cm

4 Calculate the circumference and area of the circle on the right using the approximation π ≈ 3·14.

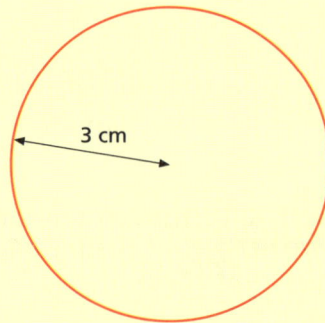

3 cm

5 Calculate the area of the shaded part of the diagram using the approximation π ≈ 3.

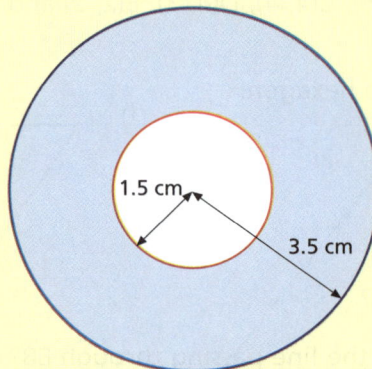

1.5 cm

3.5 cm

6 △ABC is congruent to △DBE. You can rotate △DBE anticlockwise onto △ABC.

  (a) Where is the centre of rotation?

  (b) What is the angle of rotation?

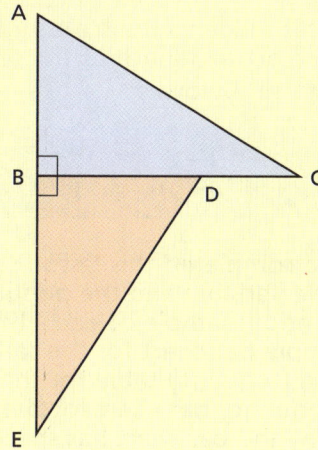

7 (a) Copy the diagram on the right and reflect triangle ABC in the mirror line *m*.

  (b) Join the points B and B′, the image of B. What is the angle made by this line with the mirror line?

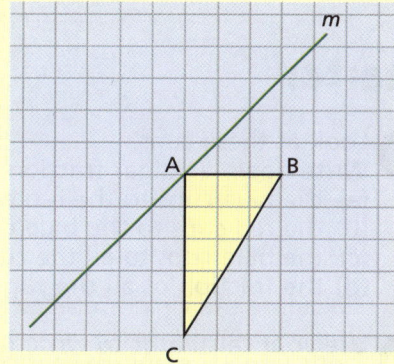

8 The points (2·5, 0) and (5, 0) are two vertices of a rectangle with area 5 cm². Write down the coordinates of the other two vertices of the rectangle. (There are two solutions.)

9 Plot the points A(1, 4), B(2, 5), C(4, 4), D(4, 3), E(2, 2) and F(1, 3), and join to form a hexagon.

  (a) Calculate the area of the hexagon.

  (b) Is the perimeter:

      (i)   less than 6 units

      (ii) equal to 6 units

      (iii) greater than 6 units?

  (c) What is the equation of the line passing through EB?

Shape and Space

Interpreting data 1

Goals

Look at the data set below.

Person	A	B	C	D	E	F	G	H	I	J	K	L	M	N	O	P	Q	R	S	T	U	V	W	X
No. of siblings	1	0	1	6	1	3	4	0	0	2	2	3	2	1	6	1	3	4	0	0	2	2	3	2

When you have completed this lesson you will be able to:
- 👁 identify the variable and the population
- 👁 select a random sample of size 11 from the population
- 👁 draw a simple bar chart for the sample
- 👁 complete a frequency table for the population
- 👁 draw a frequency bar chart for the population
- 👁 explain why the bar chart has spaces between the bars
- 👁 explain why this data set has a discrete variable
- 👁 write down the domain of the variable.

Starter

1 Look at these cups.
Write down a vulgar fraction to compare:
(a) the blue cups to the red cups
(b) the red cups to the blue cups
(c) the blue cups to all the cups
(d) the fraction of all the cups that are red.

2 Use your calculator to write down each of these fractions (a) in decimal form (b) as a percentage.

Demonstration 1

Below is a data set for all the members of Hopegate Sports Club. This is the population.

Person	A	B	C	D	E	F	G	H	I	J	K	L	M	N	O	P	Q	R	S	T	U	V	W	X
Shoe size	8	8	5	5	6	7	5	5	8	4	5	7	5	7	5	4	5	8	8	8	8	5	5	7

What is the variable?   Shoe size
Is the variable discrete or continuous?   Discrete
What is the population?   The shoe sizes of all the members of Hopegate Sports Club
What is the population size?   24

This is a random sample from the above population.

Person	B	E	M	O	T	V
Shoe size	8	6	5	5	8	5

What is the variable?   Shoe size
What is the sample size?   6

Letts I See Maths Year 7

Demonstration 2

Sample

Person	B	E	M	O	T	V
Shoe size	8	6	5	5	8	5

Simple bar chart

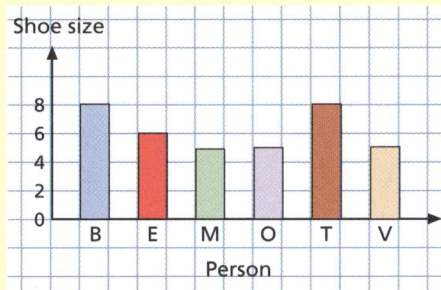

Frequency bar chart

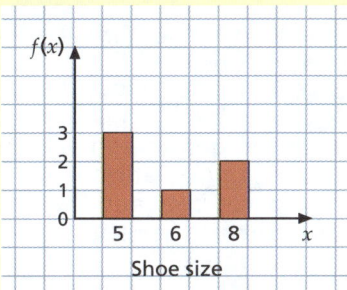

Frequency line graph

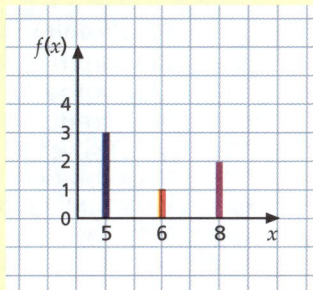

Tally chart

Variable (shoe size)	Frequency (number)
x	$f(x)$
5	III
6	I
8	II

Frequency table

Variable (shoe size)	Frequency (number)
x	$f(x)$
5	3
6	1
8	2

Key words   bar chart   data set   discrete variable   frequency   frequency distribution   frequency table   line graph   population   random sample   sample   tally chart   variable

Worked example

Variable (shoe size)	Frequency (number)
x	$f(x)$
5	3
6	1
8	2
	$\sum f(x) = 6$

Exercise bank

1 (a) What fraction of the sample was size 8? (Write a vulgar fraction.)

$\frac{2}{6}$

(b) Write this vulgar fraction as a decimal.

$\frac{2}{6} = \cdot 3 \ldots$

Use a calculator:

$\frac{2}{6} = \cdot 33$ (to 2 d.p.)

Plenary

👁 Go back to the Goals and look at the population. Select your own random sample (sample size = 11) and use it to complete all the tasks in the Goals.

Interpreting data 1

1 **Survey of cars in St George's Square car park**

Colour of car	Tally	Frequency
white	~~IIII~~ III	
blue	~~IIII~~ II	
green	IIII	
red	~~IIII~~ ~~IIII~~	
silver	~~IIII~~ ~~IIII~~ ~~IIII~~	
black	III	
yellow	II	
purple	I	
	Total	

(a) Copy and complete the table above.
(b) How many cars are in the survey altogether?
(c) What is the most common colour of car (the mode)?
(d) What is the least common colour of car?
(e) How many cars are not white?
(f) How many cars are either silver or black?
(g) What fraction of the total number of cars is silver?
(h) Write the answer to (g) as a percentage?
(i) What fraction of the total number of cars is red?
(j) Write the answer to (i) as a percentage.
(k) Discuss whether this survey can help us know about all cars.

2 **Survey of cars in Box Lane car park**

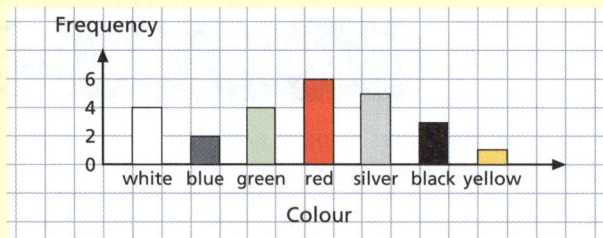

Bar chart to show the result of the survey

(a) How many cars are in the survey altogether?
(b) How many cars are blue?
(c) What is the most common colour of car (the mode)?
(d) How many cars are not green?
(e) How many cars are either black or yellow?
(f) What percentage of cars is silver?
(g) What percentage of cars is red?
(h) Which of the two car parks, St George's Square or Box Lane, has a higher percentage of green cars?

Challenging exercise

3 (a) In a survey of 50 cars, 10% were white. How many cars were white?

(b) In a survey, the ratio of blue cars to green cars was 2 : 3. If the total of green and blue cars was 15, how many cars were blue?

(c) In a survey, if the fraction of cars that are red is $\frac{3}{5}$, what percentage of cars is not red?

(d) In a survey of 25 cars, three were green. What percentage of cars was green?

Problem-solving exercise

4 **Survey of Compton School car park**

Colour	Number of cars
white	
blue	
green	
red	
silver	
black	
yellow	

= 2 cars

Pictogram to show the number of cars in the car park

(a) How many cars are in the survey altogether?

(b) How many cars are red?

(c) What percentage of cars is silver?

(d) What fraction of cars is yellow?

(e) What percentage of cars is not red?

(f) Four visitors arrive and park in the car park. One of their cars is white, one is red and two are silver. What percentage of cars is now red?

Homework

(a) Draw a bar chart to show the survey in question 1.

(b) Construct a frequency table for the information shown in the bar chart in question 2.

(c) Construct a frequency table for the information shown in the pictogram in question 4.

Interpreting data 2

Goals

Look at the sample below.

Person	B	E	M	O	T	V
No. of letters in first name	5	4	4	5	4	5

When you have completed this lesson you will be able to:

- 👁 complete a frequency table
- 👁 identify the variable and state whether it is discrete or continuous
- 👁 draw a bar chart
- 👁 draw a pie chart
- 👁 calculate the angle in the sector representing 5-letter names.

Starter

1. Object → image 1 (clockwise)
   Fraction of whole turn =
   Size of angle   =

2. Object → image 2 (clockwise)
   Fraction of whole turn =
   Size of angle   =

3. Object → image 1 (anticlockwise)
   Fraction of whole turn =
   Size of angle   =

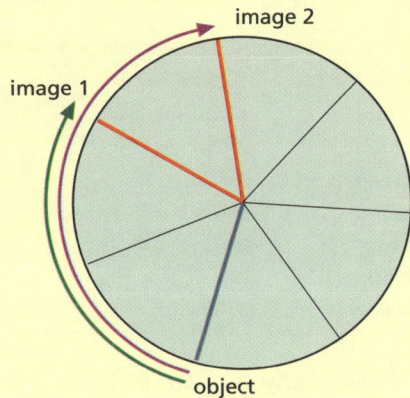

Demonstration 1

A data set was collected from all members at Hopegate Sports Club. This is the frequency table for the population of shoe sizes.

Population

Variable (shoe size)	Frequency (number)		The population is:
x	$f(x)$		
4	2		4 4
5	10		5 5 5 5 5 5 5 5 5 5
6	1		6
7	4		7 7 7 7
8	7		8 8 8 8 8 8 8
	$\sum f(x) = 24$		

The size of the population is 24. The size of the domain is 5. The frequency is distributed over the variable

Letts I See Maths Year 7

Handling Data

Demonstration 2

Bar chart for frequency distribution of population

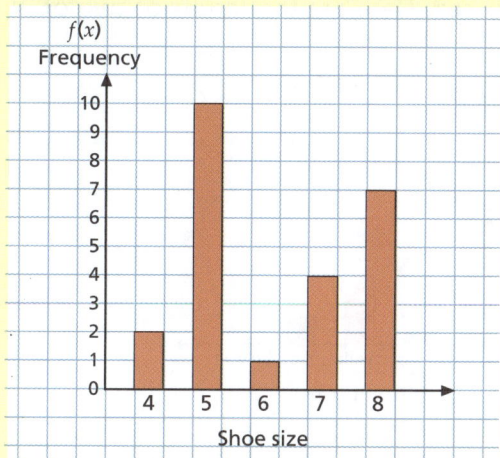

Pie chart for frequency distribution of population

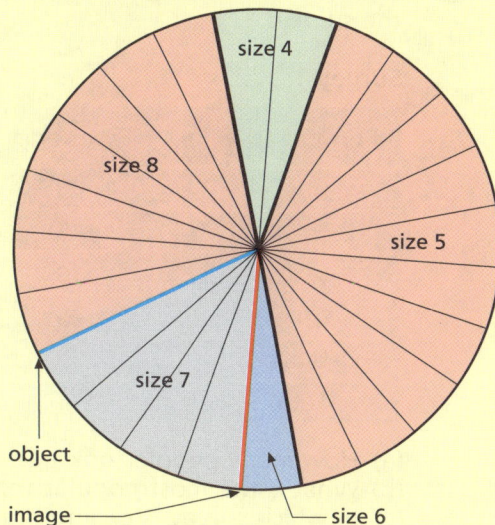

Look in the pie chart at the angle of the sector representing shoe size 7.

The image turns through $\frac{4}{24}$ of $360° = 15° × 4$
$= 60°$

Key words   domain   image   object   pie chart   sector

Worked example

Exercise bank

1. What angle does the image turn through for shoe size 6 in a pie chart for this sample frequency distribution?

Variable (shoe size)	Frequency (number)
x	$f(x)$
5	3
6	1
8	2

Angle $= \frac{1}{6}$ of $360°$
$= 60°$

Plenary

- Study the sample in the Goals and use it to complete the tasks.
- Talk about the sentence, 'The frequency is distributed over the variable.'
- Discuss what a bar chart or a pie chart tells you about a frequency distribution.

Letts **I See Maths** Year 7

Interpreting data 2

Essential exercises

1 Local businesses blamed early morning traffic congestion on the 'school run'. They conducted surveys in the local schools about the forms of travel used. Here are the results of two of the surveys.

Survey 1

Form of travel	Frequency
bus	5
train	3
walk	10
car	25
bicycle	7
Total	

Survey 2

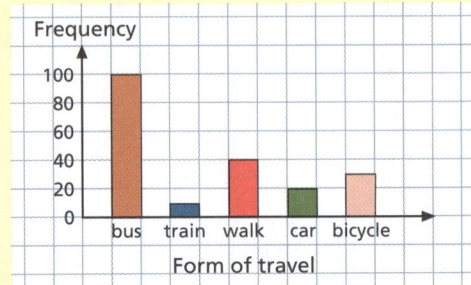

(a) How many people took part in each survey?
(b) What is the most popular form of travel in each survey (the mode)?
(c) In which survey is cycling most popular?
(d) What percentage of people walked to school in each survey?

2 Here is the result of a third survey on methods of travel to school.

Survey 3

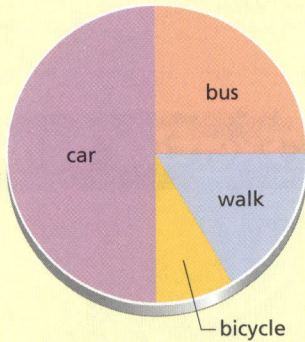

(a) What is the most popular form of travel (the mode)?
(b) What is the least popular form of travel?
(c) Copy and complete the following table.

Form of travel	Fraction of total	Percentage of total
bus		
walk		
car		
bicycle		

(d) If there were 120 children in the survey, how many travelled by car?

Letts **I See Maths** Year 7

Interpreting data 2

Challenging exercises

3 (a) On a day in September, three-quarters of the pupils in St Anne's School travelled to school by car. What percentage did not travel by car?
   (b) In two surveys, the results of travelling to school by car were 35 pupils in the first survey and 43 pupils in the second survey. Is it correct to write this as the ratio 35 : 43? Explain your answer.

4 There were 144 people in a survey. Calculate the angles needed to represent the results in a pie chart.

Form of travel	Number of people	Size of angle (in degrees)
bus	64	
walk	36	
car	40	
bicycle	4	
Total		

Problem-solving exercise

5 Two more surveys on travelling to school are shown below.

Survey 4

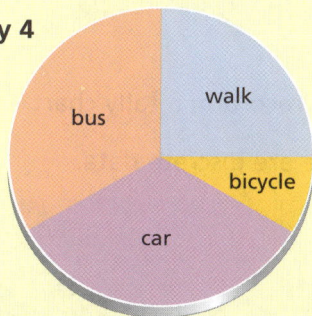

Survey 5

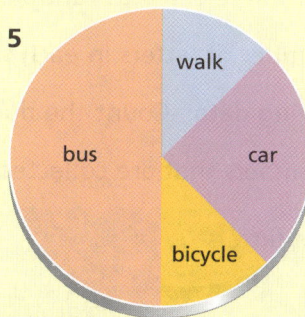

Which of the following statements are true? Explain your answers.
(a) More children travel by car in Survey 4 than in Survey 5.
(b) The percentage of children who walk to school is greater in Survey 4 than in Survey 5.
(c) A quarter of the children in Survey 5 walk to school.
(d) The number of children who cycle to school in Survey 4 is three times the number who walk.
(e) The number of children who walk to school in Survey 4 is double the number who walk to school in Survey 5.

Homework

Draw pie charts to represent the data for the two surveys in question 1.

Grouped discrete data

Goals

When you have completed this lesson you will be able to:

👁 discuss the implicit discrete information in Demonstration 1 about how the data set was collected

👁 discuss different ways of grouping the data

👁 use the grouped data to draw a bar chart.

Starter

1 Give the following fractions and decimal fractions as percentages.

(a) $\frac{1}{2}$ (b) 0·25   (c) $\frac{3}{4}$ (d) 0.07   (e) $\frac{3}{8}$

(f) $\frac{7}{10}$ (g) $\frac{5}{1000}$ (h) $1\frac{1}{2}$ (i) $\frac{9}{20}$ (j) 0·003

Demonstration 1

Sample: A paragraph selected at random from my reading book.

Data set: The number of letters in each word.

Method of collecting data: Count the number of letters and record in a tally chart.

The data set is numbers that are collected by counting. These are discrete data.

Numbers of letters	Tally	Frequency
1	II	2
2	IIII IIII	10
3	IIII IIII IIII	15
4	IIII IIII III	13
5	IIII III	8
6	IIII III	8
7	IIII	4
8	I	1
9	II	2
10		0
11	I	1
12	I	1
Total		65

The most common number (the mode) of letters is three.
The percentage of words with three letters is $\frac{15}{65}$ or 23%.

Demonstration 2

The data can be shown in a grouped frequency table.

Number of letters	1–3	4–6	7–9	10–12
Number of words	27	29	7	2

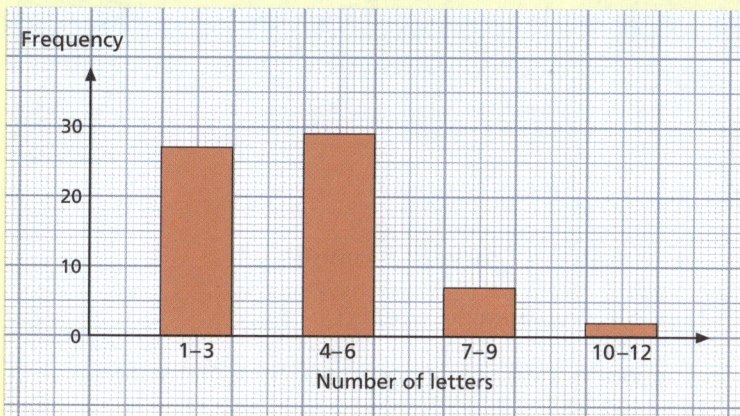

Bar chart to show the number of letters in words

The modal class of number of letters is 4–6.

Key words   discrete data   grouped frequency

Worked example

Exercise bank 👉

1 Look at the information in Demonstration 2.

(a) What is the total number of words?
    $27 + 29 + 7 + 2 = 65$

(b) What fraction of words had 1 to 3 letters in them?
    $\frac{27}{65}$

(c) What percentage of words had 10 to 12 letters in them?
    $\frac{2}{65} = 2 \div 65 = \cdot03 = 3\%$

Plenary

👁 Inspect the data set in Demonstration 1. Why is this called discrete data?

Group the data in a different way and complete a grouped frequency table.

Draw a bar chart to represent this data.

👁 Discuss reasons for grouping data.

Grouped discrete data

Essential exercises

1 Crockers' Chocolates received several complaints from customers that their packets of supreme caramels had fewer than the promised 20 sweets in them. They decided to take a random sample of the product and test it. They recorded the results in a table.

Number of caramels in a packet	11–13	14–16	17–19	20–22	23–25	26–28	29–31
Number of packets	1	2	9	24	8	5	1

(a) Draw a bar chart to represent this data.

(b) How big was the sample?

(c) How many packets of sweets fulfilled Crockers' promise?

(d) What percentage of packets of sweets fulfilled Crockers' promise?

(e) What percentage of packets contained fewer than 17 sweets?

(f) If the sample is representative of the whole population, estimate how many packets would be unsatisfactory in a batch of 3000.

(g) Did the sampling exercise support the customers' complaints?

2 A company is marketing a new type of peas. It would like its advertisements to state that the majority of pods contain more than seven peas. In order to verify this statement, the company conducts a sample survey. The results are recorded below.

Number of peas	2–4	5–7	8–10	11–13	14–16	17–19
Number of pods	2	10	10	11	5	2

(a) Draw a bar chart to represent this data.

(b) What percentage of pea pods had more than seven peas in them?

(c) Is the company's claim correct for this sample?

(d) Could the company claim, from this sample, that the majority of pea pods contained more than ten peas?

(e) If the sample is representative of the whole population of pea pods, estimate how many pods, out of a sample of 500, you would expect to have more than 16 peas in them.

Handling Data

Challenging exercise

3 Survey of pupils in Bart's Wood School who send text messages

Number of texts sent each day	1–5	6–10	11–15	16–20	21–25	26–30	Do not text
Number of girls	70	60	25	10	5	0	150
Number of boys	40	40	45	10	3	140	140

(a) Draw a bar chart to represent this data.

(b) What percentage of girls text?

(c) What percentage of all pupils text?

(d) Is the percentage of girls who send more than five texts a day greater or less than the boys?

(e) As a part of the survey, 30 of the girls who sent fewer than six texts a day decided to leave their phones at home. What percentage of girls still sent fewer than six texts a day?

Problem-solving exercise

4 Pupils conducted a survey to find out how many daisies were on the school field. They divided the field into equally sized sections and recorded the results in a table.

Number of daisies	0–9	10–19	20–29	30–39	40–49	50–59	60–69
Number of sections	4	14	25	32	29	10	6

(a) Into how many sections was the field divided?

(b) How many sections had fewer than 20 daisies in them?

(c) What percentage of sections had more than 29 daisies in them?

(d) Would it be true to say that the majority of the sections had more than 39 daisies in them?

Homework

Hypothesis: The word-length in magazines is shorter than that in newspapers so that magazines are easier to read.

Test this hypothesis by counting the word-length in a sample of words from each type of publication.

Continuous data

Goals

When you have completed this lesson you will be able to:

- inspect a frequency diagram representing continuous data
- work out the total frequency
- work out the fraction or percentage of the number in any class.

Starter

1 In the following questions, the number x is within a range of values. State whether the values given for x are correct.

(a) $55 \leq x \leq 59$	(i) $x = 57$	(ii) $x = 45 \cdot 9$	(iii) $x = 58 \cdot 9$	(iv) $x = 59$
(b) $55 \leq x < 59$	(i) $x = 56$	(ii) $x = 55 \cdot 2$	(iii) $x = 58 \cdot 7$	(iv) $x = 59$
(c) $55 < x < 59$	(i) $x = 55 \cdot 01$	(ii) $x = 59$	(iii) $x = 55$	(iv) $x = 58 \cdot 6$

Demonstration 1

Data set for population: The heights of all members of Hopegate Sports Club.
Method of data collection: Measuring all the heights to the nearest centimetre.

The data are collected by measuring. These are continuous data.

Frequency table

x (height in cm)	$f(x)$
155	2
156	0
157	0
158	1
159	0
160	1
161	1
162	1
163	3
164	2
165	3
166	2
167	2
168	1
169	2
170	1
171	1
172	1
173	0
174	0

Grouped frequency table

x (height in cm)	$f(x)$
$155 \leq x < 160$	3
$160 \leq x < 165$	8
$165 \leq x < 170$	10
$170 \leq x < 175$	3

Grouped frequency table

x (height in cm)	$f(x)$
$155 \leq x < 160$	3
$160 \leq x < 165$	8
$165 \leq x < 170$	10
$170 \leq x < 175$	3

Letts I See Maths Year 7

Handling Data

▶ Demonstration 2

Below is a frequency diagram for the population of heights of all members.

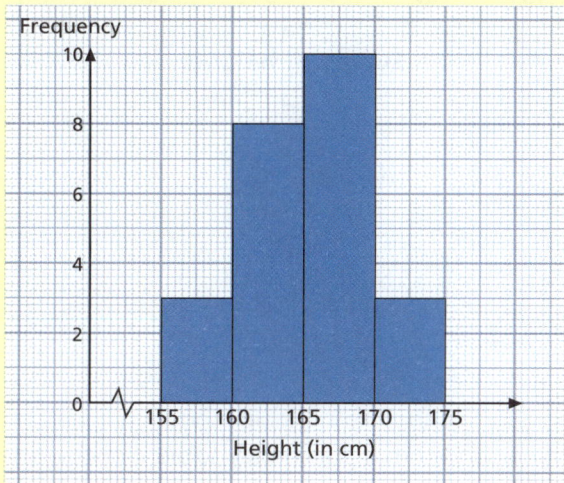

Key words   continuous data   frequency diagram   frequency table
grouped frequency table

▶ Worked example

Exercise bank 👉

1 Look at the frequency diagram in Demonstration 2.

(a) How many people had their heights measured?
$3 + 8 + 10 + 3 = 24$

(b) What is the modal class of heights?
The tallest bar is 10. The modal class is $165\,cm \leq x < 170\,cm$.

(c) What percentage of heights are greater than or equal to 165 cm?
There are $10 + 3 = 13$ heights greater than or equal to 165 cm.
There are 13 out of a total of 24: $13 \div 24 = \frac{13}{24} = 54\%$

▶ Plenary

👁 Inspect the data set in Demonstration 1. Why is this called continuous data?

Group the data in a different way and complete a grouped frequency table.

Draw a frequency diagram for your table.

👁 Discuss reasons for grouping data.

Letts I See Maths Year 7

Continuous data

Essential exercises

1 Inspect the frequency diagram below representing a survey of the heights of children in St Anne's School.

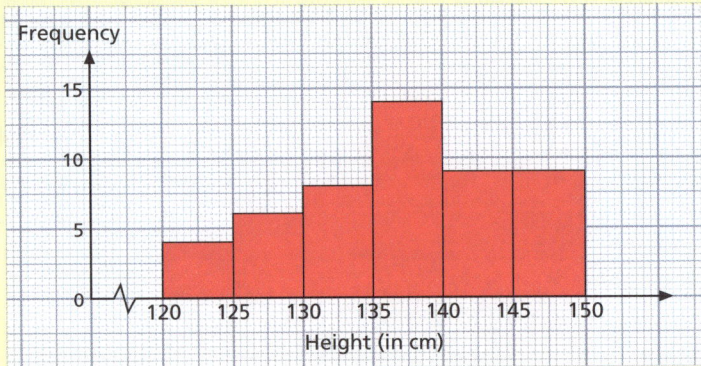

Survey of heights

(a) The frequency diagram was drawn using data recorded in a frequency table like the one below. Copy and complete the table.

Height x (in cm)	$120 \leq x < 125$	$125 \leq x < 130$	$130 \leq x < 135$	$135 \leq x < 140$	$140 \leq x < 145$	$145 \leq x < 150$
Frequency	4					

(b) How many children took part in the survey?
(c) How many children have a height of less than 135 cm?
(d) What percentage of children has a height greater than or equal to 130 cm?
(e) What fraction of the children has a height of $135 \leq x < 140$?
(f) Write the answer to (e) as a percentage.
(g) What is the modal class of heights?

2 A company tested the life of the batteries it manufactures by taking a sample and running a toy car until it stopped.

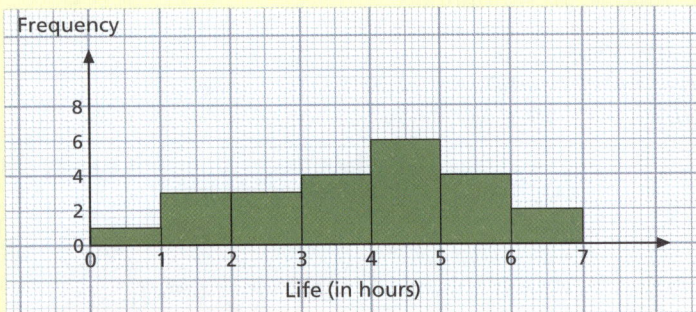

Frequency diagram to show a survey of battery life

(a) How many batteries were sampled?
(b) How many batteries lasted for less than five hours?
(c) What percentage of the batteries lasted less than two hours?
(d) Can the company claim that the majority of its batteries last more than six hours?

Letts **I See Maths** Year 7

Handling Data

Challenging exercise

3 The following marks were gained by the pupils in 7L.

| 6 | 11 | 16 | 17 | 22 | $8\frac{1}{2}$ | 14 | 15 | 20 | 19 | 22 | 21 | 17 | 16 | 8 |
| 23 | $14\frac{1}{2}$ | 13 | 12 | 18 | 17 | 12 | $17\frac{1}{2}$ | 18 | 20 | $19\frac{1}{2}$ | 18 | 13 | 10 | $12\frac{1}{2}$ |

(a) Copy and complete the following frequency table.

Marks (x)	$0 < x \le 5$	$5 < x \le 10$	$10 < x \le 15$	$15 < x \le 20$	$20 < x \le 25$
Frequency					

(b) Construct a frequency diagram to represent the data in the frequency table.
(c) What percentage of pupils gained a mark greater than 10?
(d) What percentage of pupils gained a mark greater than 20?
(e) Which is the modal class?

Problem-solving exercise

4

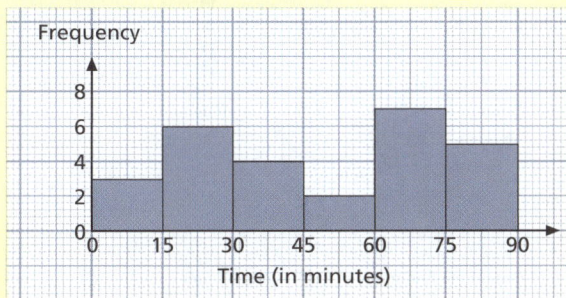

Frequency diagram to show the timing of goals scored in football matches one Saturday

Which of the following statements are true? Explain your answers.
(a) The least number of goals is scored in the 15 minutes after half-time.
(b) More goals are scored in the second half of the game.
(c) Half the goals are scored in the last thirty minutes.
(d) A third of goals are scored in the first thirty minutes.

Homework

Study this question for discussion in the next lesson.

Robert is in Class 7L and is 157 cm tall. He says, 'There are only two people taller than me in this class.' Could Robert be correct?

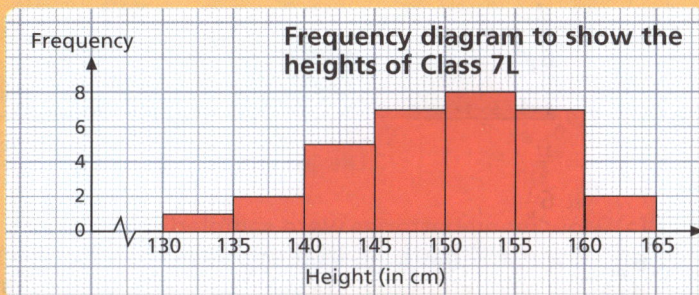

Frequency diagram to show the heights of Class 7L

Handling Data

Calculating statistics 1

Goals

When you have completed this lesson you will be able to answer questions such as this:

👁 Here are the test scores of ten people:

| 85 | 70 | 62 | 75 | 68 | 94 | 88 | 64 | 58 | 80 |

(a) What is the sum of all the scores?

(b) How many scores were added?

(c) What is the mean score?

(d) Two more scores are received late. They are 76 and 82. What is the new mean size?

Starter

1 Complete these equations.

(a) $3 \times 5 + 4 =$

(b) $7 + 2 \times 5 =$

(c) $2 \times 4 + 3 \times 5 =$

(d) $3 \times 4 + 7 + 2 \times 5 =$

(e) $1{\cdot}2 \times 3 + 2{\cdot}3 \times 2 + 3{\cdot}1 \times 4 =$

(f) $\frac{19}{6} =$

(g) $\frac{17}{6} =$

(h) $\frac{23}{9} =$

(i) $\frac{29}{10} =$

(i) $\frac{20{\cdot}6}{9} =$

2 Write $\frac{1}{6}$ as a decimal.

Demonstration 1

Person	B	E	M	O	T	V
Shoe size (British sizes)	8	6	5	5	8	5

Mean $= \bar{x} = \dfrac{8 + 6 + 5 + 5 + 8 + 5}{6}$

$\phantom{Mean = \bar{x} } = \dfrac{37}{6}$

$\phantom{Mean = \bar{x} } = 6\frac{1}{6}$

Mean $= \bar{x} = \dfrac{5 \times 3 + 6 \times 1 + 8 \times 2}{6}$

$\phantom{Mean = \bar{x} } = \dfrac{37}{6}$

$\phantom{Mean = \bar{x} } = 6\frac{1}{6}$

Simple bar chart

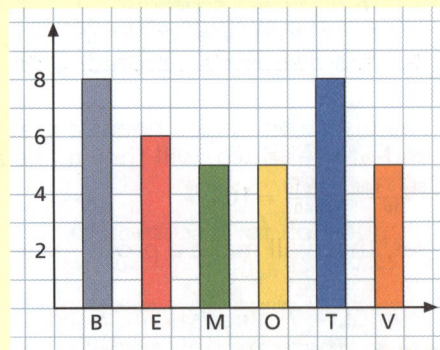

$6\frac{1}{6}$	$6\frac{1}{6}$	$6\frac{1}{6}$	$6\frac{1}{6}$	$6\frac{1}{6}$	$6\frac{1}{6}$
8	6	5	5	8	5

► Demonstration 2

Frequency table for sample

Variable (shoe size) x	Frequency (number) $f(x)$	$xf(x)$
5	3	15
6	1	6
8	2	16
	$\sum f(x) = 6$	$\sum f(x) = 37$

Mean of the sample:

$$\bar{x} = \frac{37}{6}$$
$$= 6\tfrac{1}{6}$$

Frequency table for population

Variable (shoe size) x	Frequency (number) $f(x)$	$xf(x)$
4	2	8
5	10	50
6	1	6
7	4	28
8	7	56
	$\sum f(x) = 24$	$\sum f(x) = 148$

Mean of the population:

$$\mu = \frac{148}{24}$$
$$= 6\tfrac{1}{6}$$

Key words   average   mean

► Worked example

Exercise bank ☞

1. A school holds a disco every month.
   The attendances at nine of these are 90, 105, 87, 100, 104, 98, 110, 95 and 75.

   (a) What is the average attendance?

   $$\frac{90 + 105 + 87 + 100 + 104 + 98 + 110 + 95 + 75}{9} = \frac{864}{9} = 96$$

   (b) The disco committee needs a mean attendance of 100 to break even. If 146 attend the end-of-year disco, will they make a profit?

   $$\frac{864 + 146}{10} = \frac{1010}{10} = 101$$

   Yes, they will make a profit.

► Plenary

👁 Inspect the test scores in the Goals. Answer questions (a) to (d).

👁 Give four numbers whose mean is six.

Handling Data

Calculating statistics 1

Essential exercises

1 Inspect the stacks of bricks below.

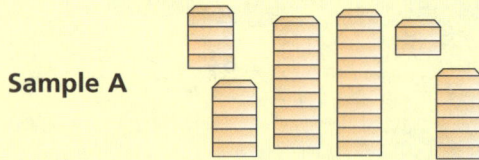

Sample A

Sample B

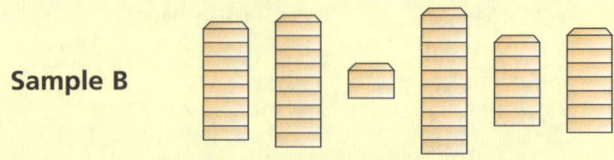

(a) Copy and complete the following summary chart for the two samples.

	Sample A	Sample B
Number of stacks of bricks		
Number of bricks in smallest stack		
Number of bricks in tallest stack		
Total number of bricks		

(b) Imagine taking the bricks apart and rebuilding them so that, in each sample, the six stacks are of equal size. How many bricks would you put in each stack:

    (i) for sample A?   (ii) for sample B?

(c) What is the mean number of bricks in the stacks in Sample A?

(d) What is the mean number of bricks in the stacks in Sample B?

2 Inspect the two sets of people below.

Set X

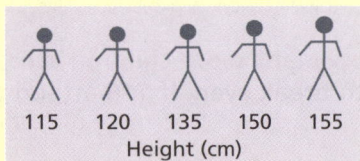

| 115 | 120 | 135 | 150 | 155 |
Height (cm)

Set Y

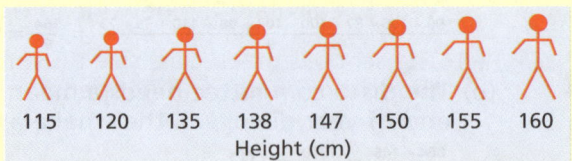

| 115 | 120 | 135 | 138 | 147 | 150 | 155 | 160 |
Height (cm)

Copy and complete the following sentences.
(a) The sum of the heights of all the people in Set X is … .
(b) The number of people in Set X is … .
(c) The mean height of people in Set X is … .
(d) The sum of the heights of all the people in Set Y is … .
(e) The number of people in Set Y is … .
(f) The mean height of people in Set Y is … .
(g) A third set of people, Set Z, has ten people in it. The mean height of people in Set Z is 138 cm. The sum of the heights of all the people in Set Z is … .

Challenging exercises

3 The heights of a set of six people are:

165 cm	170 cm	172 cm	173 cm	175 cm	180 cm

(a) What is the sum of all six heights?

(b) Calculate the mean height of the set of people.

(c) What is the range of heights of the set of people?

(d) Two people with heights of 172 cm and 181 cm join the set. Calculate the new mean height and range of the set.

4 Ten children sit a test. Their scores are:

3	11	13	15	15	16	16	17	18	19

(a) What is the total of all the scores?

(b) Calculate the mean score.

(c) The children sit the same test again and all of their scores increase by 1 point. What is the new mean score?

Problem-solving exercise

5 In a primary school there are six classes. The class sizes are:

Year 1	Year 2	Year 3	Year 4	Year 5	Year 6
24	28	31	29	30	32

(a) Calculate the mean class size.

(b) A family with two children moves into the area. One child joins Year 3, the other joins Year 5. Calculate the new mean class size.

(c) The school's mean class size must not rise above 30. How many more children can join the school before this happens?

Homework

Work out the mean values and ranges of the following sets of numbers.
(a) 6, 2, 3, 5, 1, 6, 3, 7, 5, 3
(b) 43, 27, 34, 40, 38
(c) 156, 178, 162, 159, 172, 165, 164
(d) 2·1, 3·5, 1·4, 2·6, 4·5, 3·2, 2·8
(e) $\frac{3}{5}, \frac{2}{5}, \frac{4}{5}, \frac{7}{5}, \frac{4}{5}$

Letts **I See Maths** Year 7

Handling Data

Calculating statistics 2

▶ Goals

Look at these frequency tables for the data sets of two samples.

Person	B	E	M	O	T	V
Shoe size (British sizes)	8	6	5	5	8	5
No. of siblings	0	1	2	6	0	2
No. of letters in first name	5	4	4	5	4	5

x (height in cm)	$f(x)$ (number)
155	2
156	0
157	0
158	1
159	0
160	1
161	1
162	1
163	3

When you have completed this lesson you will be able to:
- 👁 identify the variable
- 👁 calculate the median
- 👁 calculate the range
- 👁 discuss the implicit information in the median and the range.

▶ Starter

1 Write these numbers in order of magnitude (smallest first).

(a) 7 4 11 19 3 8 7 12   (b) 4 1·8 4·5 1·82 1·813 5   (c) ·4 ·403 ·41 ·413 ·431

2 These numbers are written in order of magnitude: 2 7 11 18 27 38 47 53 71
There are nine numbers. The middle number is the 5th. Discuss.

3 These numbers are written in order of magnitude: 2 7 11 18 27 38 47 53
There are eight numbers. The middle number is between the 4th and 5th. Discuss.

▶ Demonstration 1

The median gives a quick, rough idea of the general size of the variable in a data set.
The median is the 'middle number' in a data set written in ascending order.

Sample 1	B	E	M	O	T	V
Shoe size (British sizes)	8	6	5	5	8	5

5 5 5 6 8 8

median $= 5\frac{1}{2}$

Sample 2	A	B	C	D	E	F	G	H	I	J	K
Shoe size (British sizes)	8	8	5	5	6	7	5	8	8	4	5

4 5 5 5 5 6 7 8 8 8 8

median $= 6$

The range shows how spread out the variable is, and is the difference between the largest and smallest value of the variable.

Range for Sample 1 $= 8 - 5$
$= 3$

Range for Sample 2 $= 8 - 4$
$= 4$

Letts **I See Maths Year 7**

Handling Data

Demonstration 2

x (height in cm)	$f(x)$ (number)
155	2
156	0
157	0
158	1
159	0
160	1
161	1
162	1
163	3
164	2
165	3
166	2
167	2
168	1
169	2
170	1
171	1
172	1

This is a frequency table for a population of heights (in cm) of members of Hopegate Sports Club.

There are 24 heights:

12th value

155 155 158 160 161 162 163 163 163 164 164 165
165 165 166 166 167 167 168 169 169 170 171 172

13th value

The middle height is between the 12th and the 13th values.

12th value
13th value

The middle height is between 165 cm and 165 cm.

Median = 165 cm

The median gives a rough idea of the heights but the heights are quite spread out.

Range = 172 cm − 155 cm
      = 17 cm

Key words   median   range

Worked example

Exercise bank

1. The data set below has range = 11 and median = 8. What is the missing number?

   8   3 x 7   14   8

   The median is 8 so the two middle numbers will be 8.

   3   –   –   –   –   14
   3   7   8   8   –   14

   The missing number would be 8 or 9 or 10 or 11 or 12 or 13 or 14 or 11·2 or 9·7.
   So: $8 \leq x \leq 14$

Plenary

Look at this data set and discuss calculating the median, mode and mean for each sample.

Sample	A	B	C	D	E	F	G	H	I	J	K	L	M
Shoe size (British sizes)	8	8	5	5	6	7	5	5	8	4	5	7	5
No. of siblings	1	0	1	6	1	3	4	0	0	2	2	3	2
No. of letters in first name	4	5	11	5	4	5	6	7	4	4	5	8	4
Height (cm)	166	172	158	171	155	168	163	160	163	165	162	164	166
Age (years)	14	14	15	14	14	14	15	14	14	15	14	14	15

Handling Data

Calculating statistics 2

Essential exercises

1. Write the following sets of numbers in order of size and work out the values of the medians.

    (a) 6, 2, 1, 7, 5, 4, 8

    (b) 23, 14, 25, 19, 21, 22

    (c) 3·2, 3·4, 3·1, 3·5, 3·7, 3·3, 3·4

    (d) $\frac{2}{5}, \frac{1}{5}, \frac{3}{5}, \frac{2}{5}, \frac{4}{5}$

    (e) $\frac{8}{10}, \frac{3}{10}, \frac{4}{10}, \frac{6}{10}, \frac{1}{10}$

2. Copy and complete the following table.

	Set of numbers	Range	Mode	Median	Mean
(a)	7, 3, 0, 8, 4, 5, 9, 2, 6, 1				
(b)	17, 13, 10, 18, 14, 15, 19, 12, 16, 11				
(c)	117, 113, 110, 118, 114, 115, 119, 112, 116, 111				
(d)	$\frac{7}{10}, \frac{3}{10}, 0, \frac{8}{10}, \frac{4}{10}, \frac{5}{10}, \frac{9}{10}, \frac{2}{10}, \frac{6}{10}, \frac{1}{10}$				
(e)	21, 9, 0, 24, 12, 15, 27, 6, 18, 3				
(f)	35, 15, 0, 40, 20, 25, 45, 10, 30, 5				

3. The maximum temperatures (in degrees Celsius) for Sunnyside were recorded for June.

14	14	15	13	16	17	17	16	15	14
12	14	15	15	12	14	16	15	17	18
17	17	16	15	17	19	22	25	24	23

   (a) What was the range of temperatures?

   (b) What was the mean monthly temperature?

   (c) What was the median temperature?

   (d) What was the most common temperature?

Letts I See Maths Year 7

Challenging exercise

4 (a) The mean of three numbers is 12. Two of the numbers are 9 and 14. What is the third number?

(b) Six numbers have a mean of 8 and a range of 14. Four of the numbers are 4, 5, 14 and 15. What are the two missing numbers?

(c) The mean of five numbers is 7. After adding another number to the five, the mean is still 7. What is the new number?

(d) Set $A = \{x, y, 30\}$

Set $B = \{25, 30, 35\}$

Set A and Set B have the same mean.

The range of A is double the range of B.

Find x and y.

Problem-solving exercise

5 The cost of a Triple X chocolate bar was recorded for twenty different shops in Burnside:

43p	39p	45p	37p	34p	32p	40p	39p	36p	40p
42p	38p	35p	40p	42p	37p	41p	40p	40p	38p

(a) What is the cheapest price?

(b) What is the most expensive price?

(c) What is the range of prices?

(d) What is the most common price?

(e) What is the median price?

(f) What is the mean price?

Homework

Work in groups. Choose a product. Each member of the group checks out the price in at least one shop. Sort your results and answer questions 5 (a) to (f) for your data.

Letts **I See Maths** Year 7

Handling Data

Exercise Bank

Comparing distributions

Goals

Look at the data set below of two samples of shoe sizes randomly selected from members of two sports clubs.

Hopegate Sports Club	5	7	8	7	5	8	8	7
Jaunty Sports Club	2	7	6	8	8	7	9	4

When you have completed this lesson you will be able to:
- identify the variables
- calculate summary statistics for each sample
- tentatively compare the populations.
- describe the population
- compare the samples

Starter

1 Look at this data set (shoe sizes).

Sample	7	9	7	11	7	4	8	7	3	8

(a) What is the variable?
(b) What is the size of the sample?
(c) What do you know about the population?
(d) Calculate the range.
(e) Calculate the mean.
(f) Calculate the median.
(g) Calculate the mode.
(h) Write down a sample of the same size, with the same range, but with mean, median and mode that are each two more than the given sample.

Demonstration 1

A random sample of 30 sentences was selected from the first chapter of Book 1 and another random sample of 30 sentences was selected from the first chapter of Book 2. The number of words in each sentence was counted. The data sets below show the results for these samples.

Frequency table for Book 1

No. of words in each sentence	x	3	4	5	6	7	10	11	14	15	16	17	20	21	22	24	27	31	37
No. of sentences	$f(x)$	4	2	2	1	2	1	1	2	2	1	2	1	3	1	2	1	1	1
	$x \times f(x)$	12	8	10	6	14	10	11	28	30	16	34	20	63	22	48	27	31	37

Frequency table for Book 2

No. of words in each sentence	x	4	6	10	12	15	18	19	23	24	25	26	28	29	31	32	33	39	40	41	46	73	78
No. of sentences	$g(x)$	1	1	1	1	2	3	1	1	2	2	1	1	2	1	1	1	1	2	1	2	1	1
	$x \times g(x)$	4	6	10	12	30	54	19	23	48	50	26	28	58	31	32	33	39	80	41	92	73	78

Book 1   Total no. words: 427   Range: 3 to 37   Mean: 14·2   Median: 14·5   Mode: 3
Book 2   Total no. words: 867   Range: 4 to 78   Mean: 28·9   Median: 25·5   Mode: 18

Letts **I See Maths** Year 7

► ## Demonstration 2

Look again at the data sets in Demonstration 1.

For Book 1	For Book 2
The variable x is the number of words in a sentence.	The variable x is the number of words in a sentence.
The frequency $f(x)$ is the number of sentences with a particular number of words.	The frequency $g(x)$ is the number of sentences with a particular number of words.

Comparing summary statistics of the two samples:

Book 1 sample for Chapter 1		Book 2 sample for Chapter 1
range 34	<	range 74
mean 14.2	<	mean 28.9
median 14.5	<	median 25.5
mode 3	<	mode 18

The sample for Book 1 generally had much shorter sentences than the sample for Book 2, but there were bigger variations with the sample for Book 2.

If the samples are representative of the population, the number of words in sentences in Chapter 1 of Book 1 is less than the number of words in the sentences in Chapter 1 of Book 2.

Key words   population   sample   summary statistics   variable

Exercise bank 👉

► ## Plenary

👁 Inspect the two sample sets in the Goals.

Calculate summary statistics and use these to compare the two sets.

👁 Look at these two sample sets of heights (in cm).

Sample 1	166	172	158	171	155	168	163	160	163	165	162	164
Sample 2	166	170	155	159	161	167	165	167	169	164	163	165

Calculate summary statistics and use these to compare the two sets.

Comparing distributions

1 Classes 7P and 7Q take a test. The test scores are recorded below in frequency tables.

7P score x	No. of pupils (frequency $f(x)$)	$x \times f(x)$
12	1	
13	3	
14	5	
15	9	
16	7	
17	3	
18	1	
19	1	
20	0	
Totals		

7Q score x	No. of pupils (frequency $g(x)$)	$x \times g(x)$
12	1	
13	2	
14	4	
15	7	
16	8	
17	3	
18	0	
19	2	
20	3	
Totals		

(a) Copy and complete the frequency tables above.

(b) For each class, calculate the following summary statistics:
   (i) the range of scores   (ii) the mean test score
   (iii) the most common score (the mode)   (iv) the median score
   (v) the percentage of children scoring above the mean.

(c) Which class has the best mean score?

(d) Each class has been set the target of 80% of pupils achieving a score of 14 or more. Do both classes meet this target?

(e) In class 7P, two children were absent on the day of the test. They take the test a week later. Both score 16. What is the new mean score?

2 Janice takes two samples of text from two newspapers and counts the number of letters in each word.

	Sample A										Sample B												
No. of letters x	1	2	3	4	5	6	7	8	9	10	1	2	3	4	5	6	7	8	9	10	11	12	13
No. of words $f(x)$	4	5	6	5	6	8	6	4	3	3	3	3	5	4	4	7	8	6	2	4	1	1	2
Total letters																							

(a) Copy and complete the tables above.

(b) For each sample, calculate the following summary statistics:
   (i) the range of the number of letters in the words
   (ii) the mean number of letters in a word
   (iii) the most common number of letters in a word
   (iv) the percentage of words with letters above the mean.

(c) One newspaper was a tabloid and one a broadsheet. Which sample do you think was the tabloid and why?

Challenging exercises

3 Inspect these two samples of stacks of bricks.

Sample A	4	5	6	7	8	10	11	13
Sample B	4	5	5	5	8	12	13	13

(a) For each sample, calculate the following summary statistics:

   (i) the range of numbers of bricks in the stacks

   (ii) the mean number of bricks in a stack

   (iii) the median number of bricks in a stack.

(b) Use bricks to make the two samples and compare them.

   (i) Do the summary statistics describe the samples well?

   (ii) What is the key difference between the two samples?

(c) Explain why the mode is not a helpful measure in comparing the two samples.

4 Sample C is given as:

2	4	5	6	9	10

Find Sample D, which also contains six numbers but which has a mean that is two more than Sample C.

Problem-solving exercise

5 Inspect the two samples below and use summary statistics to compare them.

Survey to find out the number of pets owned by pupils

No. of pets (x)	No. of pupils (frequency f(x))	x × f(x)	No. of pets (x)	No. of pupils (frequency f(x))	x × f(x)
0	5		0	12	
1	12		1	14	
2	8		2	3	
3	2		3	1	
4	3		4	0	
Totals			Totals		

Homework

Select two newspapers or magazines. Take a sample of text from each and count the word-length. Compare the two samples.

Goals

When you have completed this lesson you will be able to do questions such as this:

👁 Sarah collected data to compare whether boys could estimate lengths of lines better than girls.
   (a) Suggest a hypothesis for Sarah.
   (b) Suggest a suitable sample size.
   (c) Suggest how Sarah might collect the data.
   (d) What sorts of diagrams might Sarah use?

Starter

1 Suggest ways of testing the following hypotheses.

   (a) Twelve-year-old boys are shorter than 12-year-old girls, based on the evidence of people in my class.
   (b) I think that the most popular colour of car is green because I see lots of green cars on my way to school.
   (c) I think that tabloid newspapers have lots more advertisements than broadsheets, based on looking at my family's newspapers.

Demonstration 1

'I think that boys are better at maths than girls.'

This is *not* a hypothesis. This is prejudice! There is no evidence yet to show that boys are better than girls, or that girls are better than boys.

A hypothesis is based on some sort of evidence.

Example
'I think that boys are better at maths than girls because the boys in my class always get better test results and always answer the teacher's questions first.'

This is a hypothesis. It needs to be tested. I could look at all the test results in my school and compare boys with girls. This would be a sample.

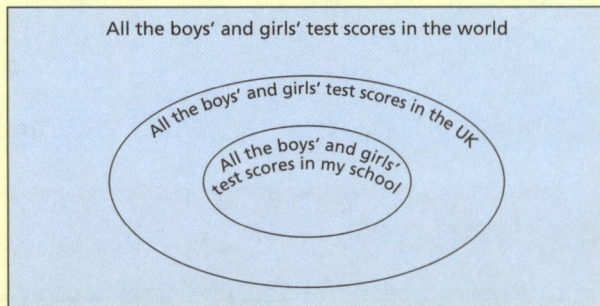

All the boys' and girls' test scores in the world

All the boys' and girls' test scores in the UK

All the boys' and girls' test scores in my school

I have to decide whether my sample is representative of the whole population.

Letts **I See Maths** Year 7

Handling Data

Demonstration 2

Setting up an enquiry

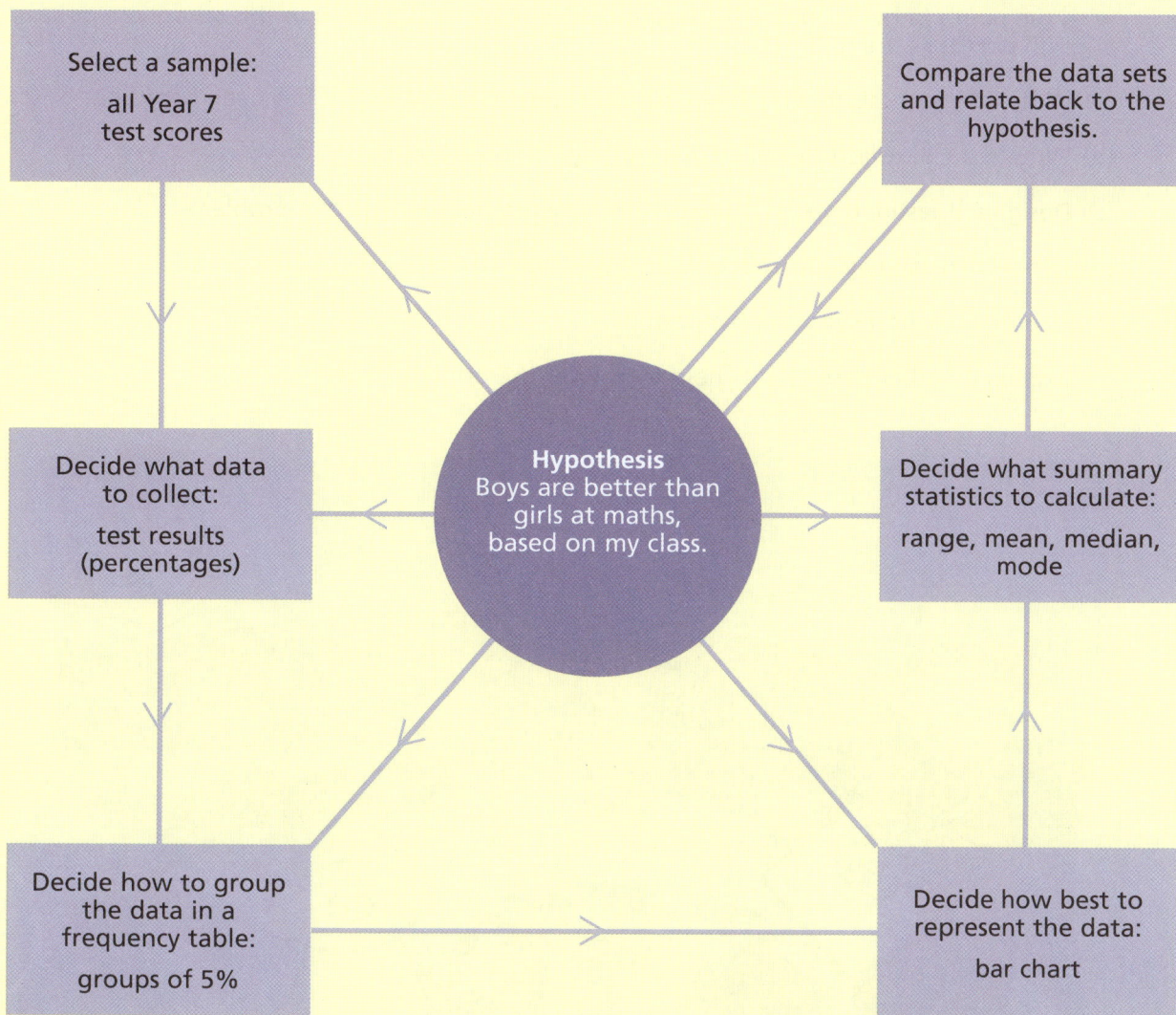

Select a sample:

all Year 7
test scores

Compare the data sets
and relate back to the
hypothesis.

Decide what data
to collect:

test results
(percentages)

Hypothesis
Boys are better than
girls at maths,
based on my class.

Decide what summary
statistics to calculate:

range, mean, median,
mode

Decide how to group
the data in a
frequency table:

groups of 5%

Decide how best to
represent the data:

bar chart

Key words   enquiry   evidence   hypothesis

Exercise bank

Plenary

👁 Consider the enquiry in the Goals and help Sarah begin her work.

👁 Suggest ideas for an enquiry and give your hypothesis.

Setting up an enquiry

Enquiries

1   A national report said that British children were not doing sufficient exercise and were becoming unfit. Mrs Jones, the headteacher of Sunnyside School, recognised some similarities with the pupils in her school. 'I must find out whether the children in this school are doing enough exercise,' she said.

(a) Write a hypothesis for this problem and state what evidence it has been based on.

(b) Write a set of questions that are posed by this problem.

(c) Design a questionnaire to use with your class to help answer the problem.

(d) Conduct the survey and collect your results together.

(e) Represent your results in a diagram.

(f) Explain whether your results help to answer the original problem.

Handling Data

Letts **I See Maths** Year 7

2 On parents' evening at Sunnyside School, several parents complained that their children were eating too many chips for lunch. They wanted their children to eat a cooked meal but felt that they would have to provide sandwiches unless the canteen started to provide healthier food. Mrs Jones, the headteacher, commented that children would not eat the healthier food and that, in her experience, they only wanted chips, beans and pizzas. The parents were very cross and said that she was wrong.

chips beans pizza   beans pizza chips   pizza chips beans

(a) Write a hypothesis for this problem and state on what evidence it has been based.

(b) Write a set of questions that are posed by this problem.

(c) Design a questionnaire to use with your class (or year group or even the whole school) to help answer the problem.

(d) Conduct a survey and collect your results together.

(e) Represent your results in a diagram (or diagrams).

(f) Explain whether your results help to answer the original problem.

Writing a report

Goals

Look at this information.

No. of times children said they would buy jacket potatoes for lunch	Frequency (%)
every day	13
at least three times a week	17
at least once a week	28
never	42

When you have completed this lesson you will be able to answer questions such as these:

👁 Write a report using the information above.
👁 Is this information sufficient for a school kitchen to make a decision on whether to sell jacket potatoes?
👁 What further information might you need?

Starter

1 Write the following results as percentages.

(a) Two in ten children say they never take exercise.
(b) A quarter of people questioned said they liked baked beans.
(c) Three people out of thirty surveyed said they went out for a meal at least once every week.
(d) Of forty-five people who answered a questionnaire, only five said they read novels regularly.

Demonstration 1

Inspect the following information.

This frequency diagram shows the actual times taken when 100 children in Y7 were asked to estimate 30 seconds of time.

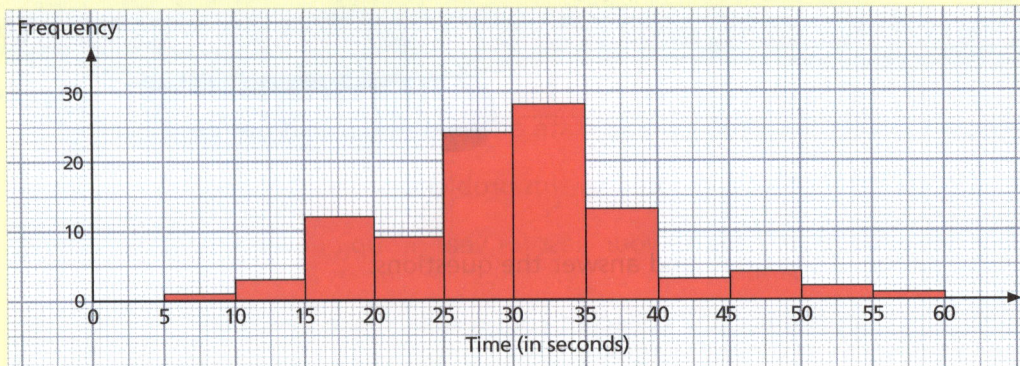

The diagram shows that $24 + 28 = 52$ children could estimate 30 seconds within an error of 5 seconds.

Demonstration 2

The original hypothesis in Demonstration 1 was:

'Based on previous surveys, I believe that children in Y7 are generally good at estimating 30 seconds but not very good at estimating one minute.'

Inspect the following frequency diagram showing the results with the same children when they were asked to estimate 1 minute.

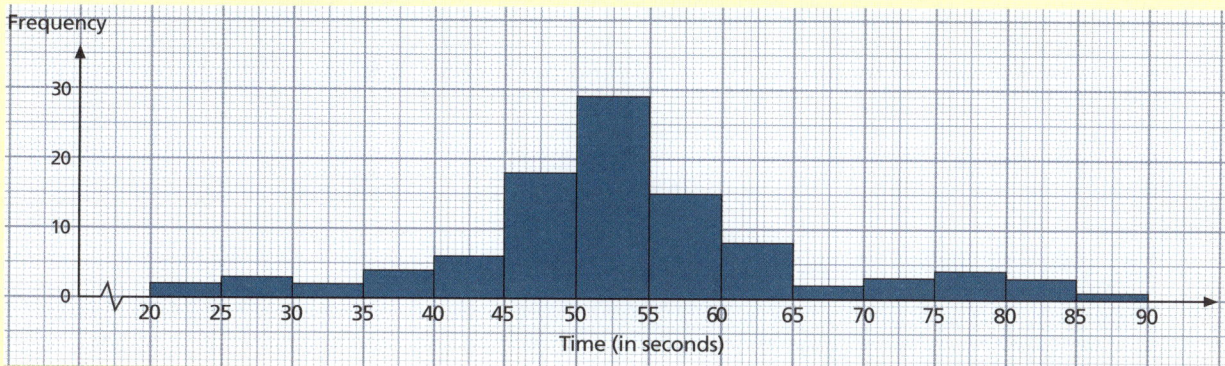

This diagram shows that 15 + 8 = 23 children could estimate 60 seconds within an error of 5 seconds.

Do these results support the original hypothesis? A yes or no answer is not enough. The report below would be better.

Report

Children were generally quite good at estimating 30 seconds: 52% of them could estimate within an error of 5 seconds and 74% within an error of 10 seconds. Only 11% were over 15 seconds wrong. When estimating a minute there was a much wider range of estimates: 25% were over 15 seconds wrong. The majority (79%) underestimated a minute, compared with 49% underestimating 30 seconds.

Key words   estimate   majority

Exercise bank

Plenary

👁 Inspect the information in the Goals and answer the questions.

👁 When you have set up an enquiry and collected your results, make sure that:
- you use relevant and appropriate diagrams and graphs
- you do not waste time duplicating information
- you interrogate the information and calculate appropriate summary statistics
- you *always* relate your results to the original hypothesis.

Writing a report

Reports

1 Fred runs a bus company in Sunnyside Town. He saw in his local newspaper that several people living on the outskirts of town had been complaining that there were no buses that they could catch to get them to the main shopping centre. Fred thought that this might be an opportunity to expand his business. He asked a market research company to conduct a survey for him. They presented him with these results.

Report
The population of the district is estimated at eight thousand people. About half of the population live in expensive executive-type homes with at least two cars. We decided to eliminate them from the survey. The remaining population lived in about one thousand households. We decided to call at every tenth house to get a sample of 100 people.

Survey
If there were a regular bus to the town centre, how often would you use it?

Number of times	Frequency
6 or 7 times a week	1
4 or 5 times a week	23
2 or 3 times a week	27
once a week	8
once a month	2
never	39

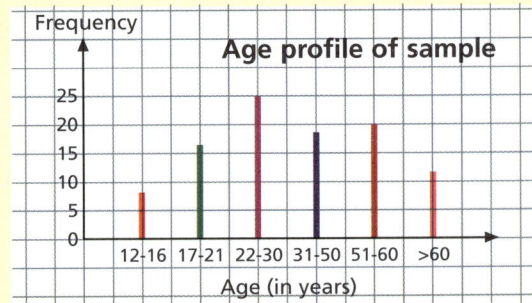

Age profile of sample

Ownership of cars in the sample

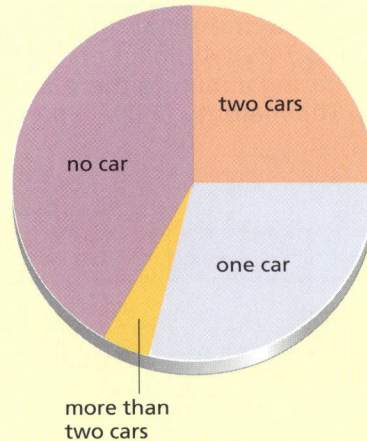

(a) How did the market research company select their sample?

(b) Why did the company eliminate people living in executive-type homes from their survey?

(c) Do you think they chose a big enough sample?

(d) Discuss the results and decide what advice you would give Fred.

Letts I See Maths Year 7

Handling Data

2 The Sunnyside Community Centre wanted to build a leisure centre with a swimming pool. They wanted to know whether people in the town would use the centre so they conducted a survey. They knew that there was not another leisure centre within a 50-mile radius.

Report on survey
We decided to sample people from different age groups:
(a) children in primary school
(b) children in secondary school
(c) late teens and early twenties
(d) parents with very young children
(e) people with jobs
(f) retired people.

We asked them how often they would use certain facilities, what time of day they would use the facilities and how much they would be prepared to pay.

Here are some of the results.

How often would you use a swimming pool?

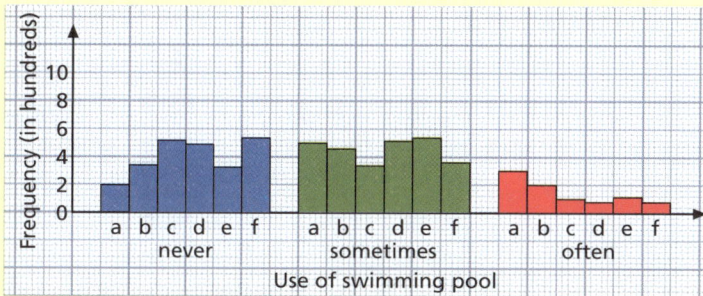

What time of day would you use it?

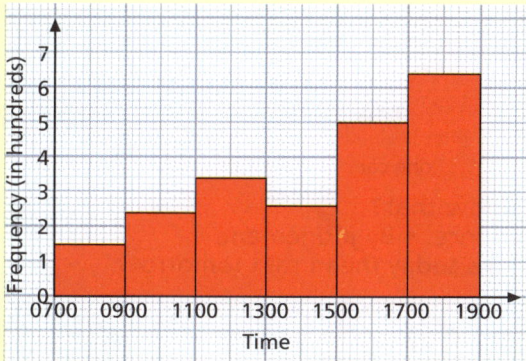

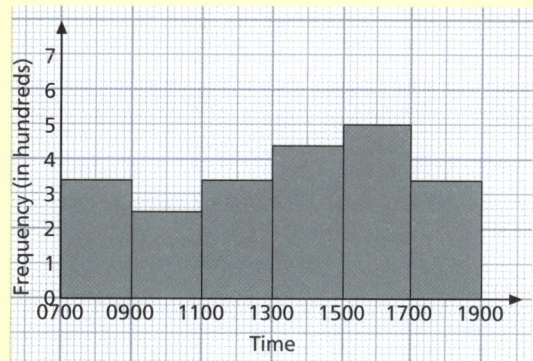

(a) Discuss the nature and size of the sample in the survey.

(b) Discuss whether the questions asked were sensible.

(c) Discuss the results shown.

(d) What further research needs to be done?

Goals

When you have completed this lesson you will be able to:

👁 say whether the statement, 'It is very unlikely I will be a millionaire' is an estimate of probability or a measurement of probability

👁 say how to make a random selection of one coin from seven coins

👁 identify all possible outcomes.

Starter

1 Speak a vulgar fraction, a decimal and a percentage for each comparison below.

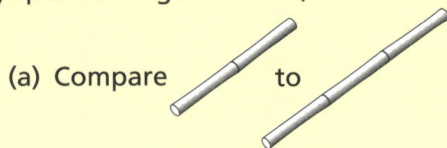

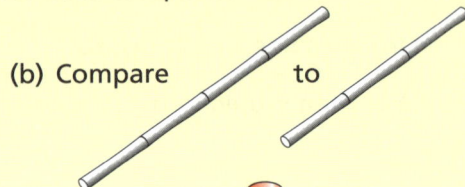

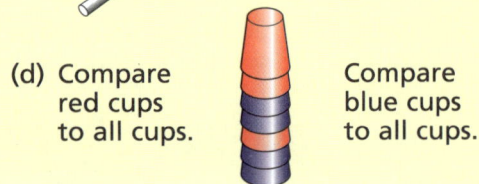

(a) Compare   to

(b) Compare   to

(c) Compare   to

(d) Compare red cups to all cups.

Compare blue cups to all cups.

(e)   Compare red cards to all cards.
Compare blue cards to all cards.

Demonstration 1

| **Everyday language**: It is very likely that it will rain tomorrow. | **Mathematical language**: The probability it will rain tomorrow is about $\frac{8}{10}$. |

How do you know that?
• By estimation. • By experience. • By judgement.
• By knowing what sort of conditions today mean rain tomorrow.

Put these counters in a bag.
Shake the bag. Without looking, take one out at random.

| It is very likely I will get a coloured counter. | The probability that I will get a coloured counter is about $\frac{8}{10}$. |

How do you know that?
• By measurement.

Demonstration 2

Select a counter at random.

There are 10 possible outcomes.

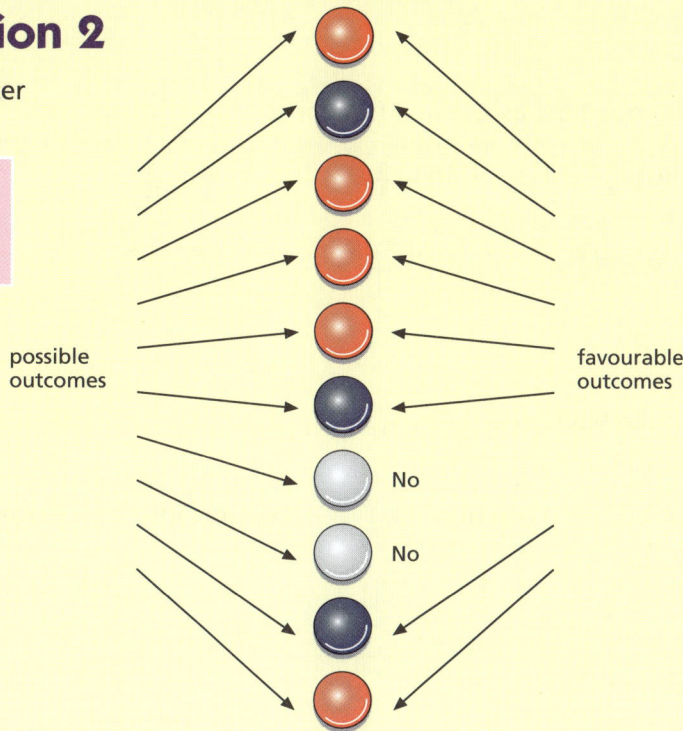

possible outcomes

favourable outcomes

You hope to select a coloured counter.

There are 8 favourable outcomes.

No

No

Compare favourable outcomes to possible outcomes: $\frac{8}{10}$

P (coloured counter) $= \frac{8}{10}$

$0 \le$ probability ≤ 1

Key words   estimate of probability   favourable outcomes   measurement of probability   possible outcomes   probability   select at random

Exercise bank

Plenary

- Is the statement, 'It is very unlikely I will be a millionaire', an estimate or a measurement of probability?

- How can I make a random selection of one coin from seven coins?

- Look at the diagram below. Discuss:
  - How many outcomes are favourable to getting a blue?
  - How many outcomes are favourable to getting a red?
  - How many outcomes are favourable to not getting a blue?
  - How many outcomes are favourable to getting a counter?

Probability 1

Essential exercises

1 Write the following numbers as decimal fractions.

(a) $\frac{1}{2}$ (b) $\frac{1}{4}$ (c) $\frac{3}{4}$ (d) $\frac{3}{10}$ (e) $\frac{45}{100}$

(f) $\frac{7}{100}$ (g) 20%   (h) 50%   (i) 5%   (j) 38%

2 (a) Complete the following probability scale.

Description		Fraction		Decimal		Percentage	
certain	—	1	—	1	—	100%	—
very likely	—					75%	—
likely	—						
equally likely	—	$\frac{1}{2}$	—		—		—
unlikely	—						
very unlikely	—		—	0·25	—		—
impossible	—	0	—	0	—	0	—

(b) Which words or phrases from the description scale match the following events?
   (i)   The probability that it will rain today is $\frac{1}{2}$.
   (ii) The probability that the sun will shine on Thursday is 93%.
   (iii) The probability that I will get a tail when I spin a coin is 0.5.
   (iv) The probability that I will get a ten when I roll a die is 0.
   (v)   The probability that I will get a number from one to six when I roll a die is 100%.

3 At the fairground, you play a game of chance. The game is to select one card from four different packs of cards. You win a prize if you select a card coloured red. Match the words from the description scale above to the chances of winning with each pack.

Pack 1	Pack 2	Pack 3	Pack 4
No red cards.	Half the cards are red.	All the cards are red.	A quarter of the cards are red.

Challenging exercises

4 When rolling a fair coin, the theoretical probability of getting a head is $\frac{1}{2}$.

(a) What is the theoretical probability of getting a tail?

(b) Estimate the number of heads you would get in one hundred rolls of the coin.

(c) Estimate the number of times you would need to roll a coin to get eighty-three heads.

5 When rolling a fair die, the theoretical probability of getting the number four is $\frac{1}{6}$.

(a) What is the theoretical probability of getting the number two?

(b) What is the theoretical probability of not getting a six?

(c) Estimate the number of times you would have to roll a die to get ten sixes.

6 A pack of playing cards has 52 cards. A card is selected at random.

(a) What is the theoretical probability of selecting an ace?

(b) What is the theoretical probability of selecting the king of spades?

(c) What is the theoretical probability of selecting a red queen?

Problem-solving exercise

7 Ten 1-digit cards are placed face down at random in a circle. Cards are turned over one at a time.

(a) The first card turned over is the number four. Is the next card likely to be higher or lower than four? Explain your answer.

(b) The second card turned over is the number seven. Is the next card likely to be higher or lower than seven? Explain your answer.

(c) The third card turned over is the number six. Is the next card likely to be odd or even?

(d) The fourth card turned over is the number eight. Is the next card likely to be a multiple of three?

Homework

Throw a coin one hundred times and record the results.

Did you get the number of heads you expected?

Goals

When you have completed this lesson you will be able to:

- 👁 discuss making a random selection from a pack of cards

- 👁 discuss a random selection from a pack of cards as a symmetrical, unbiased selection

- 👁 discuss each possible outcome of selecting a card from a pack as an equally likely outcome

- 👁 discuss theoretical probability.

Starter

1 State the values of n such that:

(a) n is even and $4 < n < 12$
(b) n is even and $4 \leq n \leq 12$
(c) n is odd and $4 < n < 12$
(d) n is odd and $4 \leq n \leq 12$
(e) n is a square number and $0 < n < 36$
(f) n is a prime and $5 \leq n \leq 11$.

Demonstration 1

A coin has a head (H) on one side and a tail (T) on the other side.
A coin on the table is either H or T.

Imagine spinning a coin and letting it land on the table. It is either H or T.
H and T are equally likely because the coin is symmetrical. (It is not biased.)

A die has six faces. It has 1, 2, 3, 4, 5, 6 on the faces.
A die on the table is either 1, 2, 3, 4, 5 or 6.

Imagine rolling a die and letting it come to rest on the table.
It is either 1, 2, 3, 4, 5 or 6.
1, 2, 3, 4, 5, 6 are equally likely because the die is symmetrical. (It is not biased.)

Possible outcomes		
H	H	H
H	H	T
H	T	H
T	H	H
T	T	H
T	H	T
T	T	H
T	T	T

Imagine spinning three coins together.

- There are 8 possible outcomes.

- Each outcome is equally likely.

- When we can measure probability by imagining what can happen, we are working out theoretical probability.

Demonstration 2

Everyday language:

When spinning a coin:
- the probability of getting a head
- the probability of getting a tail

When rolling a die:
- the probability of getting a 4
- the probability of not getting a 4
- the probability of getting a number bigger than 7

When selecting a card from a pack of playing cards:
- the probability of getting an ace
- the probability of not getting a queen

Mathematical language:

- $P(H)$ [probability of H]
- $P(T)$ [probability of T]

- $P(x = 4)$ [probability of getting a 4]
- $P(x \neq 4)$ [probability of *not* getting a 4]
- $P(x > 7)$ [probability of getting a number greater than 7]

- $P(A)$ [probability of selecting an ace]
- $P(Q')$ [probability of not selecting a queen]

Key words   bias   equally likely $P(3)$ random selection   theoretical probability

Exercise bank

Plenary

- Go back to the Goals and discuss each point in turn.

- Discuss all possible outcomes of selecting three cards from those below.

| 1 | 2 | 3 | 4 |

Handling Data

Probability 2

Essential exercises

1 (a) Write down all the possible outcomes when you roll a fair die.

(b) What is the theoretical probability of each of the following?

(i) rolling the number 2 – $P(n = 2)$

(ii) rolling an even number – $P(n$ is even$)$

(iii) rolling a number greater than 3 – $P(n > 3)$

(iv) rolling a prime number – $P(n$ is prime$)$

(v) rolling a square number – $P(n$ is square$)$

2 In a bag I have ten balls of the same size and mass. There are six red balls, three white balls and one yellow ball. I put my hand in the bag and, without looking, select a ball, note its colour and put it back.

Work out the following theoretical probabilities.

(a) P(red)   (b) P(not red)   (c) P(white)   (d) P(not white)

(e) P(green)   (f) P(not green)   (g) P(red or white)   (h) P(yellow)

3 The letters in the word MATHEMATICS are put in a bag. A letter is selected at random and replaced.

Work out the following theoretical probabilities of selecting letters.

(a) P(letter H)   (b) P(letter M)   (c) P(a vowel)   (d) P(a consonant)

(e) P(letter O)   (f) P(a repeated letter) (g) P(letter T or C)   (h) P(letter Z)

4 A fair octagonal spinner is made, like the one on the right.

Work out the theoretical probabilities of the arrow pointing to the following numbers after spinning.

(a) P(a square number)

(b) P(a prime number)

(c) P(a multiple of 3)

(d) P(an even number)

(e) P(a multiple of 11)

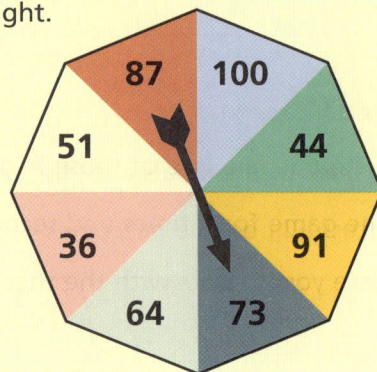

Letts I See Maths **Year 7**

Handling Data

Challenging exercises

5 Consider a pack of 52 playing cards (no jokers). A card is picked at random and replaced.

Work out the theoretical probabilities of selecting the following cards.

(a) P(red card) (b) P(king) (c) P(king, queen or jack)

(d) P(ace of hearts) (e) P(a black 4) (e) P(not an ace)

6 Consider, again, a pack of 52 playing cards (no jokers). A card is picked at random but *not* replaced.

Work out the theortical probabilities of selecting the following cards.

(a) The 1st selection is the king of clubs. Find P(2nd selection is the ace of diamonds).

(b) The 1st selection is the king of clubs, and the 2nd selection is the 3 of hearts. Find P(3rd selection is a king).

(c) The 1st selection is the king of clubs, the 2nd selection is the 3 of hearts, and the 3rd selection is the king of spades. Find P(4th selection is an ace).

Problem-solving exercise

7 Matthew conducted an experiment with a die. He threw the die one hundred times and recorded the results.

Number on die	Number of times
1	12
2	16
3	24
4	16
5	18
6	14

Use Matthew's results to work out the following probabilities with this die.

(a) $P(6)$ (b) $P(2)$
(c) P(3 or 4) (d) P(even number)
(e) P(prime number) (f) P(square number)

Homework

Make a game like one of those in questions 2, 3 or 4.

Play the game forty times and record the results.

Compare your results with the theoretical probabilities of getting the results.

Handling Data

Review of Handling Data 1

1 **Survey of 7A's and 7B's favourite colours**

Colour	Tally	Frequency
red	~~IIII~~ ~~IIII~~ II	
orange	IIII	
yellow	~~IIII~~	
green	~~IIII~~ I	
blue	~~IIII~~ ~~IIII~~ ~~IIII~~ I	
pink	~~IIII~~	
violet	II	
	Total	

(a) Copy and complete the frequency table above.

(b) How many children were in the survey altogether?

(c) What is the most popular colour?

(d) What is the least popular colour?

(e) How many children chose blue or red as their favourite colour?

(f) What percentage of children chose blue?

(g) What percentage of children did not choose red?

(h) Draw a bar chart to represent the survey above.

2

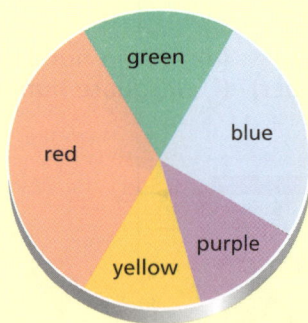

Pie chart to show the result of a survey on favourite colours

(a) What is the most popular colour?

(b) What fraction of children chose yellow?

(c) What percentage of children chose blue?

(d) If there were 90 children in the survey, how many chose red?

(e) What percentage of children did not choose red?

Letts **I See Maths** Year 7

3 Saxby's Seeds received complaints about the number of seeds in their packets. They decided to check the filling machine by sampling some packets.

Number of seeds in packet	20–24	25–29	30–34	35–39	40–44
Number of packets	52	76	48	20	4

(a) Draw a bar chart to represent this data.

(b) How big was the sample?

(c) Saxby's promised that there would always be at least 25 seeds in the packets. What percentage of packets failed to meet this promise?

(d) What percentage of packets had 40 or more seeds in them?

(e) Do you think the filling machine is faulty? Explain your answer.

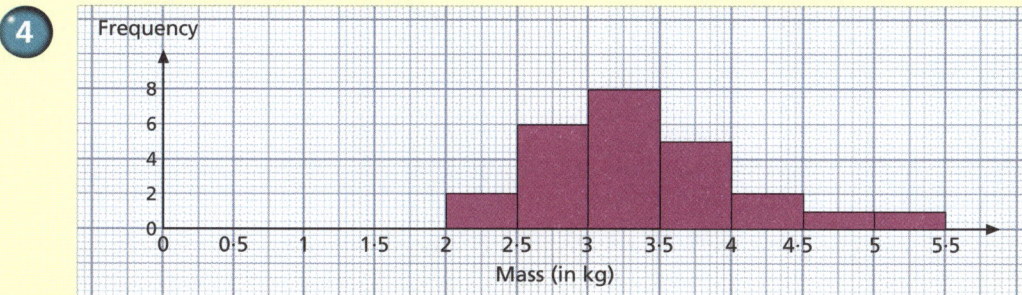

4

Frequency diagram to show the mass of new-born babies

(a) How many babies' masses were recorded altogether?

(b) How many babies have a mass greater than 3 kg?

(c) What percentage of babies has a mass greater than 3 kg?

(d) What is the modal class of masses?

(e) What percentage of babies has a mass less than or equal to 4 kg?

1 Complete the following table.

Set of numbers	Range	Mode	Median	Mean
(a) 2, 5, 3, 2, 4, 2, 3, 6, 5, 2				
(b) 0, 7, 3, 1, 0, 2, 5, 4, 3, 4				
(c) 13, 19, 15, 10, 14, 8, 9, 16, 14, 15				
(d) 362, 351, 364, 360, 359				
(e) 0·4, 0·2, 0·6, 0·2, 0·8				
(f) 0·07, 0·05, 0·01, 0·09, 0·04				

2 Two classes take a test. The test scores are recorded below.

Class A				Class B		
Score x	Frequency $f(x)$	Score × frequency $x \times f(x)$		Score x	Frequency $g(x)$	Score × frequency $x \times g(x)$
42	1			42	5	
43	2			43	6	
44	4			44	3	
45	4			45	0	
46	6			46	0	
47	5			47	1	
48	5			48	4	
49	3			49	7	
50	0			50	4	
Totals				Totals		

(a) Copy and complete the tables above.

(b) For each class, calculate the following summary statistics.
   (i) the range of scores   (ii) the mean score
   (iii) the most common score   (iv) the median score
   (v) the percentage of children scoring above the mean

(c) Describe the distribution of marks in each class.

Handling Data

3 (a) What numerical value is given to the probability of an event that is certain to occur?

(b) What numerical value is given to the probability of an event that is impossible?

(c) Explain what is meant by, 'The probability of an event is 50%.'

(d) How likely is it that it will rain tomorrow if the probability of rain is 0·2?

4 (a) I throw a fair die and get a 6.
What is the probability that,
on the next throw, I will get a 6?

(b) A fair pentagonal spinner has the numbers 0, 1, 2, 3 and 4 on it.

Work out the following theoretical probabilities of the
arrow pointing to these numbers after spinning.

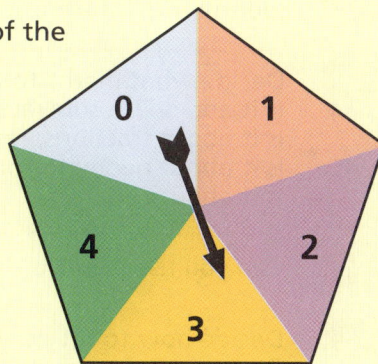

(i) P(zero)

(ii) P(an odd number)

(iii) P(a prime number)

(iv) P(a square number)

(v) P(a factor of 12)

(c) The letters of the word HAPPY are put in a bag.
A letter is selected at random and replaced.

Work out the following theoretical probabilities of selecting letters.

(i) P(letter Y)

(ii) P(vowel)

(iii) P(consonant)

(iv) P(repeated letter)

(v) P(H or P)

(vi) P(not Y)

Problem solving

Introduction

Key Stage 3 National Strategy Framework for Teaching Mathematics

- Solve word problems and investigate in a range of contexts: number, algebra, shape, space and measures, and handling data; compare and evaluate solutions.

- Identify the necessary information to solve a problem; represent problems mathematically, making correct use of symbols, words, diagrams, tables and graphs.

- Break a complex calculation into simpler steps, choosing and using appropriate and efficient operations, methods and resources, including ICT.

- Present and interpret solutions in the context of the original problem; explain and justify methods and conclusions, orally and in writing.

- Suggest extensions to problems by asking, 'What if …?'; begin to generalise and to understand the significance of a counter-example.

Helping you to solve problems using mathematics

1   Read the question very carefully.

2   Identify the information you need and write it down.

3   Decide what maths to apply:
Is it an add? A subtract? A multiply? A divide?
Is it about fractions, ratios or percentages?
Is it about geometry or statistics?
Is it about … ?

4   Can you use algebra right from the start?

5   Decide how to set out your solution:
Do you need a table for results?
Do you need a diagram or graph?
Will someone reading it understand what you have done?

6   Decide whether you can make a general statement:
In words? Using algebra?

7   Go back to the original question. Have you answered it?

8   Ask, 'What if …?'

Letts I See Maths Year 7

Example

Problem A square and a rectangle have the same area.
The sides of the rectangle are in the ratio 8 : 2.
Its perimeter is 200 cm.
What is the length of a side of the square?

Prompts	Solution
1 Read the question.	Rectangle and square – same area Rectangle – sides in ratio 8 : 2 Rectangle – $P = 200$? length of side of square?
2 Identify information and write it down.	
3 Ratio, geometry, algebra	
4 Yes.	
5 Draw diagrams.	
I know that the rectangle has sides $8n$ and $2n$.	Let n be the multiplier for the sides of the rectangle.
I don't know the side of the square.	Let x cm be the length of the square.
I use what I know about the perimeter of the rectangle.	Given: $\quad P = 200$ But: $\qquad P = 16n + 4n$ $\qquad\qquad\quad = 20n$ Therefore: $20n = 200$ $\qquad\qquad n = 10$
I work out the dimensions of the rectangle.	Therefore, the rectangle measures 80 cm by 20 cm.
I go back and look for further information.	Area of rectangle $= 1600\ \text{cm}^2$ Area of square $\quad = 1600\ \text{cm}^2$
I work out the length of the square.	Therefore: $\quad x^2 = 1600$ $\qquad\qquad x = \sqrt{1600}$
6 There is one answer so no need for a generalisation.	$\qquad\qquad\quad = 40$
7 Yes, I have answered the question.	**Answer** The length of the side of the square is 40 cm.
8 Here is another possible question.	What if the ratio of the sides of the rectangle was 1 : 9?

Using maths in everyday life

Goals

By the end of this lesson you will be able to answer questions such as this:

👁 In January a house was priced at £140 000. By April the price had increased by 6%. By August the April price had increased by 4%. What was the price in August?

Starter

1 Answer the following questions.

(a) Write 253 pence as pounds.
(b) Write £5·42 as pence.
(c) Write 7 pence as pounds.
(d) Add £3·48 and £5·07.
(e) What is 10% of £1?
(f) What is 50% of £3·60?
(g) What is the cost of three pens at £1·99 each?
(h) I spend £10·40 on four identical packets of biscuits. What is the cost of one packet?

Demonstration 1

Question

The price of a coat was decreased by 10% in a sale. Four weeks later the price was increased by 10%. Is the final price the same as the original price?

Read the question carefully. Ask yourself questions.

- What was the original price of the coat? I do not know because it is not given. Maybe it does not matter. I could *let* the price be £1, £10, £100 or £x. I think that I will let the original price be £100.

- I have to decrease the price by 10%. I know two different ways of doing this. I can either find 10% of £100 and take it away or I can find 90% of £100. The last one is easier because I can do it with one calculation.

$$\text{Sale price} = £\tfrac{90}{100} \times 100 = £90$$

- Now I have to increase this by 10%. Either work out 10% and add it on or work out 110%. Again, the latter is easier.

$$\text{Final price} = £\tfrac{110}{100} \times 90 = £99$$

- This is less than the original price. The reason the answer is different is because I am finding 10% of different sums of money.

Letts **I See Maths** **Year 7**

Demonstration 2

A recipe for onion soup uses three small onions for every half litre of soup.
How many onions do I need to make two litres of soup?
How much soup can I make from fifteen onions?

Read the question carefully. Ask yourself questions.

- What sort of maths shall I use? I think it will be ×, ÷, + or −.

  I know how to make a $\frac{1}{2}$ **litre** of soup.

$$3 \text{ onions} \to \tfrac{1}{2} \text{ litre soup}$$
$$4 \times 3 \text{ onions} \to 4 \times \tfrac{1}{2} \text{ litres soup}$$
$$12 \text{ onions} \to 2 \text{ litres soup}$$

- I can start with the same information.

$$3 \text{ onions} \to \tfrac{1}{2} \text{ litre soup}$$
$$5 \times 3 \text{ onions} \to 5 \times \tfrac{1}{2} \text{ litres soup}$$
$$15 \text{ onions} \to 2\tfrac{1}{2} \text{ litres soup}$$

- The ratio of onions : litres is $3 : \frac{1}{2}$.

  This ratio has the same value as 6 : 1.

  For n litres of soup I need $6n$ onions.

Key words   ratio   percentage (%)

Exercise bank 👉

Plenary

- 👁 Go back to the Goals and answer the question on the price of a house.
  Read the question carefully. Ask yourself questions.

- 👁 Discuss:
  An increase of 6% followed by a further increase of 4% can be calculated by multiplying the original price by 1·06 and then 1·04.
  $$1·06 \times 1·04 = 1·1024$$

Using maths in everyday life

Exercises

1 A drink and a sandwich together cost £3·70.
Two drinks and a sandwich together cost £4·90.

(a) What is the cost of a drink?
(b) What is the cost of a sandwich?
(c) What is the cost of three drinks and two sandwiches?

2 Sophie went to the shops and bought six identical packets of biscuits for her party. She spent £11·10.

(a) What is the cost of one packet of biscuits?
(b) What would be the cost of nine packets of biscuits?

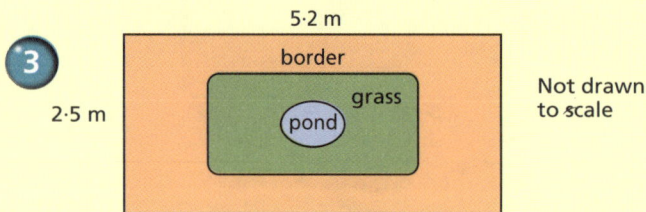

3

5·2 m

border

grass

pond

2·5 m

Not drawn to scale

(a) This is a sketch of Mary's garden. She has decided that she wants 60% of her garden laid down to grass. What area will be grass?

(b) Mary goes to the garden centre to buy grass seed for her lawn. She needs 15 g of grass seed for every square metre of lawn. How many grams of grass seed should she buy?

4 Peter and John were saving money to go on holiday. Peter saved twice as much as John and then his Granny gave him an extra £7. Together they saved £97. How much did John save?

Using and Applying

Letts **I See Maths** Year 7

Using maths in everyday life

5 Last winter there was a 'flu epidemic in Sunnyside town. The health authority said there was a 1 in 50 risk of catching the 'flu. If the population of Sunnyside was 87 500, how many people were likely to catch the 'flu?

6 Gary gets £12 a week pocket money. He saves three times as much as he spends. How much money does he save each week?

7 In January 2002, one euro could buy 62 pence. How many euros would you get for £1?

8 Ramesh is delivering boxes of books to a company on the twelfth floor of a building. He uses a service lift that can take a maximum load of 600 kg. Each box of books weighs 6.08 kg. Ramesh weighs 75 kg. What is the maximum number of boxes that Ramesh can take with him in the lift?

9 In June a pair of trainers cost £62.50. They were reduced by 15% in a sale. What is the sale price of the trainers.

10 (a) Barry's mum drives him and his sister to and from school every day. The average journey time from home to school is 17 minutes. How much time does Barry spend in the car travelling to and from school each week?

(b) Some new traffic lights increased the time of travel over a week by 25 minutes. What is the new average journey time?

Using maths to investigate

► Goals

By the end of this lesson you will:

- know that, in an investigation, you ask, 'What if ... ?'
- know how to break down a question, be systematic and record results
- know what a conjecture is
- know what a generalisation is.

► Starter

1 Answer the following questions.

(a) five squared

(b) one squared

(c) ten squared

(d) two squared

(e) four squared

(f) nine squared

(g) six squared

(h) three squared

(i) eight squared

► Demonstration 1

Question: How many squares are there on a chess board?
Inspect the chess board. It measures 8 squares by 8 squares.

Answer: 64 squares
But what if you look again?
Can you see more squares? 2 by 2 squares? 3 × 3 squares? ...
This is interesting but I keep losing track of all those squares.

• **Break down the problem.**	• **Be systematic.**	• **Record results.**
Begin with a 1 by 1 square.	No. of 1 × 1 squares = 1	Total = 1
Go to a 2 by 2 square.	No. of 1 × 1 squares = 4 No. of 2 × 2 squares = 1	Total = 5
Go to a 3 by 3 square.	No. of 1 × 1 squares = 9 No. of 2 × 2 squares = 4 No. of 3 × 3 squares = 1	Total = 14

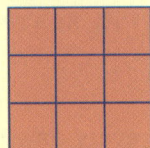

- Look at your results so far.
- What do you notice?
- Is there a pattern?

Conjecture: I think that the number of squares goes up in square numbers. I predict that for a 4 by 4 square there will be 1 + 4 + 9 + 16 squares.

Using and Applying

Letts **I See Maths** Year 7

Using maths to investigate

Test: Draw a 4 by 4 square.

No. of 1×1 squares $= 16$
No. of 2×2 squares $= 9$
No. of 3×3 squares $= 4$
No. of 4×4 squares $= 1$
Total $= 30$

No. of squares on a 4 by 4 square $= 1^2 + 2^2 + 3^2 + 4^2$
No. of squares on a 5 by 5 square $= 1^2 + 2^2 + 3^2 + 4^2 + 5^2$
Number of squares on a chess board $= 1^2 + 2^2 + 3^2 + 4^2 + 5^2 + 6^2 + 7^2 + 8^2$
$= 204$

Generalisation:

No. of squares on a n by n square $= 1^2 + 2^2 + 3^2 + 4^2 + 5^2 + \ldots + n^2$

Now ask your own questions:

• What if I look at rectangular boards?

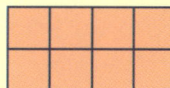

• What if I look at triangles in an equilateral triangle?

• What if I look at cubes within cubes?

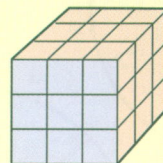

• What if … ?

Key words   conjecture   generalisation   predict

Exercise bank

Plenary

◉ When you are asked to investigate what do you do?

◉ What is a conjecture?

◉ What is a generalisation?

◉ How many squares are there on a 100 by 100 square board?

Using and Applying

Letts **I See Maths** Year 7

Using maths to investigate

Investigations

1 Matchstick shapes

Triangles are made using matchsticks like this.

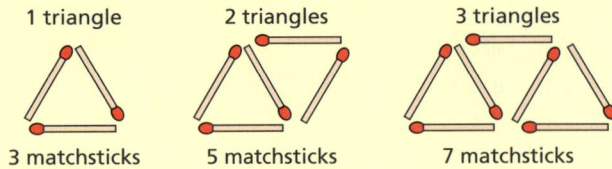

1 triangle — 3 matchsticks

2 triangles — 5 matchsticks

3 triangles — 7 matchsticks

(a) How many matchsticks do you need to make ten triangles?

(b) How many matchsticks do you need to make n triangles?

(c) Investigate other shapes you can make with matchsticks.

2 The pizza problem

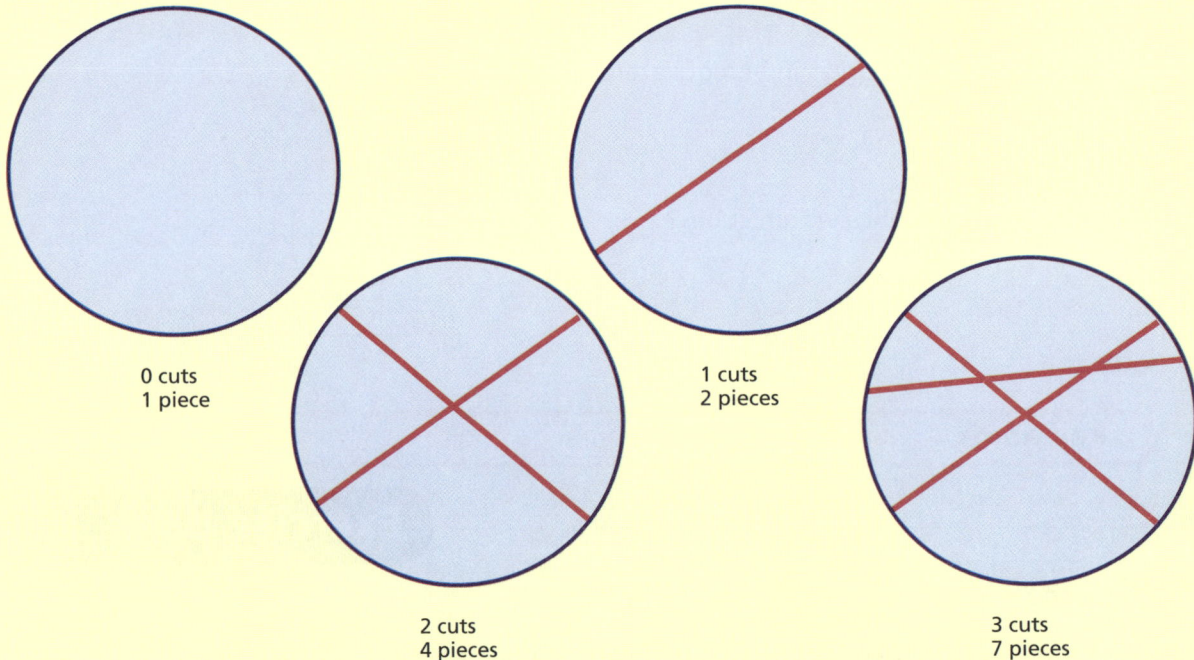

0 cuts
1 piece

1 cuts
2 pieces

2 cuts
4 pieces

3 cuts
7 pieces

Each new cut must cross all other cuts separately to get the maximum number of pieces.

(a) How many pieces will you get with four cuts?

(b) How many pieces will you get with ten cuts?

(c) How many pieces will you get with n cuts?

Using and Applying

3 Jugs

You have two jugs. One holds 5 litres of water and the other holds 3 litres of water. You are not allowed to mark the jugs in any way.

(a) How can you measure 1 litre using the two jugs?

(b) What other measures can you make with the two jugs?

(c) Investigate the problem with different sizes of jugs.

4 Branches

These shapes are made with matchsticks. They are called 'branches'.

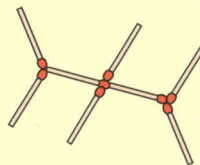

Branch A

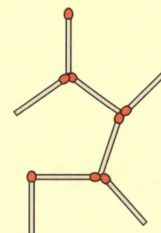

Branch B

There are no closed loops in a branch. So these are *not* 'branches'.

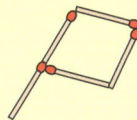

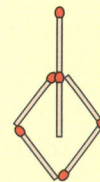

Look at this branch.
It has four ends (E).
It has four joins (J).
It uses seven matches (M).

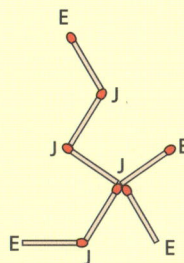

Branch C

(a) Make a table and count the number of ends, joins and matches for Branch A and Branch B.

(b) Draw some branches of your own and fill in the information in your table.

(c) **Investigate:** Can you find a relationship between the number of matches, ends and joins?

Working like a detective

Goals

By the end of this lesson you will be able to answer questions such as this:

👁 The diagram shows a rhombus. Calculate the angles $a°$, $b°$, $c°$ and $d°$.

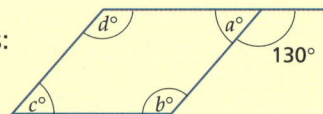

Starter

1 Use a ruler and a pair of compasses to construct all the triangles that are possible using these lengths.

(a) 3 cm   (b) 4 cm   (c) 6 cm   (d) 7·5 cm

Demonstration 1

Work out angle $a°$.

Inspect the diagram on the right. C is the centre of the circle. Look for clues.

Clue 1
The most important fact to remember about a circle is that the radius (r) is *always* the same length.

I can mark all the radii as equal.
Now I can see two isosceles triangles.

Clue 2
I know that the angles of a triangle add up to 180°.

$\hat{DCA} = 180° - 70° = 110°$
$\hat{DCB} = 180° - 50° = 130°$

Clue 3
The angle at the centre is 360°.

$\hat{ACB} = 360° - 240°$

$= 120°$

$a° = 120°$

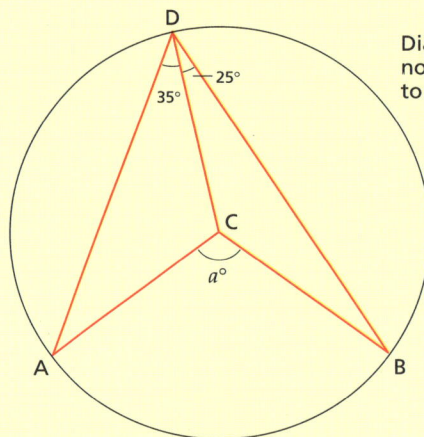
Diagram not drawn to scale

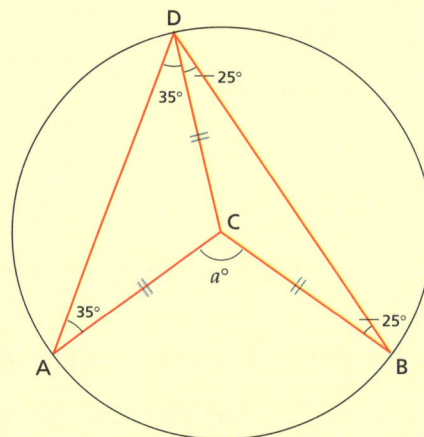

Using and Applying

Letts **I See Maths** Year 7

► Demonstration 2

Mark all the angles in the diagram that are equal to 41°.

B

41°

Diagram
not drawn
to scale

Clue 1
Lines l_1, l_2 and l_3 are all parallel.

I know that alternate angles are equal.
I know that corresponding angles are equal.

A

l_1

l_2

Clue 2
When two straight lines cross then vertically opposite
angles are equal.

C

l_3

Clue 3
Angle $\hat{B}A\hat{C}$ is a right angle.

Note
There are several different ways of doing this question.
Here is one way.

D

41°

$a°$

$b°$

$a° = 41°$ (alternate angles from parallel lines l_1 and l_2)

$b° = a° = 41°$ (vertically opposite angles)

$c° = b° = 41°$ (alternate angles from parallel lines
    l_2 and l_3)

A

l_1

l_2

$c°$

C

l_3

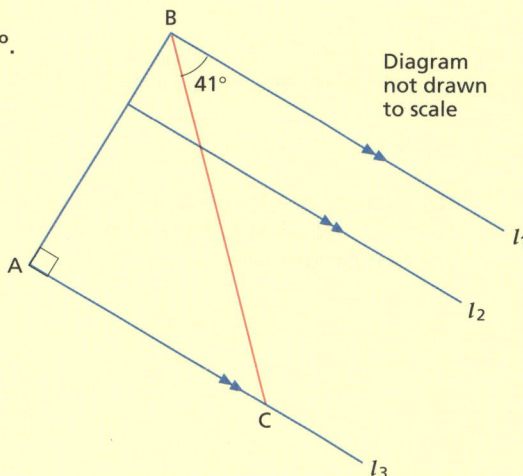

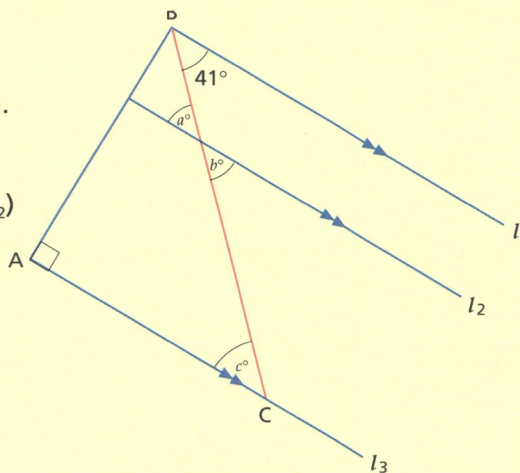

Key words   clues   inspect   parallel   radii

....

Exercise bank 👉

► Plenary

👁   Go back to the Goals and calculate angles $a°$, $b°$, $c°$ and $d°$.

👁   Look at Demonstration 1 again. What do you notice about $A\hat{D}B$ and the angle marked $a°$?
    Investigate placing D at different points on the circumference.

Working like a detective

Exercises

1 AB is the diameter of the circle.
O is the centre of the circle.

(a) Calculate $A\hat{C}B$.

(b) Investigate the size of $A\hat{C}B$ when
C is placed at different points on
the circumference.

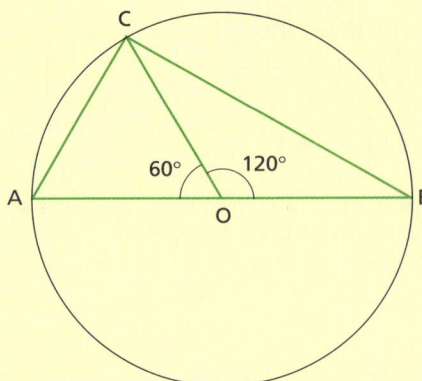

Diagram not
drawn accurately

C

60°   120°

A   O   B

2 The shapes investigated in this question are all quadrilaterals.
Inspect the statements below. Look for clues.

Name the quadrilateral from this list that matches each of the following statements.

parallelogram   rectangle   rhombus   square

(a) The diagonals are equal in length and bisect each other.

(b) The diagonals bisect each other but are *not* equal in length.

(c) The diagonals bisect each other at right angles.

(d) The diagonals are equal in length and bisect each other at right angles.

3 Shape ABCD is a trapezium.

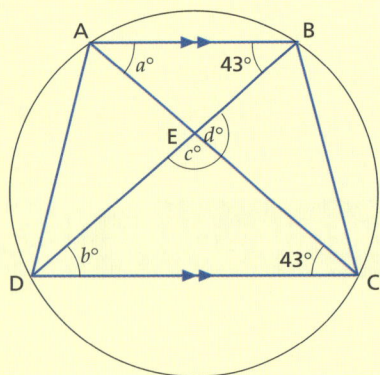

A   B
$a°$ 43°
E $d°$
$c°$
$b°$ 43°
D   C

(a) Calculate the angles marked with letters.

(b) Write down any lines that you know are equal in length.

Using and Applying

Letts I See Maths Year 7

Working like a detective

4 Lines l_1 and l_2 are parallel.

Investigate the areas of triangles ABC, ABD and ABE.

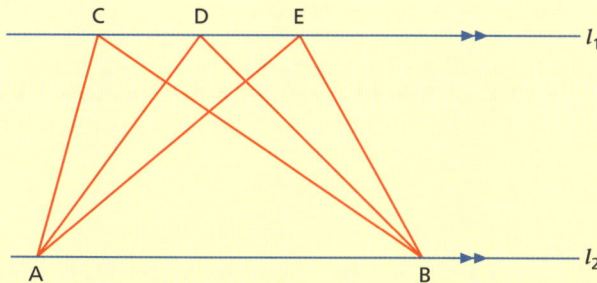

5 Lines l_1 and l_2 are parallel.

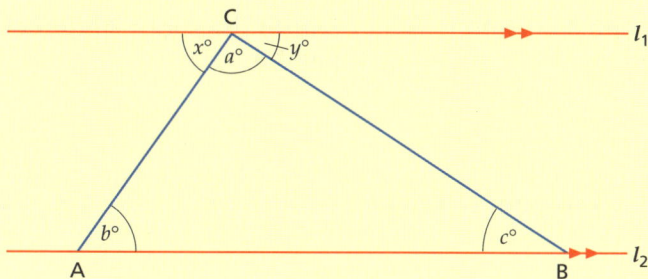

(a) State an angle equal to $x°$.

(b) State an angle equal to $y°$.

(c) What can you say about $x° + a° + y°$?
Give your reason for the answer.

(d) What can you say about the sum of the angles of the triangle ABC?

6 Draw any triangle ABC.

(a) Draw a line through the midpoint of AB
that is perpendicular to AB.

(b) Draw a line through the midpoint of BC
that is perpendicular to BC.

(c) Draw a line through the midpoint of AC
that is perpendicular to AC.

(d) Your three lines should meet in a point.
Put your compasses on this point and
draw a circle that just passes through the
vertices A, B and C.

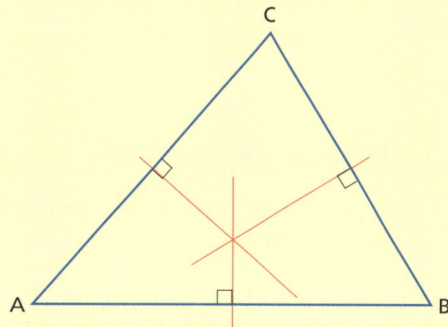

Letts **I See Maths** Year 7

Using maths to understand text

Goals

By the end of this lesson you will be able to make sense of text such as this:

👁 Jasmin went on a 3 km bike ride. When she finished it she checked her counting machine. It showed her that her bike wheel had turned 2000 complete turns since her journey began. Jasmin's dad thinks that she has probably covered about 300 km on this bike since she had it for her birthday.

Starter

Read these stories. Write the maths story for the real-life story and work out the answer.

1 Becky wanted to decorate her bedroom. She went with her dad to the shops. Together they bought a set of brushes for £5.50 and three tins of sky-blue paint at £4.20 each. How much did they spend altogether?

2 Tom wanted a special pen. He had seen it advertised for 55 pence. He went to a shop that sold the pen and found out about an offer. If he bought six of the pens he could get twelve pence off each one. He worked out how much six pens would cost him.

Demonstration 1

Read this story.

Danielle invited three of her friends to sleep over. Using her £5 pocket money she bought snacks for her friends and herself. Everyone had the same: a packet of crisps and a bar of chocolate. The crisps cost 35 pence a packet and the chocolate 45 pence a bar.

Read the text. Ask yourself questions.

- How many were in the story altogether?
    Danielle and three of her friends. That makes four altogether.

- How much was spent on each person?
    Crisps at 35 pence and chocolate at 45 pence makes 80 pence each.

- How much was spent altogether?
    Four people at 80 pence each. $4 \times 80p = 320p$
    $$= £3·20$$

Demonstration 2

Read this diary of John and Juliette's holiday.

Day 1: Arrive in San Diego. At 9 a.m. take bus 30 miles from San Diego to La Jolla Cove (1 hour 30 minutes, fare $2 each). Go snorkelling, watch seals. At 7 p.m. catch bus back. After 20 miles get off at Mission Beach. Spend hour here. At 9 p.m. take later bus back. Arrive in San Diego at 9.30 p.m.

Day 2: At 10 a.m. take 20-minute bus ride to Seaworld, 8 miles away. See dolphins and killer whales. At 5 p.m. catch return bus to San Diego. Rush-hour traffic adds 20 minutes to journey.

Day 3: Fly San Diego to San Francisco. Leave at 2.30 p.m. The 400-mile flight takes 1.5 hours. Hire car. Drive to Big Basin Redwood National Park, 150 miles away. Spend 4 hours on winding mountain roads. Trees are awesome.

Day 4: Big Basin to Kings Canyon National Park, 300-mile non-stop drive takes 6.5 hours. High mountains and huge redwood trees en route.

Day 5: Drive Kings Canyon to Death Valley (hottest place on Earth). Crossing Sierra Nevada mountains takes 8 hours. Camp in Death Valley.

Day 6: Death Valley to Yosemite National Park by car. Snow in mountains means 500-mile detour in blizzards! Takes 11 hours. Camp in Yosemite. Brown bears look round our tent for food in the night. Scary.

Day 7: Hire bikes for day in Yosemite Valley. Cycled: campsite to Mirror Lake (5 miles, 30 minutes), Mirror Lake to Yosemite Falls (4 miles, 20 minutes), Yosemite Falls back to campsite (7 miles, 1 hour).

Day 8: Drive from Yosemite to San Francisco. The 400 miles on fast five-lane roads takes 7 hours. Fly home.

Read the text. Ask yourself questions.

- What time did John and Juliette get to La Jolla Cove?
  Left San Diego 9 a.m., took 1 hour 30 minutes, arrive 10.30 a.m.

- How fast was the bus travelling on average between San Diego and La Jolla Cove?
  Distance 30 miles, time $1\frac{1}{2}$ hours, average speed 20 m.p.h.

- Can I draw a distance–time graph of John and Juliette's holiday?
  Yes. First …

Exercise bank

Plenary

- Complete the distance–time graph for John and Juliette's holiday.
- Go back and make sense of the text in the Goals.
- Write a story of your own using some mathematics.

Stories

1

Queen Elizabeth Forest Park

By the mid-seventeenth century, natural birch and oak woodlands had almost disappeared from the area of Stirlingshire in Scotland that is known today as Queen Elizabeth Forest Park. Then from 1760 to 1770, as the tanning industries developed, there was a growing demand for oak bark. By the beginning of the next century there were about 3000 acres of oak coppice in Stirlingshire. In 1809 the price for oak bark was £18 a ton. Each acre of woodland produced between 1·5 and 2 tons of it.

The amount of land under forestry continued to increase. Often, different species of tree were grown together. In one acre there might be 1000 hardwood trees, 1250 Scots pines and 900 European larches. Every day forestry workers planted about 300 hardwood trees and between 600 and 700 conifers. They received a wage of 12·5p a day. The Montrose Estate planted about 1200 acres of woodland over 20 years using this method.

In spite of the expanding forestry industry, the population of this part of Stirlingshire was getting smaller. This trend was finally halted when slate began to be quarred commercially, north of Aberfoyle. By 1858, one of the largest quarries was producing 1 400 000 slates a year. This created a need for transport and, in 1859, a rail link was opened.

More employment was provided by a project to turn nearby Loch Katrine into a reservoir. The first aqueduct was completed in 1859. With a gradient of 10 inches per mile, it supplied 40 million gallons of water a day. A more direct aqueduct, built later, had a gradient of 11·5 inches per mile and supplied 70 million gallons of water a day. But turning lochs into reservoirs had its drawbacks. Good sheep-grazing land was lost as water levels rose – in Loch Venachar by 5·75 inches and in Loch Drunkie by 25 feet.

Read the text.

(a) How long ago was oak bark sold for £18 a ton?

(b) How many trees were planted in five days?

(c) Ask your own questions to help you make sense of the story.

Letts **I See Maths Year 7**

2 **Matthew's canoeing trip**

Day 1: Leave work 5.30 p.m. (Edinburgh). Drive to Glencoe, 150 miles, 3.5 hours. Rush hour in Edinburgh (1 hour to drive 10 miles!). Camp in Glencoe.

Day 2: Up early. Rain. Good for canoeing. Drive to Glen Etive, 10 miles, 30 minutes. Winding road. Kayak down River Etive (Grade 5, big waterfalls, very scary), 2 miles, 3 hours (including time to inspect rapids). Walk back to car, 15 minutes in soggy wetsuit! Drive back for kayak, 5 minutes.

Day 3: Wet. Cold. Drive to Fort William, 30 miles, 1 hour. Have a cup of tea and some cakes in a warm café. Camp in Fort William. Rain all night.

Day 4: Rivers high. Drive to Spean Bridge, 10 miles, 20 minutes. Paddle Spean Gorge in flood, 7 miles, only 2 hours. Very fast water, big rapids. Hamish drives me back to Spean Bridge, 10 miles, 30 minutes. Camped.

Day 5: Sunny. Brilliant! Go hiking. 9 a.m. drive to Ben Nevis, 9 miles, 20 minutes. Walk up Ben Nevis (4400 feet, UK's highest mountain), 4 miles to summit, 3 hours. Snow on top. Lunch, 30 minutes. The 4 miles down take just 2 hours. Drive to Fort William, 1 mile, 5 minutes. Buy fish and chips.

Day 6: Start 8 a.m. Drive east via Loch Ness (no monsters today!) to Inverness, 80 miles, 2 hours. Then on to Perth, 90 miles, 1 hour 45 minutes on a fast road. Kayak down River Tay, 3 miles, 1 hour. Friend picks me up. We drive to Dunkeld, 10 miles, 15 minutes. Paddle River Bran, 4 miles, 2 hours. Very exciting narrow gorge. Lift back to car, 3 miles, 10 minutes. Camp.

Day 7: At 7 a.m. get cooked breakfast in Dunkeld. Then 7.40 a.m. drive back to Edinburgh via Forth Road Bridge, 50 miles, 1 hour 30 minutes. Home exhausted but happy.

Read the diary.

(a) What time did Matthew arrive in Glencoe?

(b) What was the average speed of driving from Glencoe to Glen Etive on Day 2?

(c) Draw distance–time graphs based on Matthew's diary.

(d) Ask your own questions to help you make sense of the story.

Preparing for tests

Goals

When you have completed this lesson you will:

👁 know how to do mental-arithmetic tests

👁 know how to do non-calculator tests.

Mental-arithmetic test

- You will need a pencil and pen. You must *not* use a calculator.
- Each question will be read twice.
- Try to work out the answer to the question in your head. You may jot down workings if this helps.

Test

For this first group of questions, you have 5 seconds to work out each answer and write it down.

(1) Add nought point three and two point seven.
(2) Look at $x + 5 = y$. When x equals 4, what is the value of y?
(3) Multiply nine by six.
(4) Subtract ninety-eight from two hundred and forty-three.
(5) The probability of winning a game is three-sevenths. What is the probability of not winning the game.

For the next group of questions, you have 10 seconds to work out each answer and write it down.

(6) Fifty per cent of a number is twenty-four. What is the number?
(7) What angle is between north and east, turning clockwise?
(8) The temperature was ⁻2°C. It rose by 8°C. What is the new temperature?
(9) The length of a rectangle is 5 cm and its width is 4 cm. What is its area?
(10) What is three-fifths of 20?
(11) Multiply fifteen by twelve.
(12) What is fifteen-twentieths as a percentage?
(13) In a class of 30 children, 14 are boys. What fraction of the class is boys?
(14) What is the value of x in the equation $2x + 10 = 4x$?
(15) What is the area of a triangle with base 8 cm and height 5 cm?
(16) In a bag are 30 red counters and 20 yellow counters. What is the probability of selecting a red counter taken at random?
(17) Write four-sixteenths in its simplest form.
(18) Approximately, how much is twenty-four per cent of seventy-nine?

For the next group of questions, you have 15 seconds to work out each answer and write it down.

(19) What is the next prime number after 37?
(20) Look at the numbers 2, 3, 5, 8, 10 and 16. Which of these are factors of 64?
(21) In a pie chart, 45° represented eight people in a survey. How many people were in the survey altogether?
(22) Last June I sent a mean of 10 text messages every day. Altogether how many text messages did I send?
(23) A bar chart shows that the proportion of men, women and children in a village was 6 : 5 : 1. What fraction of the village is men?
(24) Subtract a quarter from three-eighths.
(25) Square twenty, then multiply by nought point two five.

Letts **I See Maths** Year 7

Non-calculator paper

- You may need pencil, pen, ruler, protractor and a pair of compasses.
- You have 50 minutes to do the test. Do not waste time on questions that you cannot do. Make a note and come back to them if you have time at the end.
- Read the questions carefully and underline any information you want to remember.
- Show *all* your workings neatly.

Example

Work out   (a) 374 + 853   (b) 502 − 255   (c) 243 × 37   (d) 1225 ÷ 5.

Answer

(a) $374 + 853 = 1227$ ← Write like this if you can add the numbers mentally.

$$\begin{array}{r} 374 \\ + 853 \\ \hline 1227 \\ \hline \end{array}$$

← Set out neatly like this if you cannot do the sum mentally.

(b) $502 - 255 = 247$ ← Write like this if you can subtract the numbers mentally.

$$\begin{array}{r} 502 \\ - 255 \\ \hline 247 \\ \hline \end{array}$$

← Set out neatly like this if you cannot do the subtraction mentally.

(c)

×	200	40	3	
30	6000	1200	90	7290
7	1400	280	21	1701
				8991

or

$$\begin{array}{r} 243 \\ \times\ 37 \\ \hline 7290 \\ 1701 \\ \hline 8991 \\ \hline \end{array}$$

or

$$\begin{array}{r} 243 \\ \times\ 37 \\ \hline 1701 \\ 7290 \\ \hline 8991 \\ \hline \end{array}$$

(d)
$$\begin{array}{r} 5\ \overline{|\ 1000} \qquad 5 \times 200 \\ 200 \qquad 5 \times 40 \\ 25 \qquad 5 \times 5 \\ \hline 5 \times 245 \end{array}$$

or $5\,\overline{|\,1225} = 245$

Plenary

- Identify the questions in the mental-arithmetic test that you could not do and set yourself targets for improvement.
- Mark the questions in Tests A1, A2 and A3, and do corrections.

Tests ☞

Letts **I See Maths** Year 7

National Curriculum Tests

231

Calculator not allowed

1 Work out:
(a) 456 + 749   (b) 301 − 146   (c) 127 × 48   (d) 1284 ÷ 6.

2 The temperature at 3 p.m. on 2 January was 2°C. By midnight the temperature had dropped by 8°C. What was the temperature at midnight?

3

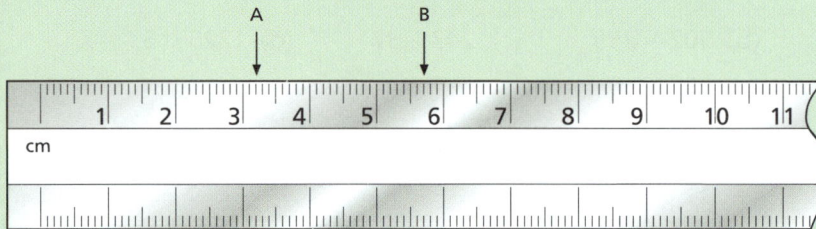

Write down the measurements at A and B in (a) centimetres and (b) millimetres.

4 Here is part of a number sequence: 5 → 14 → 41 → 122

To get the next number you   **multiply by 3 then subtract 1.**

Fill in the two missing numbers in the sequence.   ◯ → 5 → 14 → 41 → 122 → ◯

5 It takes 2 hours 50 minutes to fly from Bristol to Barcelona. If the flight leaves Bristol at 08:40, what time will it arrive in Barcelona?

6

| 65 | 65 000 | 6·5 | 0·65 | 650 | 6500 | 0·065 |

Write down which of the numbers above is:
(a) ten times as big as 65   (b) a tenth of 65   (c) one hundred times as big as 65.

7 A cuboid has measurements of length 4 cm, width 3 cm and height 6 cm.
Work out   (a) the volume of the cuboid   (b) the surface area of the cuboid.

8 Copy and complete the multiplication grid on the right.

×				6	
3	6	12			24
		10			40
				42	
			36	54	

Letts I See Maths Year 7

9 In a class of 30 children, 60% answered a question correctly.

(a) What percentage of the class answered the question incorrectly?

(b) How many children answered the question correctly?

10 Write down three numbers that have a mean of 5.

11 Look at the equation $y = x + 3$.

Which of the following equations show the same relationship as this?

(a) $y - 3 = x$ (b) $y + x = 3$ (c) $y + 3 = x$ (d) $y - x = 3$

12 Write the ratio 20 : 40 in its simplest form.

13 What quick test tells you that this division question is wrong?

2324 ÷ 9 = 258

14 Which of the following statements are correct?

(a) $\frac{3}{5} = 0 \cdot 6$ (b) $0 \cdot 7 = 7\%$ (c) $0 \cdot 25 = \frac{1}{4}$ (d) $\frac{2}{3} = 3 \cdot 2$

15 Work out the area and perimeter of the shape on the right.

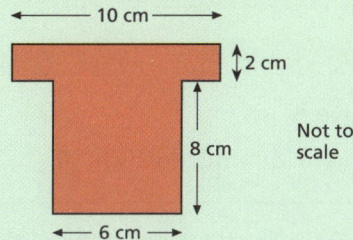

10 cm

2 cm

8 cm

Not to scale

6 cm

16 Use a pair of compasses and a ruler to construct a triangle with sides of 4 cm, 5 cm and 6 cm.

17 A sequence of numbers is generated using the rule $3n + 1$. Write down the first three terms of the sequence.

18 The following coordinates (x, y) all lie on a line.

(0, 4), (1, 3), (2, 2), (3, 1), (4, 0)

Write down the equation of the line.

19 Write down the equation of a line parallel to $y = x + 3$.

20 Work out the values of the two algebraic expressions below when $y = 5$.

(a) $(2y)^2$ (b) $2y^2$

Letts **I See Maths** Year 7

Test A2

Calculator not allowed

1 Work out:

(a) 397 + 568   (b) 490 − 182   (c) 304 × 29.   (d) 2464 ÷ 7

2 The temperature drops from ⁻2°C to ⁻11°C. By how many degrees has it dropped?

3 How much liquid is in the measuring jug on the right?

Write the measurement in   (a) millilitres   (b) litres.

4 Here is part of a number sequence:

$$4 \rightarrow 9 \rightarrow 19 \rightarrow 39$$

To get the next number you   **multiply by 2 then add 1.**

Fill in the two missing numbers in the sequence.   ◯ → 4 → 9 → 19 → 39 → ◯

5 It takes 3 hours 45 minutes to travel by train from Plymouth to London. If the train leaves Plymouth at 06:50, what time will it arrive in London?

6

| 34 | 0·034 | 340 | 3400 | 0·34 | 34 000 | 3·4 |

Write down which of the numbers above is:

(a) one thousand times as big as 34   (b) a hundredth of 34   (c) ten times as big as 34.

7 A cuboid has measurements of length 5 cm, width 4 cm and height 5 cm.

Work out   (a) the volume of the cuboid   (b) the surface area of the cuboid.

8 Copy and complete the multiplication grid on the right.

×		9		
6	30			12
			32	
	15	27	24	
		63		14

9 In a box of 20 chocolates, 75% of them had soft centres.

(a) What percentage of the chocolates did not have soft centres?
(b) How many of the chocolates had soft centres?

10 Work out (a) the mean (b) the median and (c) the mode of the following set of numbers.
12, 10, 14, 15, 15, 10, 14, 12, 14, 14

Letts   **I See Maths** Year 7

National Curriculum Tests

11 Write each expression below in its simplest form.

(a) $3 + 4t + 8t$ (b) $s + 6 + 4s + 5$ (c) $(4x + 3) + (3x - 2)$ (d) $5y - ^-y$

----

12 Write an expression for the following.

(a) the perimeter of rectangle ABCD
(b) the area of rectangle ABCD

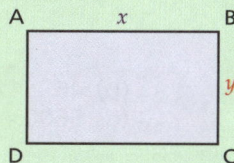

----

13 Which of the following statements are correct?

(a) $\frac{3}{4} = 0.75$ (b) $\frac{1}{3} = 0.3$ (c) $\frac{4}{5} = \frac{36}{45}$ (d) $0.08 = 8\%$

----

14 A sequence is generated using the rule $5n + 2$. Write down the first three terms of the sequence.

----

15 Look at the bar chart on the right. It shows a survey of the colour of cars.

(a) How many cars were counted in the survey?
(b) What proportion of cars were blue?
(c) What percentage of cars were red?

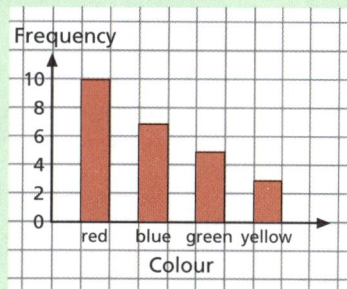

----

16 (a) Use a pair of compasses and a ruler to draw a triangle with sides of 7 cm, 5 cm and 5 cm.
(b) Name the triangle you have drawn.

----

17 The coordinates (1, 2), (3, 4) and (5, 2) are three vertices of a square. Write down the coordinates of the fourth vertex.

----

18 Write down the coordinates (x, y) of four points that lie on the line $x + y = 6$.

----

19 Work out the values of the two algebraic expressions below when $x = 3$.

(a) $(2x^2) + 5$ (b) $2x^2 + 5$

----

20 At what point on a grid does the line $y = 2x + 4$ cross the y-axis?

Calculator not allowed

1. Write one number at the end of each equation to make it correct.

   Example
   35 + 52 = 27 + 60

   (a) 340 + 290 = 180 + ...
   (b) 46 − 17 = 52 − ...
   (c) 4 × 96 = 6 × ...
   (d) 5600 ÷ 100 = 560 ÷ ...

2. Look at these three signs:

< is less than	= is equal to	> is greater than

   Put the correct sign in each number sentence.

   (a) 4 + 9 ... 10 + 1
   (b) 17 − 4 ... 15 ÷ 6
   (c) 2 − 3 ... ⁻2 + 1

3. Diane throws a fair die. What is the probability that she will get an even number? Write your answer as a fraction.

4. Here is a list of numbers:
   ⁻6, ⁻5, ⁻3, ⁻1, 0, 2, 3, 5

   (a) Choose two of the numbers from the list which have a total of:
       (i) 2   (ii) 0   (iii) ⁻1   (iv) ⁻3   (v) ⁻11.

   (b) What is the total of all eight numbers in the list?

5. You are given that 27 × 45 = 1215. Use this to write down the answers to the following.

   (a) 270 × 45   (b) 27 × 4500   (c) 2·7 × 45   (d) 2·7 × 4·5

6. Which of the following statements are always true?

   (a) A rectangle is a parallelogram.
   (b) A square is a rectangle.
   (c) A rhombus is a quadrilateral.
   (d) A kite is a parallelogram.
   (e) A pentagon is a quadrilateral.

7. Use a protractor to draw accurately angles of (a) 120° (b) 45°.

8. There were 320 people who each paid £5·20 for a cinema ticket. How much is that altogether?

9. Two numbers multiply together to give ⁻24. They add together to make 2. What are the two numbers?

Letts **I See Maths** Year 7

10 (a) Work out the areas of rectangles A, B, C and D.

(b) What is the area of the whole shape?

(c) What is 14×13?

8 cm   6 cm

8 cm   A   B

5 cm   C   D

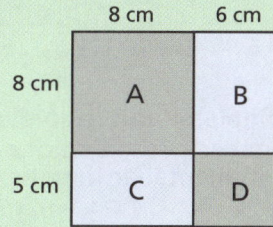

11 Write each expression below in its simplest form.

(a) $5 + t + 6t$

(b) $4x + 7 + 3x - 5$

(c) $8y - y$

(d) $2xy - 2x$

12 Which of the following statements are correct?

(a) $\frac{4}{100} = 0\cdot04$

(b) $\frac{35}{49} = \frac{5}{7}$

(c) $\frac{1}{6} = 60\%$

(d) $\cdot2 = 20\%$

13 A sequence is generated using the rule $1 + 4n$. Write down the first three terms of the sequence.

14 Look at the frequency table on the right.

(a) How many people altogether answered the questions?

(b) What proportion of people preferred to travel by train?

(c) What percentage of people preferred to travel by car?

Frequency table to show a survey of preferred transport

Transport	Frequency
walk	14
car	19
bicycle	12
train	5

15 (a) Use a pair of compasses and a ruler to draw a triangle with sides of 6 cm, 6 cm and 6 cm.

(b) Name the triangle you have drawn.

16 The coordinates (1, 1), (3, 3) and (6, 3) are three vertices of a parallelogram. Write down the coordinates of the fourth vertex.

17 Write down the coordinates (x, y) of four points that lie on the line $x + y = 10$.

18 Work out the values of the expressions below when $x = 3$.

(a) $5(2x + 3)$

(b) $10x + 3$

19 Write down the equation of a line parallel to the line $y = 3x + 7$.

20 Which of the following points lie on the line $y = 2x + 4$?

(a) (1, 6)   (b) (0, 4)   (c) (2, 9)   (d) (-1, 2)   (e) (-2, 6)

Letts **I See Maths** Year 7

Goals

When you have completed this lesson you will:

👁 know how to do mental-arithmetic tests

👁 know how to do calculator-allowed tests.

Mental-arithmetic test

- Remember you need a pencil and pen. You must *not* use a calculator.
- Each question will be read twice.
- Try to work out each question in your head.

Test

For this first group of questions, you have 5 seconds to work out each answer and write it down.

(1) Add nought point two and five point eight.
(2) Look at $x + 3 = y$. When x equals 5, what is the value of y?
(3) Multiply six by seven.
(4) Subtract ninety-nine from one hundred and one.
(5) The probability of snow tomorrow is one-tenth. What is the probability it will not snow?

For the next group of questions, you have 10 seconds to work out each answer and write it down.

(6) Fifty per cent of a number is twenty-three. What is the number?
(7) What angle is between east and south-east, turning clockwise?
(8) The temperature was ⁻4°C. It rose by 6°C. What is the new temperature?
(9) The length of a rectangle is 7 cm and its width is 4 cm. What is its area?
(10) What is four-sevenths of twenty-one?
(11) Multiply twenty-five by eight.
(12) What is eight-tenths as a percentage?
(13) At a party there were twenty children. Eight were boys. What fraction was boys?
(14) What is the value of x in the equation $3x - 5 = 7$?
(15) What is the area of a triangle with base 10 cm and height 6 cm?
(16) In a bag are forty blue counters and sixty red counters. What is the probability of selecting a red counter taken at random?
(17) Write sixteen-twentieths in its simplest form.
(18) Approximately, how much is nineteen point nine per cent of fifty-nine point nine?

For the next group of questions, you have 15 seconds to work out each answer and write it down.

(19) What is the next square number after thirty-six?
(20) Which of these numbers, 1, 2, 3, 4, 5, 6 and 7, are factors of fifty?
(21) In a pie chart, 30° represented ten people in a survey. How many people were in the survey altogether?
(22) Last April I saved a mean of £1·50 a day. Altogether, how much did I save?
(23) Mrs Jones gave her children, Anne, Brian and Chris, pocket money in the ratio 5 : 3 : 2. What fraction of the total pocket money did Anne get?
(24) Subtract a third from five-sixths.
(25) Divide fifty by a half.

Calculator paper

- You may need pencil, pen, ruler, protractor, a pair of compasses and a calculator.

- You have 50 minutes to do the test. Do not waste time on questions that you cannot do. Make a note and come back to them if you have time at the end.

- Read the questions carefully and underline any information you want to remember.

- Show *all* your workings neatly.

Example
Work out the value of the following algebraic expressions when $x = 7 \cdot 2$.

(a) $x + 8$ (b) $3x - 4$ (c) $4(x - 1)$ (d) x^2

(a) $x + 8 = 7 \cdot 2 + 8$ ← Set your work out neatly.

$= 15 \cdot 2$

Put equal signs underneath each other.

(b) $3x - 4 = 3 \times 7 \cdot 2 - 4$

$= 21 \cdot 6 - 4$

$= 17 \cdot 6$

> You may get marks for your method even if the answer is wrong.

(c) $4(x - 1) = 4(7 \cdot 2 - 1)$

$= 4(6 \cdot 2)$

$= 24 \cdot 8$

(d) $x^2 = 7 \cdot 2 \times 7 \cdot 2$

$= 51 \cdot 84$

Tests

Plenary

👁 Identify the questions in the mental-arithmetic test that you could not do. Have you improved since the last test? Set yourself targets for improvement.

👁 Mark the questions in Tests B1, B2 and B3, and do corrections.

👁 Write down the maths you are good at doing. Write down the maths you find difficult. Go back and do exercises from the book to help you with questions you find difficult.

Letts I See Maths Year 7

Calculator allowed

1 The diameter of the disc on the right is 2·45 cm.

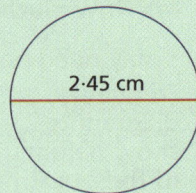

2·45 cm

(a) I put four discs in a row. What is the length of the row?
(b) I put four different discs in a row. The length of the row is 7·8 cm. What is the diameter of each disc?

2 Arrange these lengths in order of size from shortest to longest.

6 kilometres   6 metres   6 miles   6 centimetres

3 A scale drawing is made of a plan of a house. The scale used is that 1 cm on the plan represents 50 cm in real life.

A room measures 6 cm by $4\frac{1}{2}$ cm on the plan. What are the actual measurements of the room?

4 Helen hires a quad bike for four hours.

How much does this cost?

Hire of quad bike

Fixed charge £10   **£2·50 per half hour**

5 (a) What is the probability of Bob's spinner stopping on an even number?

(b) What is the probability of Bob's spinner stopping on a prime number?

(c) Is Bob's or Jo's spinner more likely to stop on a square number?

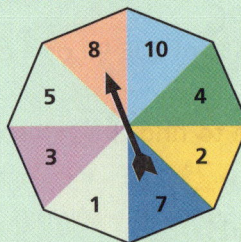

Bob's spinner

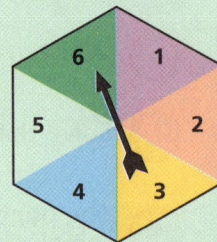

Jo's spinner

6 Work out the values of the following algebraic expressions when $x = 2.5$.

(a) $x + 1$ (b) $3x + 4$ (c) $2(x - 1)$ (d) x^2

7 Write a set of four numbers that has a median of 7.

8 Three consecutive numbers are given as n, $n + 1$ and $n + 2$. Complete the list of consecutive numbers.

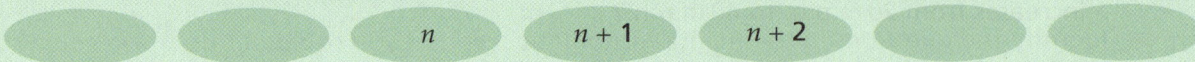

n $n + 1$ $n + 2$

9 Give the dimensions of a rectangle that has the same area as triangle ABC.

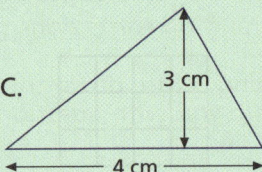

3 cm

diagram not to scale

4 cm

Letts   **I See Maths**   Year 7

10 The cost price of a television is £324. VAT of 17·5% has to be added to this before it is sold.

(a) How much VAT has to be added?   (b) What is the final price of the television?

11 Frequency diagram to show heights of girls

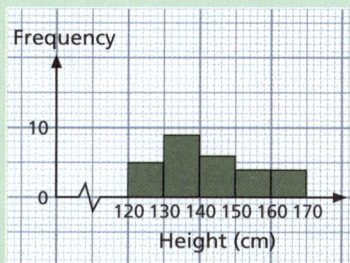

Frequency diagram to show heights of boys

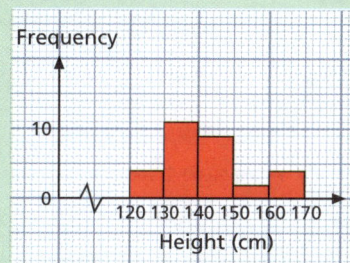

Which of the following statements are true, based on the information given in the diagrams?

(a) There are more girls than boys in the survey.
(b) There are fewer boys with a height greater than 150 cm than girls.
(c) The percentage of boys with a height greater than 160 cm is the same as that for girls.

12 Work out the angles marked with letters in the diagrams below.

(a)

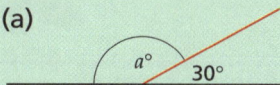

(b)

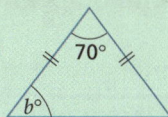

(c)

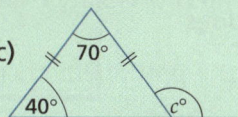

13 Which is bigger, 35% of £38·90 or $\frac{2}{7}$ of £38·90? Show all workings to explain your answer.

14 Solve this equation to find the value of y: $6y - 2 = 5y + 1$

15 The population of Sunnyside town is 216 000. The ratio of male to female is 2 : 3. How many females are there?

16 How many square centimetres are there in a square metre?

17 A triangle with vertices A(0, 0), B(0, 3) and C(2, 0) is rotated anticlockwise about the origin (0, 0). Give the coordinates of the new triangle A′B′C′.

18 The arrow on the speedometer of my car turns through 90° when the speed increases from 10 m.p.h. to 60 m.p.h. Through how many degrees does the arrow turn when the speed increases from 20 m.p.h. to 40 m.p.h.?

19 Draw, accurately, the net of a tetrahedron with side edges of 3 cm.

20 Draw a grid like the one on the right and shade it to show $\frac{1}{2} + \frac{1}{4} + \frac{1}{6} + \frac{1}{12} = 1$.

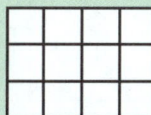

Calculator allowed

1 A box of cereal costs £2·45. What is the cost of seven boxes of cereal?

2 Angel cakes have a diameter of 3·5 cm. I pack them into boxes in seven neat rows. The two outer rows just touch the box. The box is 27 cm wide. How much space can I leave between each row of cakes?

3 A model car is made to scale where 1 cm on the model represents 40 cm on the real car. The model car measures 6·2 cm in length. What is the length of the real car?

4 Bag A contains balls of the same size and mass with numbers 1, 1, 2, 3, 4, 4, 5 and 6 on them.

Bag B contains balls of the same size and mass with numbers 1, 2, 3, 4, 5 and 6 on them.

(a) What is the probability of picking an odd number from Bag A?

(b) What is the probability of picking a prime number from Bag B?

(c) Is it more likely that you will get a six if you pick a ball from Bag A or Bag B?

5 A medicine is made by adding 2 ml of water to every 18 g of substance X.
(a) How much water is needed for 54 g of substance X?
(b) How much of substance X is needed to mix with 9 ml of water?

6 Work out the values of the following algebraic expressions when $x = 3·4$.

(a) $x + 9$ (b) $5x - 2$ (c) $3(x - 2)$ (d) x^2

7 Write a set of five numbers with a mean of 6.

8 Three consecutive even numbers are given as $2n$, $2n + 2$ and $2n + 4$. Complete the list of consecutive numbers.

$2n$ $2n + 2$ $2n + 4$

9 Give the dimensions of a triangle that has the same area as a rectangle with length 10 cm and width 5 cm.

10 Work out 39% of £460.

11 Accurately draw the net of a square-based pyramid with a square base of edge 3 cm and slant edge 4 cm.

12 Which is bigger, 68% of £72·30 or $\frac{3}{5}$ of £72·30? Show all workings to explain your answer.

13 Work out the angles marked with letters.

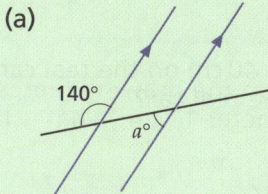

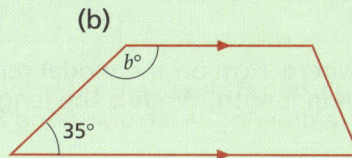

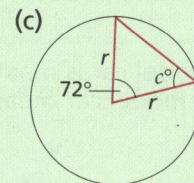

(a)

140°

$a°$

(b)

$b°$

35°

(c)

r

72°

$c°$

r

14 Solve this equation to find the value of x:
$5x + 7 = 52$

15 How many cubic centimetres are there in a cubic metre?

16 A triangle with vertices A(1, 1), B(1, 5) and C(4, 5) is reflected in the mirror line $y = 0$. Give the coordinates of the image A'B'C'.

17 A bag contains red and green counters in the ratio 3 : 5. There are 152 counters in the bag altogether. How many counters are red?

18 The two diagonals of a quadrilateral are equal and bisect each other. What sort of quadrilateral is it?

19 Look at the pie chart on the right. It shows preferred forms of travel.

(a) What fraction of all the people preferred to travel by bus?

(b) What percentage of all the people in the survey preferred to travel by car?

(c) If twenty-seven people preferred to walk, how many preferred to go by bike?

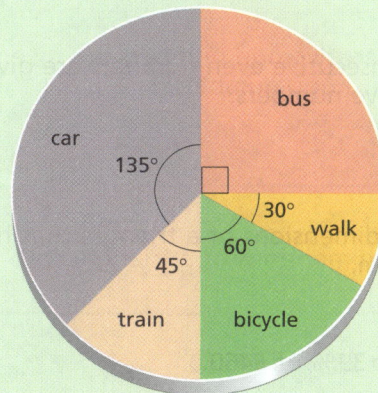

bus

car

135°

30°

walk

60°

45°

train

bicycle

20 Draw a grid like the one on the right and shade it to show:
$\frac{1}{2} + \frac{1}{4} + \frac{1}{5} + \frac{1}{20} = 1$

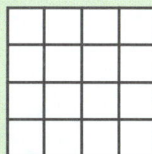

Calculator allowed

1 Some square tiles measure 9·45 cm across. Fifteen tiles are placed next to each other in a row. What length is the row?

2 Arrange these lengths in order of size.

9 kilometres   9 centimetres   9 miles   9 yards

3 A scale drawing is made of a garden. The scale used is that 1 cm on the drawing represents 25 cm in the real garden. In the drawing, a circular pond has diameter 11 cm. What is the diameter of the real pond?

4 Marie pays an annual fixed charge of £65 for her mobile phone and a monthly rental of £7 before paying for calls. How much does she pay a year before paying for calls?

5 The letters in the word

E X A M I N A T I O N

are put in a bag. I select a letter without looking and do not replace it.

(a) What is the probability of selecting a vowel?
(b) What is the probability of selecting the letter Z?
(c) If I select another letter, what is the probability that I have selected a double letter on the two draws?

6 Work out the values of the following algebraic expressions when $x = 4·1$.

(a) $x - 3·4$ (b) $5x + 2·2$ (c) $3(x - 0·1)$ (d) $3x^2$

7 Write a set of seven numbers with a mean of 10.

8 The consecutive odd numbers are given as $2n + 1$, $2n + 3$, $2n + 5$. Complete the list of consecutive odd numbers.

$2n + 1$ $2n + 3$ $2n + 5$

9 Give the dimensions of a triangle with the same area as a square of side 4 cm.

10 Work out 53% of £1260.

11 In September all the prices in Fred's shop were put up by 10%. The following January Fred reduced all the prices by 10% in the winter sale. Were the sale prices the same as those before the September increase? Explain your answer.

....

12 Solve this equation to find the value of x:

$18 - 5x = 3$

....

13 Which is the bigger, 38% of £102 or $\frac{3}{8}$ of £102?
Show all workings to explain your answer.

....

14 Work out the angles marked with letters in the diagrams below.

(a)

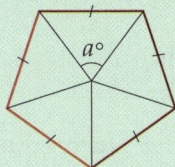

(b)

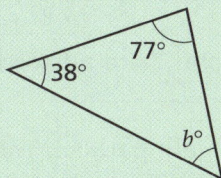

77°

38°

$b°$

(c)

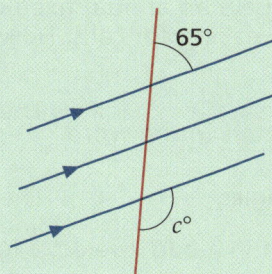

65°

$c°$

....

15 A factory makes brown chocolate and white chocolate in the ratio 7 : 2. In a year, it makes a total of 1008 tonnes of chocolate. How many tonnes of white chocolate does it make?

....

16 A triangle with vertices A(1, 0), B(5,0), and C(5, 3) is reflected in the mirror line $y = x$. Give the coordinates of the image A′B′C′.

....

17 What angle does the minute hand on a clock turn through between 06:08 and 06:15?

....

18 What is the sum of the three consecutive numbers, n, $n + 1$ and $n + 2$?

....

19 The probability of winning a game is 0·85. What is the probability of losing?

....

20 Draw a grid like the one on the right and shade it to show:

$\frac{1}{3} + \frac{1}{4} + \frac{1}{6} + \frac{1}{8} + \frac{1}{12} + \frac{1}{24} = 1$

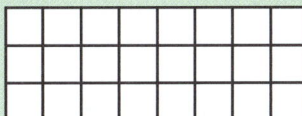

Glossary

acute angle

An angle between 0° and 90°.

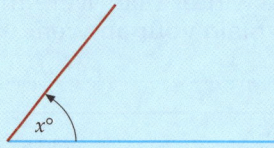

adjacent to ...

The same as 'next to ...'.
For example:
The angles $a°$ and $b°$ are adjacent to each other.

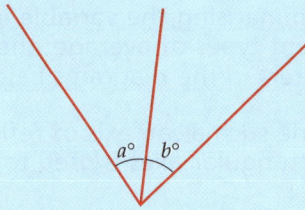

The numbers 6 and 7 are adjacent to each other.

alternate angles

The lines l_1 and l_2 are parallel. The angles $c°$ and $d°$, formed by the line T as it crosses both lines, are equal and are called 'alternate angles'.

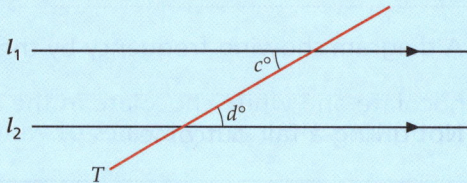

angle

An angle is a measure of turn as the object AB turns onto the image AC.

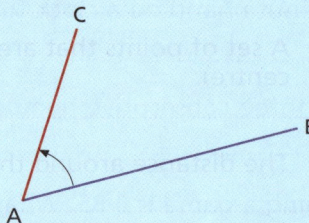

approximate

Find an expression for some quantity, accurate to a specified degree.
For example:
$57 \approx 50$ to the nearest 10
$\pi \approx 3{\cdot}14$ to 2 decimal places

Letts **I See Maths Year 7**

arc	Part of a curve. When using a pair of compasses, you might be asked to 'draw arcs' like those below.

ascending order	Quantities in order of size from smallest to largest.
average	A way of summarising the variable in a set of data. There are three different types of average: the mean, mode and median.
axis, axes	A defined line such as an axis of reflection. A pair of rectangular axes is used to define a grid for drawing graphs.
axis of reflection	The line in which an object is reflected to produce an image. It is sometimes referred to as the 'mirror line' or a 'line of symmetry'.
bar chart	A diagram showing frequency by the height of columns.
bar-line graph	A diagram showing frequency by the height of lines.
bias	Not giving a fair outcome.
bisect	Divide into two equal parts.
chord	A straight line joining two points on the circumference of a circle.
circle	A set of points that are equidistant from a single point (the centre).
circumference	The distance around the outside of a circle.
coincident lines	Lines that cross at a point.
commutative	Giving the same result whatever the order: $a * b = b * a$. Addition and multiplication are commutative. Subtraction and division are not commutative.

Glossary

complementary angle	Either of two angles whose sum is 90°.
congruent	Identical in size and shape.
conjecture	A prediction based on results.
consecutive	Following one another without interruption. For example, 3, 4, 5, 6 are consecutive whole numbers.
construct	Use given measurements to draw accurately using geometrical instruments.
continuous data	Data that has been found by measuring.
coordinates	A set of numbers defining a point. For example, (x, y) or (x, y, z).

corresponding angles

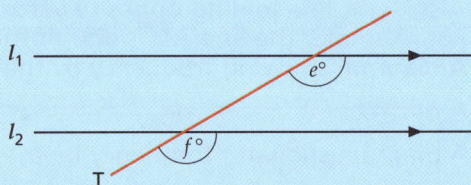

The lines l_1 and l_2 are parallel. The angles $e°$ and $f°$, formed by the line T as it crosses both lines, are equal and are called 'corresponding angles'.

cross-section	The plane surface made by cutting a solid.
cube	A solid with six identical square faces. OR The instruction to multiply a number by itself three times. For example, $5^3 = 5 \times 5 \times 5 = 125$.
cuboid	A solid with six rectangular faces. A cube is a special kind of cuboid.
data	Information that has been measured or counted.
data set	A collection of data.

Letts I See Maths Year 7

decimal fraction	A fraction whose denominator is a multiple of ten. Decimal fractions can be written, for example, as $\frac{6}{10}$ or $\cdot 6$ or $0\cdot 6$.
deduction	Using given (or implicit) information to work out new information. OR Reducing a quantity by subtraction.
degree	The unit used to measure angles.
denomination	A unit of measure such as pounds sterling, metres, litres, miles, fifths, hundredths, etc.
denominator	The number denoting the size of a fraction. For example, in the number $\frac{3}{5}$, the 5 tells you that the denomination is fifths.
descending order	Quantities in order of size from largest to smallest.
diagonals	A straight line joining opposite vertices of a shape. For example, the line AD is one of the diagonals of the rectangle ABCD.
diameter	A chord that passes through the centre of a circle.
difference	Used in mathematics specifically to mean the positive result of subtracting one number from another.
digit	Any one of the numbers, 0, 1, 2, 3, 4, 5, 6, 7, 8 and 9.
discrete data	Data that has been found by counting.
distributed	Spread over.
distributive	For example: $k(a + b) = ka + kb$　　$k(a - b) = ka - kb$ $6 \times 54 = 6 \times 50 + 6 \times 4$　　$6 \times 19 = 6 \times 20 - 6 \times 1$

Glossary

divisible	Can be divided by. Giving an integer answer to division.
domain	The set of values of the independent variable.
equally likely	Events that have an equal chance of occurring.
equidistant	Lines or points that are an equal distance apart.
equilateral triangle	A triangle that has all sides equal. The angles all equal 60°.
equivalent	Having the same value.
estimate	Use known facts to predict a measurement or value. For example, I know what a metre is so I can estimate that the door is about two metres high.
experimental probability	A measure of probability that is calculated from a set of experimental data. For example, a set of data is collected about the weather and this is used to predict the probability of future weather patterns.
explicit	Used in mathematics to describe information that is given or can easily be seen.
exterior angle	An angle outside a shape formed by extending a line segment.

factor	A number that divides exactly into another number. For example, 5 is a factor of 20.
favourable outcomes	In a set of possible outcomes, those that satisfy the criteria. For example, if I am looking for even numbers in the set of numbers, 1, 2, 3, 4 and 5, then the favourable outcomes are 2 and 4. Two of the outcomes are favourable.
formula	A way of expressing a rule using letters to denote quantities. For example, the formula for the area of a rectangle is lw, where l is the length and w the width.

fraction	A number. A part of something. A way of representing division. Types of fraction: • vulgar fraction – written in the form $\frac{a}{b}$, such as $\frac{3}{5}$, $\frac{7}{5}$, $\frac{99}{4}$ • mixed number – written as a whole number and a fraction, such as $3\frac{2}{5}$ • decimal fraction – a fraction whose denominator is a multiple of ten, such as $\frac{3}{10}$, $\frac{43}{1000}$ or $\cdot 3$, $\cdot 043$.
frequency	The number of times something occurs.
frequency diagram	A diagram representing grouped continuous data in columns.
frequency distribution	Any diagram that shows how a set of data is spread.
frequency table	A table of events showing the number of times each event occurs.
gradient	The steepness of a line.
grouped frequency	Grouping a set of data to make it more manageable.
horizontal	A line that is parallel to the horizon. On paper it is a line parallel with the top and bottom edge.
hypotenuse	The longest side of a triangle.
hypothesis	A predictive statement based on observation, experiments or theory.
image	The result of transforming an object in some way.
implicit	Used in mathematics to mean information that can be deduced about something. For example: an isosceles triangle has two equal sides and two equal angles; the radii of a circle are equal; multiplication is commutative.

Glossary

included angle

The angle between two given sides.

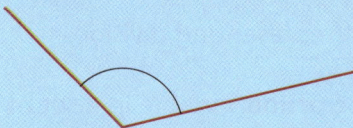

included side

A side between two given angles.

infinite

Uncountable.
For example, there is an infinite number of fractions between a quarter and a half.

information

Data that has been collected and processed systematically.

integer

A positive or negative whole number.

interior angle

An angle inside a closed shape.

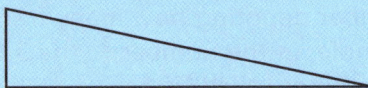

Any of the angles inside the triangle is an interior angle.

isosceles triangle

A triangle with two sides equal in length.

kite

A quadrilateral with two pairs of equal adjacent sides.

mean

The average calculated by working out the total and dividing by the number of objects.
For example, the mean of 3, 5, 2, 8 and 7 is $\bar{x} = \frac{25}{5} = 5$.

median

The average calculated by placing the values of the variable in a set of data in order of size and working out the middle value. If the set contains an even number of values, the median is halfway between the two middle values.

mirror line

The axis of reflection.

modal class	The class of values of the variable in a set of data with the greatest frequency.
mode	The value of the variable in a set of data that occurs most frequently.
multiple	A number that is the result of multiplying a number by a positive integer. For example, 40 is a multiple of 5.
multiplication pairs	Two numbers that multiply to produce a given number. For example, (5, 8) is a multiplication pair of 40.
natural number	A positive whole number or zero.
negative number	For every positive number there exists a negative number such that their sum is zero. For example: $3 + {}^-3 = 0 \qquad 2{\cdot}5 + {}^-2{\cdot}5 = 0 \qquad 99 + {}^-99 = 0 \qquad x + {}^-x = 0$
numerator	The number denoting how many fractions there are. For example, in the number $\frac{3}{5}$, the 3 tells you that there are three of those things called fifths.
object	A line, shape or number before a transformation.
obtuse angle	An angle between 90° and 180°.
parallel lines	Lines that are always the same distance apart. Parallel lines never meet. Parallel lines point in the same direction.
parallelogram	A quadrilateral with two pairs of opposite sides equal and parallel.
percentage	'Compared to one hundred.'
perimeter	The distance all the way around a shape.
perpendicular	A line that is at right angles to another line.

pi (π)	An irrational number that relates the circumference and diameter of a circle: $C = \pi d$. Common approximations for π are: $\pi \approx 3$, $\pi \approx 3{\cdot}1$ and $\pi \approx 3{\cdot}14$.
pictogram	A diagram showing frequency by using pictures.
pie chart	A circular diagram showing frequency as a proportion of a circle.
polygon	A two-dimensional closed shape with straight edges.
population	The overall set of data from which a sample is taken.
position-to-term rule	A rule that relates the position of a term in a sequence to that term. For example, the fifth square number is 5^2.
possible outcomes	An example would be, when rolling a die, all the possible outcomes are 1, 2, 3, 4, 5 and 6.
prime	A number with only two factors, 1 and itself.
prime factor	A factor that is also a prime number.
prism	A solid with a regular cross-section.
probability	An estimate of how frequently something will happen based on theory or experiment.
product	The result of multiplication.
proportional	One set of numbers relating to another set of numbers with a constant scale factor.
protractor	A scale used to measure angle.
quadrilateral	A closed two-dimensional shape formed by four straight sides.
quotient	The result of a division.

radius, radii	The distance from the centre to the circumference of a circle.
random sample	A sample taken from a population using a system or method to avoid bias.
range	The difference between the largest and smallest values in a set of data.
ratio	The comparison of quantities.
rectangle	A quadrilateral with two opposite pairs of equal sides and four right angles.
reflex angle	An angle between 180° and 360°.
regular	Used in mathematics to denote a polygon with its sides and angles all equal.
rhombus	A quadrilateral with four equal sides.
rotational symmetry	A property of a shape as a result of turning about some point. For example, a rectangle has rotational symmetry of order 2 because it can turn 180° and 360° about its centre and fit exactly into its original shape.
rounding	A method for giving an approximate answer. For example, 3.28 can be rounded to 3.3, to 1 decimal place, or to 3, to the nearest whole number.
sample	A selection of the variable of a specified population.
scale factor	The number used to multiply a quantity.
scalene triangle	A triangle with no equal sides.
sector	A part of a circle bounded by two radii and an arc.
segment	A part of a circle bounded by a chord and an arc.

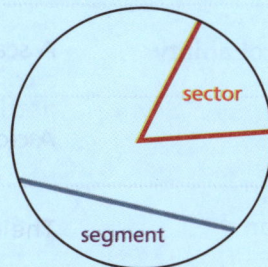

Glossary

sequence	Something that is placed in order. For example, this is a sequence of numbers: 3, 6, 9, 12.
sketch	Draw a representative diagram or graph that is not to scale.
solve	An instruction to find one or more values.
square	A quadrilateral with four equal sides and four right angles. OR An instruction to multiply a number by itself. For example, $3^2 = 3 \times 3 = 9$.
square root	The number that was squared to produce the given number. For example, $\sqrt{25} = \pm 5$.
sum	Sometimes used to denote any combinations of operations with numbers. Specifically used in mathematics to mean the result of addition.
summary statistics	Any statistic that is calculated to describe a set of data.
supplementary angle	Either of two angles that have a sum of 180°.
surd	A number containing an irrational root such as $2\sqrt{3}$.
tally	A mark made when counting frequency. The convention is to count in multiples of five: ~~IIII~~.
term-to-term rule	A method for calculating the next term from the one given. For example, in the sequence, 8, 11, 14, the rule from term-to-term is 'add three'.
tessellation	The covering of space without any gaps.
theoretical probability	Probability that is calculated using implicit information. For example, a coin has two faces and one of them is a head. The probability of getting a head when you spin a coin is therefore considered to be $\frac{1}{2}$.
transformation	A change according to some rule.

Letts **I See Maths** Year 7

translation	A transformation that moves an object from one position to another without turning, reflecting or enlarging.
transversal	A line that crosses other lines.
trapezium	A quadrilateral with at least one pair of parallel sides.
variable	Having a range of possible values.
vector	A pair of numbers $\begin{pmatrix} x \\ y \end{pmatrix}$ describing a translation.
vertex, vertices	The points where straight lines meet.
vertical	The line perpendicular to the horizontal.
vertically opposite angles	

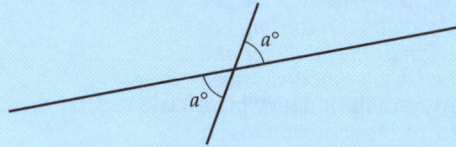

Published by Letts Educational
The Chiswick Centre
414 Chiswick High Road
London W4 5TF
☎ 020 89963333
📠 020 87428390
✉ mail@lettsed.co.uk
🌐 www.letts-education.com

Letts Educational Limited is a division of Granada Learning Limited,
part of Granada plc.

First published 2002

ISBN 184 085 6904

British Library Cataloguing in Publication Data
A catalogue record for this book is available from the British Library.

Commissioned by Helen Clark
Project management by Vicky Butt
Designed and edited by Topics · The Creative Partnership, Exeter
Diagrams by Tony Wilkins
Cartoons by Jim Peacock
Printed and bound by Ashford Colour Press, Gosport